CW00968192

THE GRAND MUFTI

Published in cooperation with

The Moshe Dayan Center for
Middle Eastern and African Studies,
The Shiloah Institute

TEL AVIV UNIVERSITY אוניברסיטת תל-אביב

THE GRAND MUFTI
Haj Amin al-Hussaini, Founder of the
Palestinian National Movement

ZVI ELPELEG

translated by
David Harvey
and edited by
Shmuel Himelstein

FRANK CASS

First published in 1993 in Great Britain by
FRANK CASS & CO. LTD.
Gainsborough House, Gainsborough Road,
London E11 1RS, England

and in the United States of America by
FRANK CASS
c/o International Specialized Book Services, Inc.
5804 N.E. Hassalo Street, Portland, OR 97213-3644

British Library Cataloguing in Publication Data

Elpeleg, Zvi
Grand Mufti: Haj Amin al-Hussaini,
Founder of the Palestinian National
Movement
I. Title II. Harvey, David
III. Himelstein, Shmuel
956.9405092

ISBN 0 7146 3432 8 (Cased)
ISBN 0 7146 4100 6 (Paper)

Library of Congress Cataloging-in-Publication Data

Elpeleg, Z. (Zvi)
    [Mufti ha-gadol. English]
    The grand mufti : Haj Amin al-Hussaini, founder of the Palestinian
national movement / Zvi Elpeleg ; translated from the Hebrew by
David Harvey ; edited by Shmuel Himelstein.
        p.   cm.
    Includes bibliographical references and index.
    ISBN 0-7146-3432-8
    1. Husaynî, Amîn, Grand Mufti of Jerusalem, 1893–1974.
2. Palestinian Arabs—Biography. 3. Politicians—Palestine–
–Biography. 4. Jewish–Arab relations—1917–   5. Palestine–
–History—1917–1948. I. Himelstein, Shmuel. II. Title.
DS125.3.H79E4413   1992
956.94′04′092—dc20
[B]   92-26148
                                                          CIP

This book was originally published in Hebrew by MOD Publishing House, Israel, 1988.

Typeset by Regent Typesetting, London
Printed in Great Britain by Bookcraft (Bath) Ltd

Contents

List of Illustrations

To NAOMI
and to our children
ORLY and OFFER

Foreword

The rise of the Palestinian national movement after the First World War was a continuation of the pan-Arab national movement that had crystallised before and during the war. The common denominator of the two movements was the fact that both had arisen primarily as responses to external challenges.

The background to the emergence of the pan-Arab movement was the weakening of the Ottoman Empire in the nineteenth century, and the tyrannical regime of Sultan 'Abd al-Hamid the Second in the last quarter of that century. Tension increased between the regime in Istanbul and groups of Arab intellectuals, primarily in Damascus and Beirut, after the 'Young Turks', who seized power in 1908, turned out to be zealous supporters of pan-Turkism, which they sought to impose on all the Empire's ethnic groups.

Criticism of the regime took on an organised character during the last years of the nineteenth century, with the appearance of clandestine groups in Lebanon.[1] The first to organise themselves were Christian intellectuals. There were two reasons for this. First, they were steeped in the political ideas brought over from Europe by missionaries active in the region. Second, it was only within the framework of the Arab nationalist idea that they could equate their status to that of the Muslim Arabs. Although this activity caused no immediate echoes outside Beirut, harassment at the beginning of the twentieth century by the regime of those suspected of 'deviating' from Turkish nationalism led to the growth of the Arab nationalist idea in other Arab provinces. What had begun as a demand for cultural autonomy for the Arab provinces developed, at well-attended conferences of regional political bodies, into a demand for independence,[2] and, eventually, in 1916, into the declaration of the Arab revolt by Sharif (later King) Husayn Ibn 'Ali.

It should be stressed that in the period preceding the First World War and during the war itself, only a few Arabs joined the nationalist movement. Religious considerations deterred Arabic-speaking Muslims from subversive action against the Muslim state, and these groups further viewed the association with the Muslim Sultan's Christian enemies as a grave sin. Many others preferred to withhold their support from either side until it became clear who would win.

Representatives from the 'District of Palestine' constituted part of the general national movement, and they participated in its various conferences, including the Arab Congress in Paris in June 1913. As in the general movement, so too in the Palestinian faction; the early activists were Christian intellectuals, particularly from Nablus and Acre. Unlike their colleagues from other countries, however, the Palestinian Arabs were concerned with the Jewish immigration to Palestine.

Long before the Balfour Declaration (2 November 1917), and many years before the outbreak of the First World War, the Palestinian Arabs faced the challenge posed by the Zionist movement, which itself greatly influenced the emergence of the Palestinian national movement. The increasing immigration of European Jews, who could now be seen in different parts of the country, the land purchase and the establishment of new settlements, all caused concern among the Palestinian political public. This concern, which was based partly on reality and partly on political propaganda, found expression in the Palestinian press published in the years preceding the First World War.

Arabic newspapers appeared in various parts of Palestine before the war, and expressed hostility to Zionism. They published exaggerated figures about the number of Jewish immigrants and land acquisitions. Especially anti-Zionist were *al-Karmil* (founded in Haifa in 1908), and *Filastin* (founded in Jaffa in 1911).[3] The publishers of both these newspapers, and of a number of others, were Christians. In addition to distributing anti-Zionist propaganda, they took part in organising political and economic campaigns against the Jewish Yishuv.

During the course of the First World War, the nationalist political organisations made great efforts to enlist Palestinian Arabs from among the Arab towns of Palestine into an anti-Turkish front. None the less, the majority of the Palestinian public and its leaders were not swept away by the nationalist propaganda, and remained faithful to the idea of the integrity of the Empire. Moreover, even among those who wished to be liberated from the tyrannical regime, there were some who preferred to wait for the outcome of the war. In any case, during the war itself, there was very little opposition to Turkish rule. In contrast, the opposition to Zionism was widespread and encompassed all of the Palestinian political factions.

Toward the end of the war, reports began to reach Palestine of both the Sykes–Picot agreement* and the Balfour Declaration. These reports greatly worried the Arab political and religious communities in Palestine. The Palestinian leaders launched a propaganda campaign in towns and villages, with the aim of arousing the masses to an anti-Zionist struggle. Within a short time, before the British had even completed the conquest of Palestine, nationalist organisations intended to fight Jewish immigration and land purchase had sprung up all over the country.

Zionist activity in Palestine increased after the British conquest, reaching a zenith with the arrival of the committee led by Haim Weizmann. On the first anniversary of the Balfour Declaration, the committee organised a procession and celebrations to mark the event, which caused a storm among the Palestinian Arabs. The latter began to establish Muslim–Christian Societies, which were to struggle against both the Zionist enterprise and the pro-Zionist policy of the British.

The Palestinian Arabs looked to Damascus to rescue them from their political distress. At the beginning of October 1918, Amir Faisal Ibn Husayn entered the city at the head of his 'Desert Army' and within a short time had announced the establishment of an independent Arab government. Palestinian leaders then issued declarations that Palestine was the southern part of Syria and that, accordingly, the government in Damascus was their government. In March 1920, the second Pan-Syrian Congress (the first had been held in July 1919, and both were attended by Palestinian activists) decided to crown Faisal king of 'Greater Syria'. This decision strengthened the Palestinian Arabs' adherence to the idea of 'Southern Syria', aroused a great deal of enthusiasm, and led to outbreaks of violence. At this stage, the Palestinian national groups enjoyed the support of those senior officials in the British military administration who viewed the Zionist policy as an obstacle to be removed.[4]

Even had the Arab independence in Damascus lasted and the competition between Britain and France been prevented, it is

---

* 1916: The agreement between France and Britain (and Russia) concerning the division of the Ottoman Empire after its collapse. The agreement was named after the chief representatives of Britain and France at the talks.

unlikely that the Palestinian Arabs could have brought about a change in the British commitment to the Zionist movement. In fact, neither of these conditions ever materialised, since, in light of the uncompromising position of the nationalist groups in Damascus, King Faisal was unable to reach an agreement with the French. As a result, the French army invaded Damascus, putting an end to the national government, and imposing the Mandatory regime by force. Faisal, who had lost his crown, left Damascus, but not long afterwards the British helped him to win another – that of Iraq. The Palestinian Arabs, who had pinned their hopes on the national regime in Damascus, were surprised and greatly disappointed. In place of the vision of a 'Greater Syria', they now adopted the idea of an 'Independent Palestine'.

At this stage, it became clear to the Palestinian Arabs that they were a separate national entity. Their national movement now began to crystallise round three challenges:

1. the British Mandatory regime in Palestine, which was committed to realising the Balfour Declaration;
2. the neighbouring Arab states, which had won their independence, if under the temporary supervision of the Mandatory powers;
3. the Jewish national movement in Palestine, which enjoyed the massive support of world Jewry.

The last-minute efforts of the Palestinian leadership to prevent the ratification of the British Mandate ended in failure, as did its attempts to alter the status of Palestine by pressuring King Husayn Ibn 'Ali, who was conducting prolonged negotiations over the British–Hejaz contract (1920–24). The king was uncompromising, partly as a result of the Palestinian demands, and the negotiations failed.

The neighbouring Arab states, which had only recently gained their independence, were concerned with safeguarding their own interests, and did not concern themselves with the question of Palestine. The Palestinian leadership was thus left to face alone challenges which were beyond its capacity. The Palestinian movement was not only disadvantaged when dealing with external opposition; it also suffered discord within its own leadership. The Mufti of Jerusalem, Shaikh Kamil al-Husayni, attempted to calm tempers and moderate the expressions of hostility toward the British; in return, the authorities granted him honours and material benefits. The rivalry which had obtained between the

leading families in the previous century went on and even worsened, as the new British administration was constituted and the
various families competed to gain its favour. The winners of this
competition were the Nashashibis, who received the office of
mayor of Jerusalem from the British Governor at the beginning of
1920. Shortly before, the office had been taken from the head of
the Husayni family, Musa Kazim al-Husayni, because of his
nationalist activities.

Aside from the internal rivalry from which this competition
sprang and from the scope of the challenges which it faced, the
traditional leadership in Jerusalem lacked both the resources
necessary to conduct the struggle, and any organisational ability.
There was dissatisfaction in the provincial towns about the way in
which the Jerusalem notables were conducting the struggle, and
resentment increased among the young; all felt a lack of direction
and a sense of hopelessness. This, then, was the background to Haj
Amin al-Husayni's arrival on the Palestinian political platform.

Introduction

The political career of Haj Amin al-Husayni, the founder of the Palestinian national movement and the Mufti of Jerusalem, stretched over almost sixty of the eighty years of his life, from the end of the First World War until his death in 1974.

During the 1920s and 1930s, Haj Amin fashioned the Palestinian national movement, founded its organisational frameworks and imbued them with his political ideas. During this period, he also strengthened his status at home, conducted the struggle against the British Mandate and Zionism, and did his utmost to turn what was then a local conflict into a regional one, by involving the masses in the Arab states in the Palestinian cause.

Between the years 1939–41 he played a part in the confrontation in Iraq between the regime of Rashid 'Ali al-Qailani and the British Army. After the failure of the Iraqis, he travelled to Italy and Germany, from where he worked to enlist the support of the Arab states for Nazi Germany. After the war he returned to the Middle East and became involved in the struggle that had already begun over the political future of Palestine. The results of this struggle, in 1948, included the establishment of the State of Israel, the creation of the refugee problem, and the annexation of Palestinian territories to the then Kingdom of Transjordan.

This marked the end of the first period of Haj Amin's political career. During the next period, he remained far from enjoying the status which he had attained previously, and was never able to come to terms with the new situation. During this period he continued to claim that he was the leader of the Palestinian Arabs, and tried to influence the fate of his people. He opposed every attempt to settle the refugees in the Arab states; he continued to persuade the masses in the Arab world that they faced danger from Israeli expansionism, and, as a result, maintained a consciousness of the regional character of the conflict; he was active in exploiting inter-Arab tensions to further the Palestinian cause and to strengthen his personal status; and he set up Palestinian units and demanded that they be integrated into the war against Israel.

Although they would never admit to it, the present leaders of the PLO are in fact continuing the struggle that Haj Amin began. Moreover, they make use of his political doctrine and the idiomatic expressions which he coined. A study of Haj Amin's political life is thus helpful in understanding the sources which nourish the present-day Palestinian national movement.

This book, the result of research undertaken at the Shiloah Institute–Dayan Centre at Tel Aviv University, is an attempt to outline both parts of Haj Amin's political biography. My intention was to present an overall picture of his political activities, while avoiding both excessive detail and the non-objective nature that has characterised a large part of the treatment of Haj Amin by both sides.

The 1948 defeat took Haj Amin away from the centre of the Palestinian and Arab political platforms. Within the Arab camp, he was both blamed for the defeat and turned into its symbol. For their part, the Arab media and Arab historiography have made little reference to Haj Amin, preferring to ignore his memory. This is explained by their desire to suppress this low point of Palestinian history and the Arab failure to prevent the establishment of the State of Israel.

This obviously hinders research into the second period of the Mufti's life. While there are numerous sources dealing with the first period, research on the second period is based on archives within Israel and abroad, and particularly on Haj Amin's own writings, published in the 1950s in the Egyptian press and some years later in his Beirut-based journal, *Filastin*.

I wish to thank Professor Uriel Dann, who advised me during this research; Professor Itamar Rabinovitz, who read the manuscript and provided important comments; and Haim Gal of the Information Centre at the Dayan Centre, who laboured to check the sources and undertook the reading of the manuscript. My special thanks to Dr Rafael Yakar, whose understanding and devotion contributed greatly to improving the content of the book. Finally, I wish to thank the director of the Ministry of Defence Publishing House, Shalom Seri, and its employees.

ZVI ELPELEG

1

Haj Amin – Maker of the Palestinian National Movement

FAMILY BACKGROUND AND EARLY STAGES

Muhammad Amin al-Husayni (subsequently Haj Amin) was born in Jerusalem at the end of the nineteenth century. There are those who maintain that he was born in 1895, while others prefer 1896 or 1897.[1]

The Husayni family of Jerusalem attributes its origins to Husayn, son of the Caliph 'Ali, and his wife, Fatma, daughter of the Prophet Muhammad. For decades, however, it was accepted, especially by Jewish writers and Amin al-Husayni's Palestinian opponents, that the Husayni family is not really descended from the Prophet's family. According to widely published reports, including a number of scholarly works, Amin al-Husayni was a descendant of the al-Aswad family. Family members claim that this family emigrated from Yemen to Palestine in the sixteenth century, and settled in a small village outside Jerusalem. At the end of the eighteenth century, one of Amin's ancestors married a daughter of the distinguished Husayni family, and, contrary to the accepted custom, the family adopted the wife's family name. From this point on, Amin's ancestors claimed to be descended from the Prophet.

In recent years, this version of events has been entirely refuted. Shlomo Ben-Elkanah discovered the family register at the East Jerusalem home of a Husayni family notable, Ibrahim Tawfiq al-Husayni. The register shows that the family is indeed descended from Husayn, the Prophet's grandson.[2] This disclosure ended claims made by its rivals about the inferior lineage of the Jerusalem Husayni family. As a result, Jewish writers, too, have stopped repeating the claim.

1

'Abd al-Latif Ibn Abdullah al-Husayni, who was born in 1694, was responsible for building the Husayni family's power base in Jerusalem. In 1745, he was appointed by the Istanbul *Naqib al-Ashraf* (head of the Sharif class) to serve as Jerusalem's *Naqib al-Ashraf*, and he held the title of *Shaikh al-Haram al-Qudsi*. When he died in 1774, the important religious offices were in the hands of his sons, and one of them, Haj Hasan al-Husayni, was appointed Mufti of Jerusalem in 1789.

In 1791, rivals of the Husayni family unsuccessfully attempted to wrest the office from Haj Hasan. However, the Husayni family succeeded in keeping it in its possession, after sending gifts to Istanbul. This shaikh died in 1809, and, since his children were still young, the office was inherited by Shaikh Tahir, the son of 'Abd al-Samad Ibn 'Abd al-Latif. In 1834, the positions of Mufti of Jerusalem and *Naqib al-Ashraf* were in the hands of two members of the Husayni family. These two, 'Umar al-Husayni and Shaikh Tahir, were involved in the revolt against Ibrahim Pasha. As a result, they were exiled by Muhammad 'Ali to Cairo, where they remained until Ibrahim Pasha's withdrawal from Syria. This exile brought about a decline in the status of the Husayni family in Jerusalem, and a rise in the power of the al-Khalidi, al-'Alami, and Jarallah families, which assumed the important offices in the city.[3]

The Mufti of Jerusalem, Muhammad Fadil Jarallah, died in 1856, and the Husayni family, with the aid of the Ottoman governor, managed to reclaim the office. Marriages at the time between the Husayni and Jarallah families also undoubtedly helped. Muhammad Amin's grandfather, Shaikh Mustafa Ibn Tahir al-Husayni, held the office of Mufti of Jerusalem from 1856 until his death in either 1893 or 1894 (the 1,311th year of the *Hegira*). The office then passed to his son, Shaikh Tahir, who had two wives. The first, Mahbubah, bore him seven daughters and one son, Kamil, and the second, Zaynab, bore him two sons, Fakhri and Amin. Tahir died in 1908, and his son, Kamil, was appointed Mufti by order of the Ottoman authorities. Amin's mother died during the First World War.[4]

During his youth, Amin al-Husayni studied in a *kuttab* (religious elementary school for the study of the Koran), and at the *I'dadi* pre-high school in Jerusalem. In addition to his school studies, which included Turkish, his father, Tahir, hired private tutors to teach him French and Arabic. At the age of seventeen, he travelled to Cairo to continue his studies at *Dar al-Dawa wa al-Irshad*, a well-known institution managed by Muhammad Rashid Rida in *al-*

Azhar. According to Biyan al-Hut, he also studied in the humanities faculty of the Egyptian University (subsequently, Cairo University).[5]

Haj Amin was later to rely on his studies at Cairo's *al-Azhar* in order to base his claim for recognition as an *'alim* (Muslim religious sage) and for his worthiness to hold the office of Mufti.[6] His stay in Cairo lasted only two years, since in 1914, when the First World War broke out, he was visiting his family in Jerusalem and was prevented from returning to Egypt. By now he already held the title of Haj, as he had travelled to Mecca with his mother the previous year, apparently during the first vacation from his studies. Because of his short stay in Egypt, Haj Amin never completed his studies in any educational institution, and obviously never received any diploma. Had he remained in Egypt, he would probably have continued his studies, but when the war broke out he enlisted in the Ottoman army. He was sent to a training camp in Astama, and, after completing an officers' course, was stationed with the 47th Brigade in the Izmir district, later serving in bases in the Black Sea area. It seems that Haj Amin never reached the front, and it is not known which position he held in the units in which he served.

A Palestinian colleague who served with him recalls that Haj Amin would express his opinions in front of the soldiers about the difficult situation of the Arabs under the Ottoman Empire, and would even speak out in favour of a struggle for Arab independence. Haj Amin himself described his relations with the division's Turkish commander, Asif Ishtif, as tense, because of his opposition to the discrimination against Arab soldiers in the distribution of food, and their inferior status in comparison with Turkish soldiers.[7]

His period of army service also lasted no more than two years. According to his diary, in November 1916 he was hospitalised in Istanbul with dysentery. With the aid of someone whom he met in the hospital, Haj Amin received three months' leave and left for Jerusalem. At the end of the three months, he remained at home and never returned to his unit.[8] Whether Haj Amin was officially discharged from the army is not known. As far as can be determined, it seems that members of his family who occupied important positions in the Ottoman administration in Jerusalem and Istanbul succeeded in persuading the authorities not to compel him to return to military service. At the beginning of 1917, as the war continued without respite, Haj Amin remained on sick leave in Jerusalem. By then, it was already clear that the Allies had the upper hand, and it was probably this factor, along with his experience of the discrimination against the Arab soldiers, which was responsible for Haj Amin's decision to leave the Ottoman military service, and not, as has been claimed, reasons of health. Indeed, not long afterwards he witnessed the British army's conquest of Palestine.

After the conquest, Haj Amin was employed by Gabriel Pasha Hadda'ad, the Arab assistant to Ronald Storrs, the military governor of Jerusalem. During the course of 1918, he occupied different positions in Hada'ad's office and helped to recruit youngsters from among the country's Arab population to Faisal's army. For a short period, he also worked as a clerk in the British military administration in Qalqilya, north of Jerusalem. At the beginning of 1919, Hada'ad was appointed director of the security department in Damascus, and Haj Amin became his assistant.[9] While in Damascus, Haj Amin became involved in nationalist groups centred around Faisal, and took an active role in the organisation of the Pan-Syrian Congress held in Damascus in July 1919. He was especially active in organising the participation of Palestinian representatives.[10]

At the end of 1919, he was dismissed from his position in Damascus by Ahmad Laham, who had replaced Hada'ad. He returned to Jerusalem where he began teaching at the *Rashidiyyah* high school, and also became a partner in the *Rawdat al-Mar'arif* school. Over the years, this institution gained a reputation as an educational centre for Arab nationalism, and as a focus for the Husayni family's struggle against Zionism.

After his return from Damascus, Haj Amin's activities were a combination of educational work and political activity. In this framework, he cooperated with his friend 'Arif al-'Arif, who was the editor and part-owner of *Suriyyah al-Janubiyyah* (Southern Syria), a Palestinian newspaper. He was also president of *al-Nadi al-'Arabi* (the Arab Club). This institution, established in 1918, included youngsters, among them members of the al-Husayni, al-'Alami, Abu al-Sa'ud, and al-Budairi families; religious leaders; and former soldiers who had served in Amir Faisal Ibn-Husayn's units. Outwardly, it functioned as a social club, although in fact, like other clubs in the years 1918–20, it was a centre of intensive nationalist activity. The club stood for the idea of Arab unity, the total rejection of Zionism, and the striving for the return of Palestine to Syria. Its central slogan was 'Our Land Is Ours'.

In addition to *al-Nadi al-'Arabi*, a literary club, *al-Muntada al-Adabi*, was established in Jerusalem in 1918. Like the club that Haj Amin headed, this club also campaigned vigorously against Zionism, and expressed the aspiration for unity with Syria. Its slogan was 'In the name of the Arabs we shall live and in the name of the Arabs we shall die'.[11] Its activists belonged to the al-Nashashibi, al-Dajani and al-Khatib Jerusalem families, which were later to constitute the opposition to Mufti Haj Amin.

Although the two clubs cooperated in their dealings with outside bodies (for example, the King–Crane Committee sent from the United States in 1919 to discuss the political future of Palestine), relations between them were tense, and there was competition to influence the Palestinian public.[12] Apart from the different family composition, the two clubs were also distinguished by the fact that *al-Nadi al-'Arabi* inclined to the British, and its leaders sought to achieve Arab unity under the British Mandate, while *al-Muntada al-Adabi* strove to achieve this same goal within the framework of the French Mandate. Under the pretext of cultural and sporting activities, the latter established secret contacts with French intelligence agents.

From the end of 1919, the opposition to Zionism and the aspiration for unity with Syria cemented the Muslim–Christian Societies. These bodies, composed of separate Christian and Muslim organisations and the two clubs mentioned above, conducted propaganda among the Palestinian population, and sent memoranda to the governors of the British military administration. Those who took part in the different delegations and contacts with representatives of the authorities were the veteran leaders, who headed the Muslim–Christian Societies, and organisations such as the club of which Haj Amin was president. However, in order to join the front rank of Palestinian leadership, Haj Amin had to wait for an opportunity to prove himself.

This opportunity came following the disturbances of April 1920 during the al-Nabi festivities. These festivities were an annual event involving Palestinian delegations from all over the country who took part in a pilgrimage to a mosque outside Jericho. According to Muslim tradition, this mosque is situated on the grave of Moses. The origin of the celebration dates back to Sala'ah al-Din's defeat of the Crusaders. After his victory, Sala'ah al-Din granted permission to the Christians to visit the holy sites during their religious holidays. Again, according to Muslim tradition, because the Muslims were afraid that the Christians would exploit

5

the Easter pilgrimage in order to re-conquer the holy sites, they introduced processions and rallies involving thousands of Muslims in order to prevent a renewed Crusader takeover.[13] This tradition was preserved over the generations in the form of an Easter procession from Jerusalem to the grave of al-Nabi Musa.

In 1920, as in previous years, thousands of Muslims gathered in Jerusalem. From there, they set off in procession in the direction of Jericho, carrying the flags of the various delegations that had arrived from all over the country. At the end of the seven-day-long celebrations, the Muslims returned to Jerusalem for the prayer marking the completion of the celebrations. Against a background of political tension, and incited by rousing speeches, the procession turned into a demonstration against the Jews. In the acts of violence that followed on 4–5 April, five Jews were murdered and 211 injured, including women and children. The procession had been directed by Kamil al-Husayni, Haj Amin's step-brother. Kamil had cooperated with the British and had hoped that the procession would end peacefully, but two youngsters did their best to create trouble. The two were 'Arif al-'Arif, who incited the crowd by means of his newspaper, *Suriyhah al-Janubiyyah*, and Haj Amin, who roused the marchers and turned the procession into a violent demonstration.[14] The fervour among the Palestinian Arabs was increased by the fact that Faisal had been made king of Syria a short time before the celebrations.

The coronation, along with rumours that the British military administration in Palestine supported the country's subordination to Faisal, served as powerful material for Haj Amin and his colleagues in *al-Nadi al-'Arabi*, in their attempts to inflame those gathered for the al-Nabi Musa festivities. The authorities issued a warrant for the arrest of Haj Amin and 'Arif al-'Arif, but the two escaped to Transjordan, and from there they made their way to Damascus. A British military court sentenced them *in absentia* to ten years' imprisonment.

Meanwhile, the military administration was replaced by a civil one and, on 1 July 1920, Sir Herbert Samuel became the first High Commissioner of Palestine. On 7 July, he announced a general amnesty for all political prisoners, although Haj Amin and 'Arif al-'Arif were excluded since they had fled before being brought to trial.

The arrival of Haj Amin and 'Arif al-'Arif in Damascus soon became known to Palestinian Arabs living there, and encouraged them to renew their activities. On 31 May 1920, Palestinian activists in the Syrian capital held a meeting, where they decided to found the Arab Palestine Society (*al-Jami'ah al-'Arabiyyah al-Filastiniyyah*). Those elected to the society's executive included 'Izzat Darwaza, Rafik al-Tamimi and Mu'in al-Madi, as well as Haj Amin and 'Arif al-'Arif. Haj Amin was appointed the association's representative for foreign relations. Apparently the reputation that he had in Damascus as having been responsible for the riots in Jerusalem during the al-Nabi festivities earned him a senior position among his fellow Palestinian Arabs. Those involved in the society saw it as an umbrella organisation for the Muslim–Christian Societies and other clubs and organisations that were active in Palestine. The association issued a protest against the San Remo decisions, and against the appointment of a Jew, Herbert Samuel, as High Commissioner. The new association also sent a memorandum to the Pope in Rome, with a request for help against the plan, contained in the Balfour Declaration, to make Palestine 'Jewish'.[15]

In August 1920, the High Commissioner visited Transjordan. In the city of al-Salt, he met notables and tribe leaders who asked him to include the two Palestinian exiles in the general amnesty. Samuel agreed to their request, and the two were indeed pardoned. Haj Amin returned to Jerusalem a hero.[16]

The Balfour Declaration, the arrival of official representatives of the Zionist movement in Palestine, the debates in the British Parliament regarding the country's political future, and the failure of the Palestinian leaders to influence the course of events, created a sense of frustration and helplessness among the Palestinian political community. Haj Amin's appearance as the hero of the attacks of April 1920 – an event which the Arabs regarded as truly heroic – his escape to Transjordan, and his prison sentence, had turned him into a national symbol. The Palestinian Arabs saw him as the first leader to have dared to fight the British and the Jews, and as the redeemer of their impugned honour. Great opportunities had presented themselves, and Haj Amin was to utilise them to the full.

APPOINTMENT AS MUFTI OF JERUSALEM

The first opportunity came when the Mufti of Jerusalem, Kamil al-Husayni, died on 21 March 1921. Known as the Grand Mufti, Kamil had achieved a position of seniority with the British military

7

authority, and the question of who would replace him now arose. In contrast to the ideological unity that generally existed within the Palestinian community at this time, there was a constant struggle between the distinguished families of Jerusalem for power. The Jarallah family saw in the death of Kamil al-Husayni an opportunity to regain the office of mufti, and put forward as a candidate Shaikh Husam al-Din Jarallah. Two other shaikhs, Khalil al-Khalidi and Musa al-Budairi, also announced that they were standing for the position. Shaikh Husam Jarallah was an *'alim*, an *al-Azhar* graduate, and inspector of the religious courts. Shaikh Khalil al-Khalidi was a well-known Islamic researcher, and president of the Shari'a appeal court in Jerusalem. The third candidate, also an *'alim*, and an *al-Azhar* graduate, held the position of religious judge. All three candidates were older men and were considered suitable for the office.[17]

In contrast to these three, Haj Amin was young and had only a limited religious education. Even among his own family, there were those who were more obvious candidates for the office of mufti. The fact that the Husayni family stood behind him and was active in securing his election would seem to show that, in this period of nationalist struggle, the political aspect took precedence over religious considerations. Politically, this enthusiastic young man had attained a strong position, which served to obscure his disadvantages. Haj Amin himself was determined to attain the office. Immediately following the death of his brother, he adopted the haj headcovering (the *'amamah*), grew a beard, and began to act as if the position was already his.[18]

However, in order to achieve office, Haj Amin had to be appointed by the High Commissioner. The commissioner had inherited the authority of the Mutasarrif of Jerusalem who, in accordance with Ottoman law, had to appoint the mufti from a list of three candidates chosen by a college of electors comprising Jerusalem *'ulama*, imams of the mosques, and the Muslim representatives of the regional council and municipality. The elections took place on 12 April, and the three candidates chosen were Shaikhs Jarallah, al-Khalidi, and al-Budairi. Haj Amin emerged at the bottom of the poll. The results were a complete surprise to the government, and obviously, to the Jerusalem Husaynis as well. The Husaynis immediately mounted a vigorous campaign aimed at preventing the loss of the office to the family. Government offices were inundated with protests and memoranda. *Qadis*, imams, religious organisations, Bedouin tribe shaikhs, *mukhtars* and even Christian religious leaders were directed by the Husaynis to demand that the High Commissioner appoint Haj Amin as Mufti. Many of them had, in fact, already made such a recommendation to the authorities when the Mufti Kamil died, and now they applied even greater pressure. They had three main arguments: first, the elections that had been held were null and void since the composition of the electoral body did not meet the requirements of Ottoman law; second, Haj Amin possessed the qualities necessary to carry out the duties of this important office; third, the majority of the Muslim population supported his appointment. A number of senior members of the British administration also supported Haj Amin's campaign, including Ernest T. Richmond, the First Secretary's political assistant, and Storrs, the Governor of Jerusalem. Both were impressed by the power of the Jerusalem Husayni family, and believed that this family, and not its rivals, was likely to reward the appointment by maintaining law and order.

The High Commissioner was inclined to support the appointment of Haj Amin, after being persuaded by Richmond and Storrs that this was the way to maintain peace in Jerusalem. He was also impressed by a conversation that he had had with Haj Amin at the time of the election. In a memorandum dated 11 April 1921, Samuel wrote:

> I saw Haj Amin Husseini on Friday and discussed with him at considerable length the political situation and the question of his appointment to the office of grand Mufti. Mr. Storrs was also present, and in the course of conversation, he declared his earnest desire to cooperate with the Government and his belief in the good intentions of the British Government towards the Arabs. He gave assurances that the influence of his family and himself would be devoted to maintaining tranquillity in Jerusalem and he felt sure that no disturbances need be feared this year. He said that the riots of last year were spontaneous and unpremeditated. If the Government took reasonable precautions, he felt sure they would not be repeated.[19]

The wave of memoranda and petitions demanding his appointment created a strong impression that Haj Amin did indeed enjoy wide public support. There was also another reason to prefer Haj Amin over the other candidates. The British sought to preserve the balance between the Husaynis and Nashashibis (the two important Jerusalem families) and the head of the Husayni family, Musa

Kazim, had been dismissed from his position as mayor of Jerusalem following the disturbances in 1920 and replaced by Raghib al-Nashashibi.

The authorities thus had good reason for wanting the office of mufti to remain in the hands of the Husaynis. The fact that the extended family stood behind and supported this young man derived from the custom of keeping the position in the immediate family. More than this, however, it would seem that the reputation that Haj Amin had already acquired among the Palestinian Arabs (and elsewhere) influenced this support. He was already regarded by the Palestinian political community and people as a representative of, and fighter for, the national cause. Although the office was a religious one, in the prevailing circumstances it had clear political significance, and it was undoubtedly Haj Amin's proven political talents that formed the basis of the wide support for his campaign to become Mufti of Jerusalem.

The High Commissioner, who by the end of April 1921 already saw Haj Amin as the preferred candidate for the office of mufti, had to contend with the election results. One of the three nominees would have to be persuaded to withdraw his candidature, thus making way for Haj Amin.

Richmond and Storrs were helped by the mayor of Jerusalem, Raghib al-Nashashibi (who was later to become Haj Amin's enemy) and by the Shari'a appeal court judge, 'Ali Jarallah – brother of the first-placed candidate. These two worked to persuade Shaikh Husam Jarallah to resign from the list.[20] This he did, and the High Commissioner was therefore able to inform Haj Amin on 8 May 1921 that he would be the next Mufti of Jerusalem. The announcement was made in person, and Haj Amin, in fact, never received an official letter of nomination, nor was his appointment ever gazetted. This did not prevent the new Mufti, at the age of twenty-six, from quickly establishing himself in this important office which was to be only the first stage in his leadership career.

PRESIDENT OF THE SUPREME MUSLIM COUNCIL

Haj Amin's success cannot be explained without mentioning the support of members of the administration's top echelon who favoured the Arab cause, and the popularity Haj Amin gained as a result of the riots of April 1920. Although the riots had been little more than indiscriminate attacks on Jewish passers-by and their

10

property, they were seen by the Palestinian population as defiance of British rule. After the relative quiet that had prevailed during military rule, largely as a result of the policy aimed at maintaining the calm pursued by Haj Amin's brother, the Mufti Kamil al-Husayni, and of the established Husayni leadership, Haj Amin seemed a champion of national heroism. The sympathy felt for him by the country's Arab population brought him to the attention of senior officials in the government. In their opinion, handing over the office to Haj Amin was a reasonable price to pay for ensuring future law and order. The future was to prove that their approach was partly justified: not only did the Husaynis prevent an escalation of tension during the 1921 al-Nabi Musa festivities, but the calm was also maintained during the following years. Referring to this, Herbert Samuel wrote that, 'with the exception of a small affray in Jerusalem in the following November, for a period of eight years no disturbances occurred anywhere in Palestine'.[21]

What lay behind the new Mufti's moderation in his dealings with the authorities was not only the promises he had made. He needed the authorities in order to consolidate his position as mufti, and to introduce into it an element of national political leadership. He demanded that the title Grand Mufti, which had been granted to his brother by the British for cooperating with them, also be given to him, and that his salary be higher than that of the other muftis. Richmond and Storrs supported this claim, arguing that since, from the spiritual and religious points of view, the status of Jerusalem was superior to that of other regions in Palestine, the Mufti of Jerusalem should be considered head of the country's Muslim community. With the establishment of the Supreme Muslim Council in January 1922, the government acceded to these demands.[22] Haj Amin's salary was increased, and he received the same status that his brother had enjoyed. He was not satisfied, however, with a position that was primarily religious in character. His ambitions went beyond this, to the accumulation of political power through the control of manpower and economic resources.

The situation created when the Christian British regime replaced the Muslim Ottoman one gave Mufti Haj Amin the opportunity to achieve his next objective: control of the Muslim community's endowments (the *waqf*), the court system, and other religious institutions that, during the Ottoman period, had been possessed by the Muslim state. The sultan, also known as the caliph, had been the supreme authority in these matters until the revolt of the Young Turks in 1908. According to a law promulgated

11

in that year, the authority had passed to parliament which, in turn, devolved it to the *Shaikh al-Islam* seated in Istanbul. Since 1914 the Minister of Justice had been responsible for the implementation of laws relating to Islamic law and religion, while the management of Muslim property throughout the country had been handed over to the *waqf*. Matters relating to non-Muslims were managed by the autonomous institutions of each community.[23]

The British military administration continued to deal with the affairs of the Muslim community as the Ottoman regime had done. By the end of 1920, however, the High Commissioner was already beginning to consider transferring the handling of the community's affairs to the Muslims themselves. He initiated the establishment of a committee composed of heads of the Muslim community, including the muftis of Jerusalem, Haifa, and Safed, the mayors of Jerusalem and Nablus, and two notables representing Acre and Gaza. Along with a number of government officials, this committee prepared recommendations that were presented to the High Commissioner in March 1921. These recommendations included the establishment of the Supreme Muslim Council (*al-Majlis al-Islami al-A'ala*), which was to have extensive authority regarding appointments to religious offices – muftis, imams, and religious judges – the appointment of officials in the legal system, and the management of the *waqf*.[24] The electoral body, which met at the beginning of 1922, was similar in composition to the body that had chosen representatives for the last Ottoman parliament. This electoral body was to choose the *Rais al-'Ulama* – president of the council – and its four members.

The Husayni family was the driving force behind preparations for the election, and Haj Amin its obvious candidate for president. Raghib al-Nashashibi, the mayor of Jerusalem, who only a year before had assisted Haj Amin in securing the office of mufti, now tried to prevent his election to the new position. When he realised that Haj Amin had a clear majority in the electoral body, which was to meet by order of the High Commissioner, al-Nashashibi tried to cancel the elections. When this failed, he, along with five of his supporters, boycotted the elections. In their absence, Haj Amin was elected *Rais al-'Ulama* by a large majority (forty against seven), and became president of the Council. The remaining four members were elected by their respective regions. The rivalry between the Husaynis and their opponents now became institutionalised: the former were known as *al-Majlisiyyun*, after the High Muslim *majlis* (council), while the latter were called *al-*

Mu'aridun, meaning opponents. Haj Amin now occupied two powerful offices. According to the law, the government was supposed to supervise the budgets and appointments that were under the Council's jurisdiction. In fact, Haj Amin did whatever he liked, using the Council in order to increase his status among the Palestinian Arabs, and to give momentum to the Palestinian struggle.

There was a struggle in government circles between those who supported Haj Amin without reservation, and those who sought to limit his influence, and it was his supporters who emerged victorious. They helped behind the scenes to secure his election and, no less importantly, ensured that the Shari'a court system, mosques, and the *waqf* were united and placed under the jurisdiction of the Supreme Muslim Council. When the Council was in the process of being set up, the government had objected to granting it the authority to appoint and dismiss employees of the Shari'a court system. Later, however, the government capitulated to Haj Amin's pressure, and as a result the First Secretary, Sir Wyndham Deedes, resigned.[25]

Some of the British officials who supported Haj Amin did so out of the belief that in this way they eased the task of the government in running the country. Others were motivated by their antipathy towards Zionism. Opponents of Zionism were especially prevalent during the period of military rule, but even after the arrival of the civilian High Commissioner there were officials who were clearly sympathetic to the Arab cause.[26] The High Commissioner had to decide whether to support Haj Amin or his rivals. His eventual decision to support Haj Amin did not indicate, however, that he favoured the Mufti's political position. Rather, it stemmed from his belief that Haj Amin was better able than his rivals to pay the price for British support: political behaviour that would ensure quiet in the country.

Haj Amin did indeed pay that price, although not out of a sense of identification with the government's interests. Simply, he needed the government. An escalation of the power struggle between the Husaynis and their opponents was inevitable after Haj Amin's success in securing the two powerful offices of Mufti and President of the Supreme Muslim Council. The source of the opposition to him was the traditional rivalry between the important families, and their struggle for positions of political and economic power. An additional reason was Haj Amin's personality: a large measure of the resentment at his meteoric rise could have been prevented had Haj Amin had the sense to include veteran leaders, such as members of the al-Nashashibi and al-Khalidi families, in the different institutions, and offer them part of the resources and offices. However, the concepts of cooperation, coordination, and the decentralisation of power were foreign to the political tradition of Arab society. In addition, Haj Amin had a particularly dominant personality, and demanded that others acquiesce in his opinions.

Haj Amin depended on his widespread family and supporters, and he knew how to bind them to him by distributing positions of power and other benefits. Under Haj Amin's leadership, the Supreme Muslim Council, which the High Commissioner had intended to deal with property and institutions of a religious character, became involved primarily in fortifying Haj Amin's status and furthering political issues. *Qadis*, imams, officials, and other office holders in the two systems – the mosques and religious legal institutions, and the *waqf* – were appointed and dismissed according to the measure of their loyalty to Haj Amin, or their connection with opposition circles. This was also the case regarding the use of *waqf* property, such as the lease of buildings and land. Nepotism, always acceptable in Arab society, assumed especially wide dimensions. Members of the Husayni family who held senior positions in the Supreme Muslim Council and institutions under its aegis made use of their status whenever a political question was raised. They took an active part in the campaign for a boycott of the Legislative Council elections in 1922–23, and helped organise the opposition to the Advisory Council (which the High Commissioner sought to set up after the failure to establish a Legislative Council). They also defended the Palestine Arab Executive (*al-Lajnah al-Tanfiziyyah al-'Arabiyyah al-Filastiniyyah*), which had been controlled by Musa Kazim al-Husayni since its establishment in 1920, when it was attacked by the opposition.

As for the British, they continued to assist Haj Amin in the face of these pressures. When the situation reached crisis point, with the opposition's demand in 1926 to hold elections for the Supreme Muslim Council, the Mandatory government came to Haj Amin's aid. With the government's intervention, an agreement was reached between the two sides, according to which some members of the Council were replaced while Haj Amin retained his position, thus confirming his claim that, as president of the Council, he had been elected for a life term. In the future Haj Amin was to describe the Mandatory regime as the root of all evil, and as the principal partner in an English and Jewish conspiracy directed against the Palestinian Arabs and the Arab world. Nevertheless, this did not prevent him from relying on the authorities in the struggle against his Palestinian rivals.

RESTORATION OF AL-HARAM AL-SHARIF MOSQUES

Having secured the two senior offices, and while still involved in repelling the attacks on him by the *al-Mu'aridun*, Haj Amin embarked on a project to restore the *al-Haram* (Dome of the Rock) and *al-Sharif* (al-Aqsa) mosques. The two structures were in a state of neglect, and restoration was necessary to prevent the collapse of certain parts. Jerusalem's importance had declined during the period of Ottoman rule, and the authorities in Istanbul had almost completely ignored the two mosques. Restoration was thus vital for the physical preservation of the buildings. In addition, Haj Amin saw this project as an opportunity to achieve other objectives: to bring the Islamic holy sites (and through them the Palestinian cause) to the attention of millions of Muslims; to create a commitment on the part of the Muslim states to support the Palestinian national struggle; and to raise his own status in the Muslim world.

Delegations of the Supreme Muslim Council left for Hejaz, India, Iraq, Kuwait, and Bahrain in 1923 and 1924 in an attempt to raise money for the restoration work. At the same time articles appeared in the local press exalting the project's initiator – Haj Amin al-Husayni. A team of technical experts arrived from Turkey to carry out a survey of the condition of the mosques and to submit proposals for their restoration. The Council's delegations made a strong impact abroad, emphasising not only the mosques' dilapidated physical condition, but also the supposed threat to them from the Zionists who planned to take over the Islamic holy sites of Jerusalem.

In 1923, during the period of the Haj, a Supreme Muslim Council delegation visited Hejaz. Emphasising the danger from the Jews, the delegation made use of propaganda material that Jews in Palestine had disseminated abroad for fund-raising purposes. Efforts by Zionist leaders to purchase the Western Wall area from the *waqf* served as 'proof' that the Jews were planning to take over the mosques and build the next Temple on their site.[27] The delegation's appeal was well received, and wealthy Muslim rulers contributed large sums of money. By the end of 1924, between £85,000 and £95,000 sterling had been collected, a huge amount at that time. The money was used to finance the restorations, which continued until the end of the 1920s. The climax of the project was the gold covering on the Dome of the Rock.

The opposition looked on helplessly as Haj Amin succeeded in establishing his reputation in the Muslim world. His opponents criticised the whole project and roused suspicions about the expenditure involved.[28] It is doubtful if these rumours had any foundation in fact. In any case, such criticism paled against such an impressive project: the two mosques were completely restored, and, in addition, a religious library and Islamic art museum were built on the site. Haj Amin restored *al-Haram al-Sharif* to its former glory, transforming an abandoned and neglected site into one evoking inspiration and glory. In the following years, Haj Amin would make continual use of the restoration of the two mosques in his political struggle to appear as the defender of Islam.

There was another aspect to the project: the opposition's stronghold was the Jerusalem municipality, at the head of which stood Raghib al-Nashashibi. The importance of the municipality derived from the fact that Jerusalem was the seat of the various government offices and foreign diplomatic missions. At the time of the establishment of the Supreme Muslim Council, the municipality was already a powerful institution. Its leaders had direct contact with the authorities and with the representatives of the different states. In contrast, the Council, despite its future importance, was little more than a local institution responsible for religious questions and the personal law of the country's Muslims. The financial resources of the municipality were also far greater than those of the Council,[29] which meant that Raghib al-Nashashibi was able to maintain a large administration and attract individuals and families by distributing offices and other benefits. This control exercised by the mayor presented a challenge to the Supreme Muslim Council and its president, Haj Amin. The restoration of the mosques was intended, among other things, to meet this challenge.

THE 1928 WESTERN WALL INCIDENT, THE 1929 RIOTS, AND THEIR CONSEQUENCES

The incident at the Western Wall on the Day of Atonement (Yom Kippur) in 1928 was influenced to a large degree by the increase in the status of the two mosques in the eyes of the country's Muslims.

Disputes regarding the right of Jews to the Wall had been continuing for hundreds of years, during which time Jews would visit the site in order to pray. Although situated outside the area of the *al-Haram al-Sharif* mosques, the Western Wall was also considered to be holy by the Muslims by virtue of its being part of the Wall of the al-Aqsa mosque. To them it was known as *al-Buraq*, after the name of the legendary horse on which Muhammad ascended to heaven. According to legend, before ascending, the prophet had stabled his horse in a pit alongside the Wall. The country's Muslims, especially those living in Jerusalem, have always displayed religious sensitivity toward the site. Quarrels between Jews and Muslims would break out periodically, especially when Jews attempted to bring religious articles, benches and partitions (to separate men and women) to the site, and to pave the alleyway adjacent to the Wall. Those arguments that were brought before the Ottoman authorities for adjudication were almost always decided in favour of the Muslims.[30] In theory, then, Jews were forbidden to introduce benches and religious articles to the holy site, although in practice they continued to do so by bribing the *waqf* guards.

The *al-Haram al-Sharif* mosques have been in Muslim possession since the Muslim conquest, while the Western Wall site had become *waqf* property approximately 500 years ago. At the end of the nineteenth century and the beginning of the twentieth, Jewish philanthropists had tried unsuccessfully to purchase the site in front of the Wall from the managers of the *waqf*. The status quo, according to which the right of Jews to go to the Wall was (in theory) restricted to prayer alone, was maintained until the British conquest during the First World War. Under British military rule, Jews began to bring their religious objects, including partitions, to the Wall on the Sabbaths and Jewish festivals, against the wishes of those responsible for the site. The Muslims saw this as an attempt to alter the status quo, having always regarded the presence of Jews at the Western Wall as a privilege and not a right. They now feared that the Jews were trying to turn the privilege into a right and, with the assistance of the British authorities, take over the *al-Haram al-Sharif* site.

A few months after its establishment, the Supreme Muslim Council decided to demand that Jews be forbidden to bring any objects to the Wall. This was one of Haj Amin's first initiatives in his new position, and he arranged to have the Council's decision publicised by conducting a propaganda campaign in the country and throughout the Muslim world. The campaign emphasised the danger of a Jewish takeover of the Islamic holy sites, and as proof photographs were distributed that had been taken by heads of *Yeshivot* (Jewish centres of learning) in Jerusalem. These were photomontages showing the Dome of the Rock upon which the flags of Zion and the Star of David had been superimposed. The heads of *Yeshivot* in the Old Yishuv (Jewish settlement in Palestine) would send requests for money to Diaspora Jews, along with such photographs which they believed were likely to persuade potential contributors. Delegations of the Supreme Muslim Council were able to use these photographs to persuade Muslims throughout the world of the necessity to dispel the threat to *al-Haram al-Sharif*.[31]

In the years immediately following its establishment, the Council was very active on the Western Wall issue. Over the course of time, however, the tension lessened, and there were no real incidents until 1928. On 23 September of that year, the eve of Yom Kippur, Jewish worshippers set up a partition, between men and women, next to the Wall, in addition to benches and religious articles. When members of the Supreme Muslim Council learned of this, they alerted the British authorities. The British ordered the Jews to dismantle the partition. When they refused to comply, a fight broke out, during which the partition was removed by British officers.[32]

Tempers ran high in both communities during the following days. In general, the British authorities supported the Muslim version of the status quo, and Haj Amin drew encouragement from this in his struggle against the Zionists. He organised meetings all over the country at which members of the Supreme Muslim Council stirred up the crowds, arranged delegations, and issued protests warning of the Jewish conspiracy to take over the country and holy sites by various designs. One of Haj Amin's arguments was that Jewish claims regarding the holiness of the Western Wall had been invented by their leaders in order to make the site a focal point for Jews all over the world, 'with the aim of returning and building the Temple on the site of the al-Aqsa mosque'.[33]

The Council's propaganda campaign was a response to the effort by Jews throughout the world, following the incident at the Western Wall, to persuade the British government to recognise the right of Jews to this holy site. There is no doubt that even Haj Amin was taken aback by the sharpness of the Jewish response, which included protest rallies and demonstrations demanding that the British government act to protect Jewish rights. This activity justified his long-held fears about the Zionists' determination gradually to take control of the holy sites in Jerusalem.

Haj Amin's connections with the leaders of the British administration were particularly strong at this time. It was widely accepted among members of the administration that the British Mandate, as stipulated, could not be carried out, and that it would have to be amended so as to satisfy at least some of the demands of the Palestinian Arabs. The administration sought to influence the decision-makers in London along these lines, and it appears that Haj Amin was anxious not to harm this process. This probably explains the absence of hostile propaganda in Haj Amin's mouthpiece, *al-Jami'ah al-'Arabiyyah*, and other Palestinian newspapers on 24 September, immediately after the incident at the Wall. 'Izzat Darwaza, who managed the *waqf* property on behalf of the Supreme Muslim Council, claimed that Haj Amin exploited a basically religious incident for his political propaganda campaign – a campaign designed to awaken the dormant Palestinian national movement. Philip Mattar rejects this claim by pointing to Haj Amin's silence during the six days from 24 to 30 September, 1928.[34]

It would appear that Mattar is correct, since Haj Amin had good reason for preventing a real controversy. First, he was well aware that the Mandatory administration was inclined to accept the Palestinian position, that is, to maintain the status quo that had been acceptable under Ottoman rule. Second, he did not want to harm the political process that was under way for the establishment of a legislative council. Finally, he was at pains to prevent any development that was likely to lead to a confrontation with the authorities, since he needed their support against the opposition's attempts to undermine him. Why then did Darwaza claim that Haj Amin sought to exploit the situation? The explanation would seem to lie in Darwaza's desire to refute opposition claims that Haj Amin preferred quiet cooperation with the British to vigorous activity by the Palestinian nationalists.

On 30 September, a week after the incident, the Council called a meeting of Muslims from Jerusalem and the surrounding areas at the site of the al-Aqsa mosque, in response to Jewish claims regarding the Western Wall. Speeches were made calling on those assembled to join the struggle against the Jewish plans to take over *al-Haram al-Sharif*. Haj Amin's involvement in these events is clearly indicated by the fact that the three speakers, Shaikh 'Abd al-Ghani Kamlah, 'Izzat Darwaza, and Shaikh Hasan Abu al-

Sa'ud, were his associates. For a time, this involvement remained covert, although tempers very quickly flared, and various groups began to demand more forceful action. At this stage, Haj Amin came out into the open and took his place at the head of the growing movement.

On 1 November 1928, he held a Muslim conference (the Islamic Congress) with the participation of almost 700 representatives from all over the country, and observers from neighbouring countries. Haj Amin ran the conference himself, and assumed the leadership of the newly established Society for the Protection of al-Aqsa and the Muslim Holy Places.[35] The Congress sent a delegation to the First Secretary, Sir Harry Charles Luke (who was standing in for the High Commissioner, Sir John Chancellor, until the latter's arrival in December), with a demand for a declaration promising that there would be no change in the status of the Western Wall. It was also decided to set up branches of the Congress in the Islamic states, and memoranda were dispatched, including one to the Arab delegation in Geneva. The memoranda emphasised the need for unification in the Muslim world over the issue of the Western Wall, and included a warning to the British government that if the Arab demands were not met, the whole Muslim world would embark on an all-out struggle.[36] The Congress also dealt with issues other than the dispute over the Western Wall, as, for example, the prohibition on the sale of land to Jews, and the demand that the government dismiss from his position the legal secretary and 'Zionist leader', Norman Bentwich.

It is reasonable to assume that when Haj Amin led the struggle to defend *al-Buraq*, he intended to direct it into political channels, thus maintaining a measure of control over events. In fact, these events quickly gathered momentum, and a few months later they deteriorated into bloodshed.

After the Muslim conference in Jerusalem, Haj Amin was active in two areas. He continued his contacts with government leaders in Jerusalem regarding the Legislative Council, and put pressure on the British Government over the issue of the Western Wall. As a result of these pressures, the Colonial Office on 19 February 1928 published a White Paper expressing support for Haj Amin's position, namely, that the Jews had access to the Western Wall only for purposes of prayer, this being the position that had existed, in theory, under the Ottoman Empire. Haj Amin greeted the Colonial Office's declaration with undisguised joy, but faced by the opposition that it aroused in the Jewish Yishuv and Zionist movement, the government did nothing to force the implementation of the status quo.

In an attempt to force the authorities' hand, Haj Amin increased the pressure on them by protesting at the Colonial Office in London and at the League of Nations, and by organising frequent protest rallies at the al-Aqsa mosque. He also provoked incidents at the Western Wall in order to sharpen the conflict and force the government to act. At the instigation of the Supreme Muslim Council, the *muezzin* at the Dome of the Rock (situated close to the Western Wall) interfered with Jewish prayers at the Wall by his cries calling the Muslims to prayer, and by holding the noisy *zikr** ceremony, with its drum accompaniment.

In order to intensify the dispute, the Council began to build a new wing for the Shari'a court overlooking the Wall, and also opened a section of the Wall's courtyard for use as a thoroughfare for the residents.[37] However, despite all these actions during the summer of 1929, no order was published giving legal backing to the Muslims' claim about their rights to the Western Wall. The growing tension undoubtedly formed the background to the riots of 23–24 August.

On Tisha B'av (a Jewish fast day commemorating the destruction of the Temple), which fell on 15 August, members of the *Betar* movement marched to Government Office in Jerusalem, in a demonstration against the government's support of the Muslims on the issue of the Western Wall. (A similar demonstration had taken place in Tel Aviv the previous day.) The group then made their way to the Wall itself, where the demonstrators flew the Zionist flag and sang *Hatikvah*, the Jewish national anthem, before the hostile eyes of the Muslims who were positioned above them. Tempers ran high during prayers in the al-Aqsa mosque on the following day, a Friday, and a demonstration was organised headed by Muslim religious leaders. Tension among the Muslims rose, reaching its peak a week after the Jewish demonstration and Muslim counter-demonstration. On Friday, 23 August, an unusually large number of *fallahun* arrived from the villages around Jerusalem, armed with clubs and knives. They gathered in and around the mosque, and after the prayers listened to speeches by Haj Amin and other members of the Supreme Muslim Council. Rumours had already been spread about a Jewish plot to seize *al-*

---

* A prayer ceremony in which the faithful recite the name of Allah at a steadily increasing tempo while in a state of religious fervour.

Haram al-Sharif, and after the speeches the inflamed mob burst into the Western Wall area. It smashed a table used to support a *Sefer Torah*, and burned notes containing prayers and supplications that Jews had left in crannies in the Western Wall. Within a few hours Jewish passers-by and businesses were set upon and attacked.

The riots spread to the Jewish quarters of Jerusalem, and then to other parts of the country. Settlements between Jerusalem and Tel Aviv were attacked, but the worst incident of all took place on the following day in Hebron, where sixty Jews were murdered and about a hundred wounded, all of them members of the Old Yishuv, who did not even try to oppose their murderers. The violence and destruction continued for another week, and on 30 August the massacre of Jews in Safed took place. Twenty were murdered, many wounded, and approximately 100 houses were robbed and destroyed. In total, 133 Jews were killed and more than 300 wounded in the violence across the country.

On the day before the massacre in Safed, the High Commissioner, Chancellor, returned from London where he had been on home leave, in order to deal with the situation. On 1 September he published a notice strongly denouncing the 'acts of wild murder' that had been perpetrated on helpless members of the Jewish community. He put the blame on the Palestinian Arab leaders, and threatened to halt the discussions being conducted with the government in London about changes in the constitution of Palestine.[38] His remarks caused a storm among the Muslims, and in the wake of a wave of protests an effort was made to assuage their anger. Indeed, the High Commissioner published a different notice a few days later, which stated that an inquiry into the behaviour of both sides would be conducted as soon as possible.

The commission of inquiry that was appointed to investigate the causes of the August riots, headed by Sir Walter Shaw, went even further in its effort to placate the Muslim leaders. It held that the violence had resulted from tension caused by the continuing Jewish immigration into the country and Jewish land acquisition.[39] In October 1930, following the appearance of the commission's findings, the British Colonial Secretary, Lord Passfield, published a White Paper. This document was largely based on the report of the delegation headed by Sir John Hope Simpson that had investigated the question of immigration and land acquisition after the Shaw conference. His report, too, inclined to meet Arab demands – a restriction on Jewish immigration, settlement, and land acquisition in the country. It also added a recommendation for the constitution of a legislative council.

The authorities' sympathy, in the years 1928–29, with Arab claims in the dispute over the Western Wall, did not become actual policy. Zionist pressure on the government in London ensured that the recommendations hostile to Zionism were not implemented. Nevertheless, the events of August were to have an effect on the future. First, they greatly intensified the Arab-Jewish conflict. It was no longer a local outburst, but rather an onslaught on Jews throughout the country, including those of the Old Yishuv who had no connection with the Zionists. The leaders of the Zionist movement could no longer doubt the depth of the enmity that this violence revealed, nor the fact that it encompassed the vast majority of the Arab population. One of the principal lessons drawn from the riots was the need to build a Jewish defence force, and this was begun a few days later. Second, with this change in the nature of the conflict, Muslim communities in other countries began to feel a sense of involvement in it. The riots themselves, which the Arabs termed the 'revolt' (*Tawrat al-Buraq*), the commissions of inquiry that were sent to the country, and the propaganda that the Supreme Muslim Council had been conducting since the beginning of the 1920s, awakened the Arab and Muslim world to the question of the defence of Palestine and the holy places. Third, Haj Amin, who stood at the centre of these events, ostensibly religious in character but with a basically political intent, succeeded in manipulating them in order to further his own status. Fourth, Haj Amin had for some time had his eyes on the senior political office in the country's Arab community, chairman of the Arab Executive, headed by one of his relations, the aged Musa Kazim al-Husayni, who was almost in his eighties. Haj Amin saw in this body a rival to the Council, and at times disputes between the two had erupted into open quarrelling. The events of 1928–29 were to bring Haj Amin closer to overcoming this obstacle.[40]

The year that had begun with the incident at the Western Wall (September 1928), and ended with the bloodshed of the August pogrom (August 1929), was fully exploited by Haj Amin. Since embarking on his political career ten years before, Haj Amin had himself initiated the different stages in his rise in the political–religious leadership. This was true in April 1920, when he orchestrated the riots during the al-Nabi Musa celebrations; in 1921, when he fought for the title of Mufti; and in his struggle in

1922 to be *Rais al-'Ulama* and president of the Supreme Muslim Council. He also initiated, planned and carried out the fourth stage of his career, the project to restore the *al-Haram al-Sharif* mosques. However, the next development, the incident at the Western Wall in 1928, happened almost by chance. Haj Amin was presumably worried by Jewish aspirations to perpetuate, and possibly even extend, the custom which they had introduced during British military rule of bringing benches and religious articles to the Wall, a holy and sensitive site. It even appears that he was convinced that the Jews wanted to rebuild the Temple on the site of *al-Haram al-Sharif*.[41] Beyond this, however, he sought to exploit the conflict over the rights to the Western Wall in order to deepen the identification of the Muslim world with the struggle for Palestine, and to strengthen his position, both at home and abroad.

During this same year there were a growing number of confrontations between Haj Amin and the opposition and other groups in the Arab Executive, which contained approximately forty of the heads of the important families. It was widely accepted by the opposition that these disputes were primarily a result of Haj Amin's unrestrained ambitions. None of the leaders lacked personal ambition, but the struggle against the government showed the difference between the two sides. While Haj Amin supported a policy that reached – although never crossed – the threshold of violence, the opposition and leaders of the Arab Executive inclined toward a more moderate approach, and were prepared to compromise with the British. In response to criticism that he had used the national struggle to further his personal ambitions, Haj Amin stated that the two were identical, a claim which, in his mind, was perfectly legitimate. Referring to this criticism in his diary, he wrote, '... I have a share in a company, and each time the shares of the company rise, my profits ... increase as well'.[42]

If the 'company' was the Palestinian national movement, then the Arab Executive was its board of directors. At the end of 1929, the Executive discussed the composition of a delegation that was to go to London. Pro-Arab British circles believed that events in the recent past had led members of the government to doubt the possibility of continuing a pro-Zionist policy, and they encouraged the idea of dispatching a delegation to London.[43] The aim of the delegation was to exploit this sympathy to the Arab cause, and foil the efforts of Zionist leaders in Britain.

The extent to which Haj Amin's position had been strengthened as a result of the events of the immediate past is illustrated by his success in overcoming Musa Kazim during the Executive's discussions about the delegation. From the beginning of the 1920s, Musa Kazim had always led the delegations that the Executive had sent abroad. Now, in a decision taken on 9 January 1930, he was actually excluded from the delegation. This was a result of the stratagem successfully adopted by Haj Amin to openly oppose the Executive's president, and in fact Haj Amin almost managed to capture his office. A few days later, however, the Executive was forced to reverse its decision when Musa Kazim's supporters formed a coalition with the opposition, and Musa Kazim was appointed as head of the delegation.[44] The other members of the delegation were Haj Amin, Raghib al-Nashashibi, Jamal al-Husayni, 'Awni 'Abd al-Hadi and Alfred Rok.

Musa Kazim was supported by the Nashashibis and associated with their moderate line; Haj Amin's supporters were therefore concerned that the delegation would agree to far-reaching concessions. Accordingly, they made him pledge not to back down from the demand for the establishment of representative national institutions in Palestine.

The delegation arrived in London on 21 March 1930, at the same time that the Shaw Commission published its report recommending the establishment of an independent government in Palestine. In the course of talks with British Government leaders, including the Prime Minister and Colonial Secretary, it became apparent that the British were prepared to accommodate the delegation's demands regarding immigration and land. Haj Amin and his supporters remained firm, however, over the demand for a 'national government', a demand to which the British Government could not agree. As a result, the negotiations reached an impasse,[45] and, at the beginning of June, the delegation returned home.

At this time, the British Government would have been prepared to acquiesce to some of the Arab demands. However, as with the rejection in 1922–23 of the proposal to set up a legislative council, Haj Amin's rejectionist position once again determined the course of events. With the aid of Alfred Rok and Jamal al-Husayni, he overcame Musa Kazim and his supporters in the delegation. Haj Amin was also helped by the extremist mood then prevalent among wide sections of the Palestinian public. Many believed there was no longer anything to be gained by hoping for a change in the British position, and that the Palestinian Arabs should seek support from the Arab and Muslim worlds in their struggle.[46] The

25

events of the next few days showed the signs of this belief, and of the internal struggle for positions of power.

THE 1931 ISLAMIC CONGRESS IN JERUSALEM

After the return of the delegation from London, Haj Amin devoted himself to increasing Muslim support for the Palestinian issue, and to institutionalising that support in an organisational framework. With this purpose in mind, he planned a general Islamic congress, an event that was likely to raise his status even higher, making him a pan-Muslim leader.

The idea for a congress, which arose during a meeting of Muslim leaders in Jerusalem in mid-1931, was a result of British reluctance to implement the pro-Arab recommendations of the committees which had visited the country following the 1929 disturbances. When it finally became clear that the British Government was not going to carry out the recommendations contained in the various reports (the Shaw Commission, the Hope Simpson recommendations, and the 1930 White Paper) these Muslim leaders decided to turn to the heads of the Muslim states and demand aid for the safeguarding of the Islamic holy sites and the preservation of Palestine's Arab character. Haj Amin's Islamic congress initiative was a continuation of this appeal. In an effort to ensure that the congress would encompass the large Muslim communities, Haj Amin enlisted the help of two influential and wealthy individuals – 'Abd al-'Aziz al-Tha'alibi, the Tunisian Muslim leader, and Shawkat 'Ali, one of the leaders of the Muslims of India. Through their influence, many in the Muslim world expressed a readiness to come to Jerusalem. At the beginning of September 1931, the preparatory committee issued a notice about the congress, and immediately afterwards invitations signed by Haj Amin were dispatched. It is interesting to note that on the invitations Haj Amin added to his title, 'President of the Supreme Muslim Council', the words 'Mufti of the Holy Land' (*Mufti al-Diyar al-Qudsiyyah*).[47]

The initial intention of the organisers was that official representatives of the Muslim states would participate in the congress. However, members of some of the Arab governments feared that Haj Amin and the other organisers planned to go beyond their declared aims, namely defence of the holy sites, the establishment of a university in Jerusalem, and the restoration of the Hejaz railway. The Muslim rulers especially feared that the congress

26

would attempt to revive the institution of the Muslim caliphate that had been abolished in 1924.

Before taking measures to dispel these suspicions, Haj Amin had to deal with a problem closer to home. The Mandatory government feared that the congress would stir up nationalist feeling among the country's Arab population; the government in London was anxious lest the congress harm diplomatic relations with those countries which objected to it being held. With all this in mind, the authorities considered withholding entry permits from foreign Muslims. Haj Amin assured the High Commissioner, Sir Arthur Wauchope, that the congress would not discuss any subjects that could embarrass the British authorities.[48]

Haj Amin's rivals among the Nashashibi and Khalidi families looked on with alarm at his growing strength, and predicted, correctly, that Haj Amin would use the congress to increase his prestige. They rejected the idea of the congress, claiming that Haj Amin and his supporters did not have the right to represent the whole Muslim population of the country. Shawkat 'Ali and another Muslim activist, the Egyptian 'Abd al-Hamid Sa'id, tried to bring about a reconciliation, but without success. As a result, the opposition held a rival Muslim congress at the King David Hotel in Jerusalem, the Congress of the Palestine Islamic Nation (*Mu'tamar al-'Umma al-Islamiyyah al-Filastiniyyah*), with the participation of hundreds of Muslims from throughout the country. The Congress was headed by Raghib al-Nashashibi, along with Fakhri al-Nashashibi, As'ad al-Shuqairy, and 'Umar al-Salih al-Barghuthy.[49] Haj Amin's colleagues on the preparatory committee were not pleased by this rival congress. Figures such as Shawkat 'Ali attributed the split in the Palestinian camp to Haj Amin's uncompromising character, and took a dim view of his egocentric behaviour.[50]

A number of governments also viewed the Islamic congress with displeasure. The attempt to bring the deposed Turkish sultan, 'Abd al-Majid (who was in exile in France), to the congress was seen by the new Republic of Turkey as a move to revive the caliphate, and it objected to this vehemently. The declaration made by Shawkat 'Ali in an interview, that he saw this same sultan as the caliph of the Muslims, was hardly calculated to assuage this fear. The Egyptians reacted with hostility to the idea of reviving the caliphate in this manner, as King Fu'ad saw himself as a candidate for the position. Additional Egyptian opposition to the congress came from the heads of *al-Azhar*, who feared the estab-

27

lishment of a rival Islamic university in Jerusalem. Haj Amin rushed to Egypt in order to reassure the Egyptians. He assured them that the issue of the caliphate would not be discussed at the congress, and that the proposal for an Islamic university was in no way directed against *al-Azhar*, but rather against the Hebrew University in Jerusalem.[51]

These were not the only difficulties that stood in the way of the congress. Saudi Arabia saw itself as a contender for the leadership of the Muslim world. King Husayn's sons – Abdullah, Faisal, and 'Ali – demanded assurances that no decisions would be made at the congress that could block their future claim to the caliphate. Haj Amin travelled to Amman in order to persuade them that, despite remarks made during the preparatory stages of the congress, the issue of the caliphate would not be discussed.

Haj Amin did not, however, succeed in gaining the confidence of the Arab states, and the congress opened, on 7 December 1931, in the absence of their official representatives. Nevertheless, it was an impressive occasion, attended by Muslim figures from twenty-two countries, including Rashid Rida and 'Abd al-Rahman Azzam of Egypt, Shukri al-Quwwatli of Syria, and Muslim figures from Lebanon, Tunis, Morocco, India, and Iran. Haj Amin opened the congress with a long political speech. He kept the promise that he had made to the British not to speak out against them, and concentrated on the danger that 'the establishment of a Zionist national home on the holy Muslim Arab land' presented to the Islamic holy places and to Arab Palestine.[52]

Haj Amin was very active in the plenary during the ten days of discussions, especially in the sub-committees, in an effort to neutralise his opponents, carry through decisions favourable to him, and turn the congress into a permanent body with him at its head. The discussions came to an end on 17 December 1931. The resolutions passed included the convening of the congress every two years; the establishment of the University of al-Masjid al-Aqsa; a commitment to keep *al-Buraq* in Muslim hands; and the establishment of an institution for Islamic education, a company to save land and protect the *fallahun*, and branches of the congress in Muslim countries.[53] The congress elected an executive, and chose Haj Amin as its permanent president.

To judge by the implementation of its decisions, the congress was a failure. The attempt to raise funds for the protection of land was unsuccessful. The planned Islamic university in Jerusalem never materialised due to lack of funds, and the congress never reconvened in its original format. From Haj Amin's point of view, however, the congress was a success. First, he had managed to direct the attention of the congress to the Palestinian issue, despite Shawkat 'Ali's attempts to focus on general Islamic issues. Second, he had gained the upper hand in his struggle with the Nashashibi–Khalidi opposition. Third, despite the many difficulties involved, he had succeeded in manoeuvring the congress away from any resolutions that would endanger his relations with the British authorities. Most importantly, he had deepened his contacts with figures throughout the Muslim world, and intensified their involvement in the Palestinian cause.

Despite the differences of opinion that existed between Haj Amin and the Muslim leaders from India, the latter were, in fact, the only group from abroad to carry out the decision to establish branches of the congress in Muslim countries. The official organ of the Supreme Muslim Council announced that such a branch had been set up in India in March 1932. At its founding conference, the branch called on the Mandatory government to 'grant the residents of Palestine the right to establish a free government composed of Muslim and Christian Arabs'.[54] The Islamic congress also led to local branches being set up in the Arab settlements of Palestine. A conference of the heads of these branches was held in Jerusalem in August 1932, and the head of the Islamic Congress Office, Diya' al-Din al-Tabataba'i (the one-time Prime Minister of Iran), informed those assembled of the intention to establish the *Jam'iyyat al-Masjid al-Aqsa* university.[55]

Haj Amin now held three offices and bore three titles: The Grand Mufti, President of the Supreme Muslim Council, and President of the General Islamic Congress. Although this last office had no real, day-to-day, substance, it did give its holder the status of a central personality in both the Muslim world and the international arena. Haj Amin later exploited this status in Middle Eastern politics, including during his stay in Europe at the time of the Second World War. In his struggle within the Palestinian camp, however, it brought him immediate benefit; although the rivalry did not cease, Haj Amin's supremacy was an established fact.

EXTREMISM IN THE PALESTINIAN CAMP

The early 1930s were heavily influenced in a number of areas by the events of the late 1920s. The failure of the Arab Executive's efforts to change British policy in Palestine damaged its prestige and hastened its decline. At the same time, and as a result of this process, Haj Amin's standing increased, as did that of the Supreme Muslim Council. Disappointment with the attempt to influence the British by political means prepared the ground for the evolution of militant, non-establishment organisations which were to influence the course of future events. Within the Palestinian-Husayni leadership, the inclination to look to the Arab states for support became stronger, and a process began which was to broaden the scope of the Jewish–Arab conflict.

The events of that period also had far-reaching influence on the Jewish Yishuv. The Jews organised the defence of their settlements, to a certain extent with the assistance of the authorities. Zionist movements and non-Zionist Jews throughout the world reached a consensus over the issue of Palestine, resulting, among other things, in the establishment of the extended Jewish Agency in 1929.

Among the country's Arab population, especially in the provincial towns, the Arab Executive, headed by Musa Kazim, symbolised the failure of the political option. Although Haj Amin had participated in the political moves in 1930 and had not given in to pressures to discontinue his cooperation with the authorities, he was not held to blame. In the public consciousness, he was seen as representing the militant line. Members of the Arab Executive faced criticism from the general public for having chosen to lobby the British, and they were condemned for having abandoned armed organisation.

When it became clear that the British Government intended to ignore the recommendations to modify its policy, and that it indeed seemed likely to continue its support of the idea of a Jewish national home, tempers flared in the country's Arab community. An accusing finger was pointed at those leaders considered moderate. On 31 June 1931, the National Arab Society (*al-Jami'ah al-'Arabiyyah al-Wataniyyah*) in Nablus, which took the place of a Muslim–Christian Society in the town, called for an emergency conference. The idea was initiated by 'Izzat Darwaza and, according to Haj Amin's newspaper, this was the first time that a national political conference had been called by a body other than the Arab Executive.[56] The conference demanded the setting up of a defence organisation and the acquisition of weapons in view of the assistance that the British were extending to Jewish defence measures. The policy of the Arab Executive was denounced by some of the speakers, particularly the younger ones, and the established leadership was criticised for its helplessness. The most serious accusation related to the struggle against the sale of land to Jews. Certain of the leaders of the campaign, it was claimed, could not resist the temptation to make money, and were themselves involved in land sales. Such rumours had long been widespread among the public, and later received confirmation in the report of Lewis French, who headed a development project that had been established in accordance with the recommendations of the 1930 White Paper. French's report included the following:

> References are made from time to time in the Arab press to the part played by some members of the Supreme Muslim Council or Arab Executive in sales by Arabs to Jews; from which it is not unfair to infer that in some leading Arab quarters such disposals of surplus lands are viewed with no disfavour.[57]

When this was revealed to the public, it caused a major storm.

Although a number of veteran activists, such as Sabri 'Abidin of Hebron, were present at the Nablus conference, it was Haj Amin's younger supporters who set its mood. At the close of the conference, a decision was taken to demand that the authorities arm the villages and Arab tribes to the same extent that they were arming the Jewish settlements. The established leaders, members of the Arab Executive whose power was declining, were quick to join the wave of extremism. At the end of August, a few of them, including Jamal al-Husayni, led a demonstration to Government House. A fight broke out, leading to the arrest of a large number of the younger members of the National Arab Society, some of whom received prison sentences.[58]

The stream of Jewish immigrants from Europe increased at the beginning of the 1930s, adding momentum to the activity of the country's Arabs against the government. Extreme elements demanded that the Arab Executive pursue a policy of non-cooperation with the government, including the resignation of Arab mayors and the president of the Supreme Muslim Council. It did not escape Haj Amin's attention that members of the extreme *Hizb al-Istiqlal* (Independent Party) had aligned themselves with his rivals among the Nashashibi family in the campaign for resignations. Accordingly, he dismissed the demand for his resignation, claiming that he was serving the nation by remaining in his powerful office, and that his resignation would be counter to the

31

national interests.[59] At a number of conferences held at the beginning of the 1930s, including those of the Arab Youth Congress (*Mu'tamar al-Shabab al-'Arabi*), discussions on the severing of contacts with the British authorities, the resignation of public office-holders, and civil disobedience continued. The national conference held in Jaffa in March 1933, known by the Arabs as the Non-Cooperation Congress (*Mu'tamar al-Lata'awun*), was the high point of the propaganda campaign organised by the Arab Executive. However, the decisions that were taken at the conference regarding non-cooperation with the government were never implemented. The primary reason for this was the stand taken by Haj Amin. His address to the conference included the following statement:

> I am no stranger in this nationalist movement ... I became immersed in the nationalist movement before the war, and I have been active in it ever since. Were I a clerk, as some think, I would not be among you now. Were I a clerk, I would not have taken upon myself the burden of the nationalist movement from start to finish, nor would I now be judged and sentenced because of the national predicament ... Were the country to benefit from my resignation, then the issue of resignation would be a simple matter. And if the day comes when my resignation will be of benefit, I will have no difficulty in submitting it. At such a time I will not only resign from the office, but from life as well ... since man's fate is decreed, whereas principles and the land are eternal.[60]

At the conference, Haj Amin candidly presented his opposition to civil disobedience and resignations, while his rivals came out enthusiastically in support of measures against the government, without believing that they had the capability actually to carry them out. The gap between word and deed left the Palestinian political public with a sense of gloom. In October 1933, however, the national mood rose again. Under pressure from members of the *al-Istiqlal* party and groups of militant youngsters, the Arab Executive called for demonstrations against the government in Jerusalem, Jaffa and other towns. The demonstrations led to clashes with the British security forces, and a number of demonstrators were injured. Haj Amin was spared having to face a difficult dilemma, since he was in India at the time, heading a delegation of the General Islamic Congress.

The demonstrations reunited the rival factions. At the sight of the demonstrators, frustration gave way to fervour among the masses that had gathered from all over the country. They marched in the streets, with the aged Musa Kazim and other dignitaries in the front ranks. The unity, however, was only temporary. The Palestinian camp was shaken in 1934 by two events that restored the hostility between the rival factions: the death of Musa Kazim, chairman of the Arab Executive Committee; and the local municipal elections.

Musa Kazim al-Husayni died in March 1934. For many years he had adopted political positions similar to those of the opposition, and from time to time relations with his relative, Haj Amin, had been tense. Despite this, Haj Amin had avoided severing contact with his old and distinguished relative. When he died, Haj Amin strove to secure the vacant office for one of his close supporters, Jamal al-Husayni, who for years had managed the office of the Arab Executive. In the meantime, Musa Kazim's position was filled by the vice-chairman of the Arab Executive Committee, Ya'qub Farraj, who was identified with the opposition Nashashibi faction. In order to elect a permanent chairman, a meeting of the eighth National Conference had to be called. The Nashashibis objected to the conference being held, thereby preventing the election of Jamal al-Husayni as permanent chairman of the Executive. All this happened before the local municipal elections. When the date for the local elections approached, tempers rose, the rift between the factions widened, and the Executive all but disappeared from the political map.

Haj Amin now sought to remove the head of the rival faction, Raghib al-Nashashibi, from the position of power which he had held for fourteen years as mayor of Jerusalem. This was the goal that Haj Amin set himself for the 1934 local municipal elections. Since the relative strengths of the parties in the city could not ensure a victory for the Husaynis, Haj Amin became reconciled with Dr Husayn al-Khalidi, whose family held the balance of power between the two principal rival families. (Although Jews constituted a majority of the city's population, some held foreign citizenship and thus did not possess voting rights.) The Husayni–Khalidi coalition won the election, and Dr Husayn al-Khalidi was appointed mayor by the government. In a number of other towns (for example, Lydda, Jericho, Majdal, Tulkarm, Beit Shean and Beersheba), Husayni candidates also won the mayoral elections.[61] After his election, however, the new mayor of Jerusalem adopted a neutral position towards the rival factions. By concentrating most of his efforts on municipal affairs, al-Khalidi ended the political significance that the office of mayor had always possessed.

The political vacuum left by the demise of the Arab Executive Committee on the one hand, and the de-politicisation of the municipality on the other, was later filled by the emergence of new political parties. In addition to the *al-Istiqlal* party, founded on 4 August 1932, the National Defence Party (*Hizb al-Difa al-Watani*) was founded at the end of 1934, the Palestine Arab Party (*al-Hizb al-'Arabi al-Filastini*) in March 1935, the Reform Party (*Hizb al-Isla'ah*) in June 1935, and the National Bloc Party (*Hizb al-Kutlah al-Wataniyyah*) in October 1935.

The appearance of these parties in the middle of the 1930s was an expression of the changes taking place in the Palestinian arena at that time for:

1. with the death of Musa Kazim, nothing remained to hold the Husayni and Nashashibi factions together;
2. the inflexible personality of Haj Amin (the only remaining Husayni leader of substance) increased the polarisation;
3. the allegiance between the al-Khalidi and Husayni families during the municipal elections further increased the rifts within the ranks of the opposition;
4. losing the office of mayoralty of Jerusalem weakened Raghib al-Nashashibi's status, and damaged his ability to lead the opposition faction.

Despite the fierce rivalry which divided the factions, as long as the Executive continued to exist it was possible to display, at least outwardly, a sense of national unity under Husayni hegemony. However, when the leaders of the Nashashibi opposition dismantled the national framework by founding the National Defence Party, Haj Amin was compelled to meet the challenge and set up his own party, the Palestine Arab Party.

The opposition might have posed a realistic threat to Haj Amin's leadership had it preserved a measure of unity. Instead, it split into three separate parties (in addition to the *al-Istiqlal* and Youth Congress parties), in contrast to the single party of Haj Amin and his ally, Jamal al-Husayni. Although all the parties had in common a hostility to Zionism, each was unique. The *al-Istiqlal* party evolved as a result of the disgust felt by political activists and academics from outside Jerusalem at the incessant rivalry between the leading Jerusalem families. It was hostile toward the British and toward imperialism, attacked both the established leadership

34

and Haj Amin for their connections with the British, and called for a policy of non-cooperation (non-payment of taxes) with the Mandatory government. The party was pan-Arab in ideology, and sought the liberation of all the Arab countries from foreign rule. It persisted in regarding Palestine as 'Southern Syria', and in general did not cooperate with either the party headed by the Husaynis or the parties established by the Nashashibi–Khalidi opposition.

The National Defence Party was founded by the Nashashibis in December 1934, in the shadow of the rift with the Khalidis and the defeat of their leader, Raghib al-Nashashibi, in the Jerusalem municipal elections. The party fought Haj Amin, and spoke out in favour of an independent Palestine which was to be achieved through cooperation with the British authorities; when the Nashashibis declared a policy of non-cooperation they did so as a tactical move against Haj Amin. The party rejected the pan-Arab idea, and was prepared to compromise with the British Government over its demands. In the initial period after its founding, the party also had a cordial approach to the institutions of the Jewish Yishuv. Favourable relations were also established with the ruler of Transjordan, Amir Abdullah.

As mentioned earlier, the Palestine Arab Party was set up by the Husaynis after the Nashashibis had taken the initiative by founding their own party. The Husaynis had refrained from such a move until then because they saw themselves as leading all the country's Arab population. In its manifesto, the new party stressed its demand for full independence in Palestine, its total rejection of Jewish rights to Palestine, and its attachment to the idea of pan-Arabism.

The ruling force in the Reform Party was the Khalidi family. The mayors of Ramallah, Bethlehem, Acre, and Gaza, and other figures in the opposition camp were also active. Despite its anti-Zionist, pan-Arab nationalist manifesto, the party in practice adopted a moderate line. Like the Nashashibi party, it also inclined toward a dialogue with Abdullah.

The National Bloc Party was also founded by a member of the opposition, 'Abd al-Latif Sala'ah, of Nablus. This party did not stand for pan-Arabism, and pursued a moderate policy in its dealings with the Mandatory government. Its principal base of support was, and remained, Nablus and its surroundings.[62]

Mention must also be made here of the Youth Congress Party. Originally established in January 1932 as a non-party organisation, it later became a political party in the fullest sense. Its first leader was Rasim al-Khalidi, who was later replaced by Ya'qub al-Ghusayn. The party was pan-Arab in ideology, and pressed for an extreme anti-government position. In the summer of 1935, its activities broadened. Branches were set up throughout the country, and its members took an active part in the clashes with the Jewish population.

In the mid-1930s, Haj Amin increased his anti-Zionist activity, while at the same time continuing negotiations with the British in the hope of persuading them to alter their policy toward Palestine. However, a series of events which took place at this time led him, unavoidably, toward confrontation.

THE DEEPENING OF THE JEWISH–ARAB CONFLICT

The increase in Jewish immigration at the beginning of the 1930s was the principal cause of the rise in tension among the Palestinian Arabs. Between 1933 and 1935, 134,500 Jews immigrated with the approval of the authorities, and many thousands of others arrived illegally. As a result, the percentage of Jews in the population increased from 17 per cent in 1931 to almost 30 per cent in 1935.[63] The Arabs were taken aback by this huge influx. The media's exaggerated reports of the number of immigrants led to fears that the Jewish population of the country would soon become the majority.[64] It was the illegal immigration which particularly alarmed the Arabs, since, in the absence of exact figures, there were wild rumours of its extent. 'The day is not far off when the Zionists will succeed in wiping out any trace of the Arabs from the country', wrote one newspaper. 'Will the establishment of the Jewish national home end when the number of Jews in Palestine reaches 500,000, a million ... or ten million, or ... after the Jews have purchased every piece of land in Palestine, Transjordan and, afterwards, Syria and Iraq?', asked another.[65]

This period was characterised by a new awareness of the conflict among the Arab masses. The problem of the 'Zionist invasion' was no longer an abstract issue restricted to the press and radio. The European dress of the newly arrived Jewish immigrants could already be seen in every part of the country. Moreover, the mass immigration brought about an acceleration in land acquisition, and an increase in the demand for places of employment for Jewish labourers. Disputes with villagers over land, and with Arab labourers over 'Hebrew labour', became much more common.

There was an increase in the number of incidents involving new settlers and Arab *fallahun* – usually caused by land disputes, and by the fact that Jewish labourers were 'taking away' work from Arab labourers.[66] The illegal immigration also became a focus for clashes. Arab leaders held the authorities to blame for allowing these immigrants in. The Youth Congress, headed by Yaq'ub al-Ghusayn, decided to act by itself. It set up a watch along the Netanya coast, manned by its members, in order to prevent the disembarking of new illegal Jewish immigrants. The attempt did not last very long, however. It was stopped after fights broke out between members of the party and Jewish youngsters.[67]

These incidents heightened the agitation and frustration among widespread parts of the Palestinian Arab community, and increased sympathy toward the militant groups. Since the end of the 1920s, these groups had been organising with the aim of attacking Jews and the British in different parts of the country. This organisation began in the hilly areas away from the centres of government, and included the Safed band, known as the 'Green Hand', headed by Ahmad Tafish and the 'Black Hand' led by Shaikh 'Izz al-Din al-Qassam.[68]

More than any other individual at the time, it was al-Qassam who contributed to the process which was to lead Haj Amin and the Palestinian leadership into confrontation with the British. Born in 1871 in the town of Jabla near Ladhikiyyah in Syria, al-Qassam was a pupil of Muhammad 'Abduh at *al-Azhar*. On his return to Syria, he founded an academy in the *al-Sultan Ibrahim* mosque in his home town. In 1920, he joined the 'Alawi revolt against the French. The authorities tried to court favour with him by offering him the office of *qadi*, but he refused. He was sentenced to death, but, on 5 February 1922, escaped with two others to Haifa. He joined the Young Men's Muslim Association, whose most prominent figure was Rashid al-Haj Ibrahim, and became its leader. He later founded the secret society known as the 'Qassamites'. After his death, his followers were known as *Ikhwan al-Qassam*.[69]

From the beginning of the 1930s, the Qassamites and other armed gangs carried out a series of violent operations in various parts of the country. Jews were murdered, railway lines sabotaged, trees uprooted, and fields set on fire. These developments, over which Haj Amin had no control, caused him some anxiety, although they won the sympathy and support of the *al-Istiqlal* party. Al-Qassam himself spoke out, both in the party's club and at the al-

Nasir mosque in Haifa, against the moderate line of the traditional leadership. On a number of occasions he asked Haj Amin to appoint him as an itinerant propagandist so that he could incite rebellion throughout the country. During the course of 1935 he sent his emissary, Mahmud Salim (known as Abu Ahmad al-Qassam), to Haj Amin with a proposal to begin preparations for the revolt. He proposed that Haj Amin should lead the revolt in the south of the country, while he did the same in the north. Haj Amin replied that the time for such action had not arrived, and that political measures were sufficient to secure Arab rights in Palestine.[70] Indeed, during 1934–35, Haj Amin's political contacts with the British authorities continued, and he feared any development which might jeopardise them.

Al-Qassam, however, did not accept his argument. Along with ten of his companions, he armed himself, and at the beginning of November 1935 set off for the hills of northern Samaria. The gang succeeded in killing a Jewish sergeant named Rosenfeld before being surrounded, on 20 November, by a British police force in the Jenin area. The gang refused to surrender, and the police opened fire, killing al-Qassam and three of his men.[71] Al-Qassam's funeral turned into a mass political demonstration. The Arab press was full of descriptions of the shaikh's heroism, and his name became a symbol of the national struggle and of self-sacrifice.[72] During his lifetime, al-Qassam had been known only in the northern area in which he was active, and his influence on national events had been marginal. However, the circumstances of his death – a battle with the British – were to have a far-reaching influence on the morale of the country's Arabs, and lead to greater extremism in their national struggle. After al-Qassam's death, the gang led by Shaikh Farhan al-Sa'adi, continued to operate in the area of Samaria, following in the tradition of al-Qassam's doctrine. During the course of 1931, 'Abd al-Qadir al-Husayni, the son of Musa Kazim, organised a group of youngsters from the Jerusalem area to prepare themselves for armed struggle. This group called itself the al-Jihad al-Muqaddas (Holy War). It purchased arms and carried out military exercises. In the following three years the organisation broadened its ranks, but maintained strict secrecy. Its leaders only revealed the fact of its existence to Haj Amin al-Husayni in the summer of 1934. He gave them his blessing and, at a later stage, secretly became their leader. Al-Jihad al-Muqaddas was active in the events of 1936–39, until the British army put down the revolt. 'Abd al-Qadir and Haj Amin became very close, and in the following years they spent time together in both Iraq and Nazi Germany. With the outbreak of hostilities at the end of 1947, the units that Haj Amin had established in order to fight the partition plan bore the same name, *al-Jihad al-Muqaddas*, and 'Abd al-Qadir al-Husayni returned as commander.[73] Other armed groups, although smaller in size, were organised in Nablus and Tulkarm, usually at the initiative of leaders of the *al-Istiqlal* party and local leaders of the Young Men's Muslim Association and Youth Congress.

A short time before the death of 'Izz al-Din al-Qassam, a large shipment of arms was discovered at Jaffa port. It had been sent from Belgium, disguised as barrels of cement, to a Jewish merchant (who was never traced) in Tel Aviv. The discovery of the weapons caused a great storm among the Palestinian public. At the same time, news arrived about anti-British strikes in Egypt and a general strike in Syria in support of the demand for independence. This combination of events aroused the radical younger elements, as well as some members of the *al-Istiqlal* party, to a pitch of feeling that threatened to engulf the whole country.

Haj Amin faced a dilemma: how, on the one hand, to maintain his image as a militant leader in the eyes of the youngsters and the various radical groups, while on the other to continue to utilise his positive relationship with the Mandatory government. He met frequently with the High Commissioner, who on his part pressed London to accommodate the Arab demands. Nevertheless, support for the radicals strengthened among the general public and in the local press. These demanded that the parties break off their contacts with the government, put an end to internal factionalism, and work as a united front in the struggle against the British.

Under pressure from these developments and from delegations that arrived in Jerusalem from other parts of the country, representatives of the five parties (excluding the *al-Istiqlal* party) met in the second half of October 1935 to decide on joint action.[74] The immediate cause of the meeting was the discovery of the Jewish shipment of weapons at Jaffa port. The delegates delivered a joint protest to the High Commissioner, Wauchope, and called for a general strike. Another step aimed at unifying the parties was undertaken a few days after Shaikh al-Qassam's stormy funeral in Haifa. On 25 November, the five parties submitted a memorandum to the High Commissioner that included three demands – the creation of independent government institutions, the cessation of Jewish immigration, and the prohibition of the transfer of Arab

39

land to Jews. The leaders of the parties emphasised that they would be unable to restrain the people if their demands were not met.

The undertaking given by the British Government in the 1930 White Paper to establish a legislative council was still on the agenda during the first half of the 1930s. The British authorities in both London and Jerusalem put forward different ideas for such a council, in an attempt to assuage the tension with the Arabs. The opposition parties inclined toward a compromise with the government, whereas the Palestine Arab Party and, at times, the Youth Congress party continued, despite internal arguments, to reject any proposal that did not meet their maximalist demands. The Jewish response to the proposal for a legislative council was totally negative, and hardened even further following the persecution of Jews in Nazi Germany.

The proposal for a legislative council was debated, and rejected, in both the House of Lords and the House of Commons in London in February and March 1936. The High Commissioner's efforts to honour the commitment to establish the council came to nothing. As an alternative, the Colonial Secretary invited the representatives of the Palestinian parties to come to London for negotiations on 2 April 1936.[75]

The contacts between Haj Amin and the High Commissioner continued throughout this period. When it became clear that the Jews would not even agree to the formation of a parity council, Haj Amin was inclined to make his position more flexible, in an attempt to force the government to reach an agreement with the Arabs alone. Although there was little chance of him succeeding, this did allow him to demonstrate a greater degree of moderation toward the British, and even to seek to prevent a deterioration in the situation. However, the attacks on Jews in mid-April in the Tulkarm area, and later in Jaffa, led to the outbreak of the general strike. The timing of these acts of violence suggests that militant groups may have decided to put an end to their leaders' contacts with the British, thus forcing them to choose the option of armed struggle. Haj Amin still preferred not to adopt this option openly, and contacts among the Palestinian Arabs continued concerning the composition of the delegation which was to travel to London. However, against the background of the outbreak of violence at the end of April, a coalition of parties convened and informed the High Commissioner that it was pointless to dispatch a delegation in the prevailing circumstances.[76] A separate decision of the party

40

leaders called on the Arabs to persevere in the strike, while maintaining law and order. By this stage, however, there was nothing that could prevent the situation from deteriorating.

THE BEGINNING OF THE REVOLT

The activities of the radical groups, such as *al-Istiqlal* and the Young Men's Muslim Association, were centred in Nablus, where, on 19 April 1936, a conference of nationalist activists was held. The conference called for a general strike against the government, and decided to set up a National Committee. It also called on other towns to follow Nablus' lead and to 'declare a strike until the nationalist demands are met, or at least until Jewish immigration is totally halted'.[77] A few days before the conference in Nablus, an armed Arab group murdered two Jews in the Tulkarm area, and on the following day two Arabs were murdered close to Yarkona. Three days later, an inflamed Arab mob attacked Jews in Jaffa, killing nine and wounding fifty-seven.[78]

This violence formed the background to the national conference in Nablus, and during the following days the same drama was played out in other towns. A study of the related sources reveals that these developments took Haj Amin and the other party leaders, with the exception of the leaders of the *al-Istiqlal* party, by surprise. Haj Amin tried to halt this process while it was still possible. On the evening of 19 April he was summoned to the High Commissioner, to whom he expressed his hope that peace would be restored, and that the party leaders would still succeed in forming the delegation that was to set out for London.[79] In response to the appeal from Nablus, the shaikhs of the Negev Bedouin tribes met in Beersheba on 20 April. The participants sensed the lack of clarity in the positions of the party leaders, and telephoned Haj Amin in Jerusalem to ask him how to proceed. He avoided giving a clear reply, stated that a final decision had not yet been made on the political line, and advised that each individual decide for himself which should be the best course of action to adopt.[80]

In the six days following the strike declaration in Nablus, the party leaders had still not agreed on a coordinated response to events. At this stage, Rashid al-Haj Ibrahim, one of the leaders of the *al-Istiqlal* party in Haifa, came to Jerusalem with three other local leaders to demand the establishment of a high committee, comprised of representatives of the six parties, which would lead

41

the strike and the struggle.[81] Haj Amin tried to avoid membership in the proposed committee, in order to prevent a breach with the authorities. However, Raghib al-Nashashibi insisted that Haj Amin become its head, which meant that his nationalism, which even at this stage he sought to hide from the British,[82] would be revealed. Eventually, the Arab Higher Committee (*al-Lajnah al-'Arabiyyah al-'Ulia*) was established. It was composed of ten members, including the leaders of the six parties and representatives of the Christians. Haj Amin was elected president. On 25 April, the new committee published an announcement calling on the Palestinian Arabs to continue the strike until the government agreed to meet the three demands that had been presented to the High Commissioner five months previously.

Now, as in 1933, members of the *al-Istiqlal* party and the Nashashibis – each for their own reasons – had sought to bring Haj Amin to oppose the government. The establishment of the Arab Higher Committee marked the achievement of this aim. On 7 May 1936, at the conference of the National Committees attended by the Arab Higher Committee, Haj Amin gave an impassioned speech. He addressed a call to the Arabs and to Muslims throughout the world to extend assistance to Palestine, 'so that it will not turn into a second Andalusia'. Although the address was characterised by anti-Jewish incitement, there was also a marked effort to prevent further confrontation with the British. Nevertheless, most of those at the conference were inspired with a spirit of radicalism, and it was this radicalism which prevailed and which was reflected in the decision to continue the strike and to stop the payment of taxes. Some delegates even called on Arab government employees to join the strike.[83]

The High Commissioner understood the difficult situation in which Haj Amin was now placed. Extreme groups, particularly the younger militant organisations, were pressuring him to step-up the struggle, as were the Nashashibis – the latter for reasons of their own. The High Commissioner faced a dilemma: to recommend that the British army intervene by force to put an end to the strike and the revolt, or to rely on Haj Amin's ability to prevent a deterioration in the situation and to try to moderate the extremists. For the time being, the High Commissioner chose the second option. On 11 May, he announced on the radio that severe measures would be taken if the strike and revolt continued. On 14 May, he met twice with leaders of the Arab Higher Committee in an attempt to resolve the situation. However, the radical organisations and younger elements swept the Palestinian public toward an exacerbation of the revolt. On 15 May, the Committee called on the public to carry out the decision taken at the conference of National Committees: continuation of the strike and the non-payment of taxes.[84]

Until the end of June, Haj Amin continually attempted to prevent an aggravation of the anti-government campaign. He directed the strike from behind the scenes and spoke publicly in favour of stepping up the struggle, but refrained from declaring a *jihad* (holy war). In the meantime, the government began to act: at the end of May, the police arrested dozens of Palestinian activists and issued orders restricting their movement. In June, a few of the leaders, including 'Awni 'Abd al-Hadi and 'Izzat Darwaza, were arrested and interned in the Sarafand military camp. At the same time, the Nashashibi opposition continued to pressure Haj Amin to break off his contacts with the government, or else be exposed as a collaborator. It did this by escalating activity against the British.[85] The opposition put additional pressure on Haj Amin, by demanding that the Supreme Muslim Council join the strike. Had Haj Amin acceded to this demand, he would have lost the position of strength which he had gained as the head of this powerful institution. To avoid being dismissed by the government, Haj Amin refrained from involving the Council in the strike. The opposition made much of his anomalous position: on the one hand, Haj Amin was president of the Arab Higher Committee, the body organising the strike, and on the other, he was president of the Supreme Muslim Council, which, by continuing to function, was breaking the strike. Nevertheless, Haj Amin possessed a personal authority which enabled him to override those who disagreed with him.

Six weeks into the strike, religious leaders associated with the Council began to speak out in its favour, and even encouraged villagers to join the revolt. A clear turnabout in the Council's attitude occurred at the end of June, when it came out in support of the nationalist struggle.[86] From what Haj Amin said and did during this period, it seems that he was still trying to avoid confrontations with the government. He explained to Musa al-'Almi that he objected to violence, 'because violence will not bring any positive results, and because in regard to violence the government is more powerful, and it will put us down since it has the power to do so'. Musa al-'Alami added that 'the Mufti conceived of a peaceful strike'.[87] This was not the whole truth. Haj Amin was interested in a violent struggle against the Jews in Palestine, and his colleagues on the Council and Committee were involved in agitation in this direction. The Mufti did, however, try to ensure that the struggle would remain under his control, and, at least until spring 1937, that it did not lead to clashes with the British security forces. He hoped, by virtue of his good relations with the High Commissioner, Wauchope, to continue the political pressure on the government in London, to prevent any massive military action by the British army, and to prevent the internal opposition from defeating him. Even the leaders of the Jewish Yishuv[88] took note of his efforts to prevent a further radicalisation of the situation.

Throughout the duration of the strike, a period of almost six months, Haj Amin was compelled to manoeuvre between contradictory constraints: the British put pressure on him to display a moderate line; the Arab extremists and the young militants demanded that he stand at the head of the armed revolt; the citrus growers and merchants demanded an end to the strike; and his principal rival, Raghib al-Nashashibi, strengthened his ties with Amir Abdullah, with the aim of creating sufficient problems for Haj Amin to cause him to lose his standing either with the British or with the radicals among the Palestinian Arabs. Yet, Haj Amin managed to steer a safe course between the contradictory demands. By virtue of his contacts with the High Commissioner, he appeared to the authorities to be the only guarantee for preventing an all-out war between the British army and the country's Arabs, and the last hope for reaching a settlement which would bring about a return to law and order. The radical and militant groups generally viewed him as the leader of the revolt, issuing orders for the continuation of the struggle from his stronghold in *al-Haram al-Sharif*. His rivals, meanwhile, regarded his talent for survival with impatience.

The strike ended on 10 October 1936, in response to an appeal from the leaders of the Arab states, formulated in conjunction with the Arab Higher Committee. This paved the way for the arrival of a royal commission, headed by Lord Peel, a month later. Until the end of December, Haj Amin adopted a hard-line approach, making his appearance before the commission contingent on a temporary halt in Jewish immigration. At the beginning of January, however, again at the instigation of the Arab states, the Committee decided to appear before the commission which, in turn, extended its stay in the country in order to collect evidence from the Arabs.

In the course of Haj Amin's evidence to the commission, in the context of his demand to establish an Arab government, the question of his attitude to the Jews arose. In her book, al-Hut includes the following extract from the evidence:

Lord Peel: Since you demand the establishment of a national government in Palestine, what will you do with the 400,000 Jews already living there?

Mufti: It will not be the first time that Jews have lived under the aegis of an Arab state. In the past it has been the Arab states which were the more compassionate to them. History shows that, during all periods, the Jews only found rest under the protection of Arab rulers. The East was always a shelter for Jews escaping from European pressure.

Lord Peel: You stated that the number of Jews has increased steeply, so that the number of Arabs, which during the time of the conquest was approximately 90% of the total population, has now dropped to 70%.

Mufti: That is correct.

Lord Peel: Notwithstanding this, if you reach agreement with the English, will you be prepared to allow the Jews to remain in the country?

Mufti: That is a matter for the government that will be formed to deal with at the appropriate time. Its principle will be justice, and above all else it will concern itself with the interests and benefit of the country.

Lord Peel: Do you think that the Jews will accept this declaration without receiving something more substantial? Such an oral declaration will not convince them.

Mufti: Jews living in the other Arab states currently enjoy freedoms and rights.

Lord Peel: I feel that I can safely assume what the Jews will have to say on this matter.[89]

A different extract from his evidence, which al-Hut omitted from her book, gives a clearer picture of Haj Amin's approach to the Jewish problem under Arab rule in Palestine:

Question: Does His Eminence think that this country can assimilate and digest the 400,000 Jews now in the country?

Answer: No.

Question: Some of them would have to be removed by a process kindly or painful as the case may be?

45

Answer: We must leave all this to the future.

Following the Mufti's evidence, the committee noted ironically:

> We are not questioning the sincerity or the humanity of the
> Mufti's intentions and those of his colleagues, but we cannot
> forget what recently happened, despite treaty provisions and
> explicit assurances, to the Assyrian minority in Iraq; nor can
> we forget that the hatred of the Arab politician for the
> National Home has never been concealed and that it has now
> permeated the Arab population as a whole.[90]

From the commission's report, it seems that its members did not
give much credence to the extent of Haj Amin's sincerity or
compassion. His refusal to provide guarantees for the safety of the
Jewish population in the event of the establishment of an Arab-
Palestinian state left a grave impression on the committee concerning the likely fate of the Jewish minority.

The Peel Commission's recommendations were published in
July 1937. Parts were leaked a few weeks before. Rumours were
rife that its members were of the opinion that the realisation of the
aims of the Mandate in its current form was an impossibility, and
that they therefore inclined toward partitioning the country between Jews and Arabs. This was indeed the principal recommendation of the commission, and, as expected, it caused a real
storm.

The Husayni leadership, along with most of the Palestinian
camp, rejected the idea of partition outright. Abdullah, who,
according to the plan, was to receive the Arab parts of Palestine,
saw the recommendation as an opportunity not to be missed.
Immediately following the publication of the recommendations,
the majority of the Nashashibi family's National Defence Party
supported the partition plan. However, when Haj Amin and his
supporters travelled around the country denouncing partition and
its supporters, the Nashashibi opposition suddenly fell silent.

The end of the summer of 1937 brought a radical change in the
course of events. The National Defence Party, which had with-
drawn from the Arab Higher Committee, lost much of its influence
among the Palestinian public. Its leader, Raghib al-Nashashibi,
lost his power base, and was no longer considered a serious threat
to Haj Amin. In the meantime, it became known that the government in London supported the Peel Commission's recommendations. As Haj Amin's field of manoeuvre rapidly decreased, he
gave up his efforts to persuade the British to alter their policy. It

became clear that he could no longer continue remaining neutral. From this point on he moved rapidly, severing his contacts with the authorities and clarifying his stance of unequivocal identification with the revolt which now threatened to break out anew.

THE REVOLT AT ITS HEIGHT

The prolonged strike created a sense of pride and power in the Palestinian camp. After one hundred days, it was described as 'one of the wonders of the world'.[91] When it finally ended in October, there was a feeling of a real victory, and the Arab press was full of praise for the leaders, fighters and masses.[92] There were two other sources of satisfaction at the time: a sense that the Palestinian issue was now the concern of the leaders of the Arab states, and the belief that the Royal Commission that had been appointed as a result of the strike and acts of violence would decide in favour of the Arabs.

When news arrived of the recommendation to partition Palestine, anger against the government flared up again, and the call was heard to renew the armed revolt. In mid-August, there were acts of violence against Jewish settlements and public transport. This time, however, unlike the previous period of the revolt, rival Arabs were also targets of attack.[93] The background to this was the rift within the Palestinian camp, which had deepened and now took the form of an armed struggle. Many members of the opposition were weary of the revolt and openly supported partition. In addition, discontent had spread, especially among the rural population, who suffered at the hands of local bands. The phenomenon of informers, which was to continue throughout the revolt, sprang from this resentment. Villagers and members of the opposition volunteered information to the authorities about the bands and their movements. In response, some commanders issued death sentences against informers, and the cycle of murders grew rapidly.[94]

Haj Amin felt that he was losing control of the revolt. From *al-Haram al-Sharif*, he tried to calm the situation, although most of his effort was expended on the attempt to mobilise the Arab world against the partition plan. He organised an all-Arab conference on 8–9 September 1937 in Baludan, Syria, which was attended by 400 delegates, including unofficial representatives from Arab countries and 124 Palestinian Arabs. The conference's chairman was Naji al-Suwaydi, the former Iraqi Prime Minister, and among those present were Muhammad 'Ali 'Alubah from Egypt, and Shakib Arslan and Riyad al-Sulh, members of the Syrian–Palestinian delegation to Geneva. Haj Amin did not attend the conference, since he was worried that the British might arrest him if he left the mosque to travel to Syria. In his absence, the delegates at Baludan elected him honorary president.[95] At the close of the conference, a decision was taken, as expected, to oppose partition and to enlist help from the Arab states in the Palestinian struggle.

During this conference, the belief still held that the British could be influenced by political pressure, and that the armed struggle could be limited to one against Jews and moderate Arabs. However, a short time later, on 26 September, Lewis Andrews, the Acting District Commissioner of the Galilee, was murdered in Nazareth.[96] The murder was carried out by members of the extreme Ikhwan al-Qassam band, under the command of Shaikh Farhan al-Sa'adi. This was the signal for the resumption of violence throughout the country. The Arab Higher Committee made another attempt to assuage British anger by issuing a condemnation of the murder, but the authorities ignored it.

On the day after the murder, scores of suspects and inciters were detained. On 30 September, the British Military Commander ordered the dissolution of the Arab Higher Committee and the arrest of its members. The National Committees were designated illegal organisations. Several members of the Arab Higher Committee – Ahmad Hilmi 'Abd al-Baqi, Dr Husayn al-Khalidi, Fu'ad Saba, Ya'qub al-Ghusayn, and Rashid al-Haj Ibrahim – were arrested and deported to the Seychelles islands. Jamal al-Husayni escaped to Lebanon.[97] Four other members of the Arab Higher Council who were abroad at the time were prohibited from returning, while Haj Amin remained in the sanctuary of *al-Haram al-Sharif*. In accordance with a military order, he was dismissed from his office as president of the Supreme Muslim Council.

Although officially he now retained only the title of Mufti (following the Ottoman practice, this had been granted for life), his authority as leader of the country's Arabs and head of the revolt had been strengthened. The entrances to *al-Haram al-Sharif* were guarded by police troops, but they did not dare violate the holy place by entering. From this sanctuary, Haj Amin maintained contact with the band leaders throughout the country and with the outside world. On 13 October, he succeeded in evading the police,

48

and made his way to Jaffa port disguised as a Bedouin. From there he was taken by his associates to Lebanon.[98]

After the arrest and deportation of so many leaders, the mosques in the Old City of Jerusalem would have been a convenient place from which Haj Amin could continue to lead the country's Arabs. His flight left the way clear for the leaders of the opposition. Why then did the Haj Amin flee? Perhaps because he felt that the liberty of action that he would enjoy abroad was more important than being close to the scene of events. He probably also feared that if the siege of *al-Haram al-Sharif* were to tighten, he would become a prisoner in the al-Aqsa mosque and be unable to operate further. It may also be true, as Haj Amin claims in his memoirs, that he discovered that the British had brought a Muslim army unit from India to break into the mosque and arrest him.[99]

In any case, even if Haj Amin had been doubtful about his escape, it became clear after the event that the decision to leave was a wise one from his point of view. The Arabs saw his escape as a successful evasion of the British enemy. His standing among the country's Arab population was so high that his rivals did not dare to try to take his place. All eyes were now on the Damascus-based Central Committee of the Jihad, and especially on Haj Amin, who was controlling events from the Lebanese town of Dhauq Mika'il.

The revolt flared up with greater violence at the end of 1937, and increased during the first half of 1938. Tolerated by the French, and out of reach of the British, Haj Amin could direct the gang leaders to extend their attacks to Jewish civilians and property, and to disrupt installations of the British military administration. All of this activity was carried out in accordance with orders that the local commanders received directly from Haj Amin, by means of the central committee in Damascus. These commanders had been operating independently in the different parts of the country since Fawzi al-Qawuqji had left in October 1936.[100]

The situation worsened in autumn 1938. Rail tracks were sabotaged, and trains stopped operating between towns. Police stations were closed after bands of rebels took over a number of them and stole large quantities of arms. In some of the Arab towns and rural areas, the rebels were in complete control, collecting taxes and establishing law courts which heard both political and civil matters. A situation ensued in which the British were compelled to recapture areas that had been taken over by the rebels. Military reinforcements were dispatched to the country, and on 18 October the army began to reconquer the Old City of Jerusalem. It was under army control again a few days later, and a Military Government was declared throughout the country. Army units continued their attacks in an attempt to drive out the bands and retrieve the areas which they had controlled. By the end of 1938, the army had overcome the rebels. Apart from *al-Haram al-Sharif*, which the British army refrained from entering, and a handful of places in the hills to which access was difficult, law and order had been restored throughout the country.

At the beginning of the revolt, the opposition, many of whose members supported the partition plan, looked on helplessly as Haj Amin's power grew, following the successful acts of hostility against the British and Jews. This was also true when the revolt was renewed after the publication of the report of the Peel Commission. However, as a result of the successes of the end of 1937 and the beginning of 1938, acts of punishment were carried out against members of the opposition. A civil war quickly developed, in which many on both sides were murdered.[101] These mutual acts of murder went beyond political differences of opinion to feuds and the settling of personal scores. Many of the murders were carried out in accordance with instructions from Haj Amin, or with his agreement. This situation especially worried Palestinian intellectuals. In Haifa, a group of young intellectuals initiated an appeal to Haj Amin, urging him to publish a *fatwa* (a legal opinion concerning the conformity of an action with Muslim law) or other order calling for an end to the acts of murder. They decided to send Dr 'Umar al-Khalil to meet Haj Amin in Lebanon, with a request that he issue a statement making it clear that the murder of an Arab by an Arab would be considered an unpardonable offence. Haj Amin received the emissary in the town of Dhauq Mika'il at the end of September 1938, but firmly rejected his appeal.[102]

END OF THE REVOLT

In the final period of the revolt, the bitterness of those in the towns and villages at the pressure exerted on them by the commanders of the gangs began to increase. The towns suffered because of the extortion of money and murder threats, and the villages, as well as sustaining damage to property and sources of livelihood, suffered the cruelty of the commanders. Opposition groups that had previously operated covertly against the revolt now openly opposed it.

They assisted the British army, and received arms from it to equip their own armed gangs, known as the 'peace bands'.

By the summer of 1939, the disintegration in the rebels' ranks was complete. The army, helped by members of the opposition, extended its control to the remote hilly areas. Those rebel commanders who did not manage to escape to neighbouring countries were caught and tried. From a military point of view, the revolt was a total failure. On the political plane the results were no better: the British refused to meet the demands set by Haj Amin as a condition for ending the revolt. Amir Abdullah's pro-British policy and his personal ambitions deepened the animosity between himself and Haj Amin, and intensified the competition between them for influence over the country's Arab population.

Nevertheless, the revolt had a far-reaching effect on the events of the following years. In practice, the British Government abandoned its partition plan. In April 1938, a committee headed by Sir John Woodhead arrived in the country and reported on the obstacles preventing the implementation of the plan. The committee was boycotted by the Arabs, following an order sent by Haj Amin from Lebanon. He and the Arab Higher Committee gave themselves the credit for having brought about this change in British policy.[103]

The process that Haj Amin had begun during the 1920s – drawing the attention and commitment of the Arab world to the problem of Palestine – gathered momentum as a result of the revolt. This is illustrated by such facts as the efforts of the Iraqi Foreign Minister, Nuri al-Sa'id, and Amir Abdullah to mediate between the government and the Arab Higher Committee; the intervention of Amir Abdullah and the kings of Iraq and Saudi Arabia in October 1936, in the efforts to bring about a cease-fire; and the participation of Arab states in the Round Table conference in London at the beginning of 1939.[104] The invitations extended by the British Government to Arab leaders to participate in this conference caused deep controversy in the Palestinian leadership. One of the problems was the refusal of the British to include Haj Amin in the Palestinian delegation. A further problem was Haj Amin's demand that delegations from the Arab states adopt his maximalist position, namely, insistence on an end to the building of a Jewish national home and the granting of independence to Palestine. The first problem was solved when Haj Amin was compelled to concede his place in the delegation, after being formally elected its president.[105] However, in regard to the second problem, he prevailed; at a conference initiated by the Egyptian Prime Minister, Muhammad Mahmud Pasha, in April 1939, the Arab governments adopted his extreme position regarding the British proposals. Haj Amin's success was the major reason for the failure of the Round Table conference at St. James' Palace in London.[106]

On 17 May 1939, Britain published the White Paper. Its principal recommendations provided for the cessation of the building of the Jewish national home, and the establishment, within ten years, of a state with an Arab majority. This was the most important achievement that Haj Amin's military and political struggle over the previous twenty years had produced. However, his extremism ensured that the Palestinian Arabs would not benefit from this success. It is true that the contents of the White Paper were problematical for Haj Amin on a number of counts. The commanders of the revolt, who did not accept the authority of the political leadership, were adamant in their refusal to accept the White Paper. They were not prepared to accept anything less than full independence, and they demanded, as a condition for ending the revolt, the release of the hundreds of their imprisoned colleagues. In addition, Haj Amin was troubled by the possibility that his rivals in the leadership might exploit the situation to reap the benefits of his struggle, and, with the assistance of the British, assume the central positions in any new arrangement. Beyond these problems, however, Haj Amin continued a policy based on the demand for full independence after the transitional period of ten years, or after law and order was restored in the country, but without the conditions that appeared in the White Paper. Haj Amin may also have considered that British efforts to seek Arab friendship – in view of the approaching war in Europe – could be exploited to gain something beyond what the White Paper offered. On the day following the White Paper's publication, Haj Amin held a meeting of the Arab Higher Committee in Lebanon, in order to decide on the Committee's response. The four members of the Committee who objected to the rejectionist position – 'Awni 'Abd al-Hadi, Ahmad Hilmi 'Abd al-Baqi, Ya'qub al-Ghusayn, and 'Abd al-Latif al-Sala'ah – were absent from the meeting, and the remaining six members decided to reject the White Paper[107] (see Appendix A). Biyan al-Hut claims, on the basis of the diary of Dr 'Izzat Tannus, that the majority of those present at the meeting supported the White Paper after 'submitting it to a strict examination', but Haj Amin was adamant in rejecting it since a number of the sections were vague. It was decided to send Dr 'Izzat Tannus to London to obtain clarifications. Tannus met the Colonial Secretary, Malcolm Macdonald, in London, and at the close of their talks the minister told him 'to return to the Arab Higher Committee and advise it that the White Paper must be accepted immediately, since the new British policy toward Palestine has been accepted by the House of Commons only with difficulty ... and the Arabs must not miss such a golden opportunity'. Tannus passed on Macdonald's message to Haj Amin, but the latter was not convinced, and forced his opinion on the other members of the Arab Higher Committee.[108]

After 1948, many people criticised Haj Amin for having rejected every solution, and thus bringing about the 'Palestine catastrophe'. In response, he published a different version of events. In a collection of his articles which appeared in Egypt in the mid-1950s, Haj Amin wrote:

> From the beginning the Arab states accepted the White Paper with resentment and reservations, because of the contradiction that it contained. Later, however, they accepted it, as did the vast majority of the Arab Higher Committee and the Arab League. In its meeting in 1945, the League demanded that the British Government carry out [the provisions of the White Paper]. Thus, the Arabs did not adopt a negative position. The Jews, however, rejected the plan, and continued to reject it, and Britain did not implement it. This despite the fact that, at the time of the White Paper's publication in 1939, Britain undertook on its honour, and on the honour of the Empire, to implement it whether or not the Arabs and Jews agreed.[109]

In 1945, the Arab leaders were, indeed, inclined to accept the White Paper as the lesser of the evils, in view of the worst possible alternative from their point of view: when the extent of the Jewish Holocaust in Europe became known, there was a wave of sympathy among world opinion for those who had survived. Political figures and intellectuals throughout the world demanded that the country's gates be opened, and even that a Jewish state be established. In the extract quoted above, Haj Amin omitted the background to the Arab states' demand after the war that Britain discharge the recommendations of the White Paper, just as he tried to conceal his total rejection of this document before the outbreak of the war.

In 1967, however, he was prepared to admit that he had taken a rejectionist stand to the White Paper at the time of its publication. He wrote in his memoirs that:

> Following the White Paper, the Arab Higher Committee published a statement expressing reservations about the document and the principles contained in it.* The Arab governments' rejection of this policy [reflected by the White Paper] at their conference expressed a similar feeling. The Jewish Agency also issued a statement rejecting the White Paper, claiming that its policy contradicted the human and natural rights of the Jewish people in Palestine – [a country that is] an eternal religious trust [*waqf*].[110]

A few years before his death, further evidence of his negative stand toward the White Paper appeared in Haj Amin's memoirs. This time, however, he emphasised the supposed support his position received from most of the members of the Arab Higher Committee. He concealed the fact, mentioned above, that four members of the Committee refused to participate in the vote during that same meeting of 18 May 1939, and also that, even among those present, Haj Amin's position was not accepted willingly.[111]

A study of the sources makes it clear that Haj Amin threw his full weight against the pro-White Paper stand of the Arab states and his colleagues in the Arab Higher Committee. In my opinion, his later contradictory versions of events can be explained as a defence against the opinion that prevailed in the Arab camp after the Second World War. There was a general feeling that an opportunity to put an end to the Jewish national home had been missed in 1939, and accusatory fingers were pointed at Haj Amin.

The revolt of 1936–39 convinced many in government circles in London that it would be difficult, perhaps even impossible, to carry out the Mandate. The rise of fascism in Europe and the sympathy with which it was greeted in the countries of the region endangered British interests and led Britain to a renewed effort to seek the friendship of the Arab world. The White Paper was the price the British were willing to pay for this friendship. Haj Amin's objection to the White Paper was thus one of the factors that

---

* Namely, the postponement of the establishment of a Palestinian state for ten years, Jewish immigration (if limited), and the prohibition on the purchase of land by Jews in certain areas.

removed the threat that an increasing cordiality between the British and the Arabs could have posed to Zionism.

2

Haj Amin in the Second World War

INVOLVEMENT IN IRAQ

The freedom of political activity enjoyed by Haj Amin in Lebanon between 1937–39 was largely a result of the continuing competition between Britain and France for influence in the region. However, when the two countries declared war on Germany on 3 September 1939, the British requested his extradition from the French authorities in Lebanon, in light of his connections with Italy and Germany.[1] The French refused, but proposed instead to increase their supervision of his activities. A number of figures in the Arab world now suggested to Haj Amin that he publish a declaration in support of the Allies. He was prepared to agree to this, but only on condition that the British authorities allowed him to return to Jerusalem. This, however, they refused to do. On 13 October he escaped from Lebanon disguised as a woman, after having bribed the French commander of the Lebanese police force with £500 sterling. Three days later he arrived in Iraq.[2]

In Baghdad, Haj Amin was welcomed by the leaders of the Iraqi regime with all due ceremony and was cheered by the masses. The enthusiasm with which he was received was due partly to the fact that Baghdad was then a centre of pan-Arab activity and partly to the general sense of hostility toward the British then prevalent in Iraq. Beyond this, however, Haj Amin was now reaping the benefit of twenty years of efforts to involve the masses in the Arab world in the Palestinian issue, and to establish himself as protector of the holy sites and a pan-Arab and pan-Islamic leader.

At the time of Haj Amin's arrival, the political leadership in Baghdad was divided over the issue of cooperation with the British, and the pro-British leaders in the regime – the Prime Minister, Nuri al-Sa'id and the regent 'Abd al-'Illah – were not particularly pleased to see him in Iraq. Nevertheless, his popularity left them with no choice but to greet him with the appropriate

56

pomp and ceremony. Someone writing about the period noted that 'the Mufti's arrival was embarrassing to the Government; but such a renowned Arab leader, who had become a popular idol in the eyes of the Arabs, was bound to be received as the welcome guest of the Iraqi Government'.[3]

This reception constituted a dramatic change in Haj Amin's position. For a period of months, until his escape from Lebanon, he had been witness to the deterioration and decline of the Arab revolt in Palestine. Many of the local commanders had refused to accept any authority and had simply done as they pleased. There had been many murders whose motives were purely personal which Haj Amin had been powerless to put an end to; there had also been political murders which Haj Amin had not only allowed, but even encouraged. The 'great revolt' had become a civil war, degenerating into an orgy of hate and bloodshed. Haj Amin had apparently felt an overwhelming sense of helplessness and deep depression during this period, and there was even a rumour that he had considered suicide. Perhaps what Haj Amin was really seeking in Baghdad was security and rest.[4] However, the Iraqi capital gave him, in addition, honour, praise, and a platform for renewed political activity. Furthermore, Baghdad was a convenient place for him to stay while he looked forward to a victory of the Axis powers.

Shortly after his arrival in Baghdad, Haj Amin promised the Prime Minister that he would refrain from political activity, and especially from intervention in Iraq's internal affairs.[5] However, when Nuri al-Sa'id resigned on 31 March 1940 and Rashid 'Ali al-Qailani turned down the offer to replace him as prime minister, Haj Amin openly reneged on this undertaking. In fact, Rashid 'Ali had made his acceptance of the position conditional on receiving the support of the four political officers known as the 'Golden Square'. Haj Amin had already acquired a measure of influence over senior politicians and generals in Iraq, and he now came to the aid of Rashid 'Ali. He succeeded in persuading these four officers, who had previously supported Nuri, to transfer their support to the new candidate for prime minister.[6]

Originally a distinguished guest in Iraq, Haj Amin quickly became the controlling force in the country's internal politics, acting both behind the scenes and openly. There were a number of anti-British Arab politicians in Baghdad at the time, as well as Palestinian Arabs who had taken part in the revolt in Palestine. In an effort to unite these individuals into a pan-Arab force with an orientation toward the Axis powers, Haj Amin organised the Arab National Party (*Hizb al-Umma al-Arabiyyah*) in the course of the first few months of his stay in Iraq. This was a secret organisation, whose aim was first to fight to free the Arab states of the burden of imperialism, and then to bring about their unification. Besides Haj Amin, who assumed the leadership of the party, other founding members included Amin al-Tamimi, Ishaq Darwish, Shaikh Hasan Abu al-Sa'ud and Rasim al-Khalidi.

At this point, a dispute broke out between Haj Amin and Jamal al-Husayni, the latter refusing to join the new party because Haj Amin demanded a right of veto and had 'become a dictator'. But those who did join included politicians, members of the Iraqi army, and figures from throughout the Arab world.[7] The new party, which was in fact more of a skeletal political leadership, aimed to unite pan-Arab activists from Syria, Palestine, Transjordan and Iraq. These activists needed an organisational framework and a leader, and Haj Amin offered both.

In addition to the Arab National Party, Haj Amin organised and headed a headquarters for Palestinian activity that enlisted support for the Palestinian cause in government institutions and among the Iraqi population. A 'Secret Committee', composed of Haj Amin, Rashid 'Ali, Yunis al-Sab'awi, Naji Shawkat and three of the Golden Square officers – Sala'ah al-Din al-Sabbagh, Fahmi Sa'id, and Mahmud Salman – met in Haj Amin's home on 28 February 1941 (the fourth Golden Square officer, Kamil Shabib, was not included in the Secret Committee). All assumed false names and swore on the Koran to struggle to oust the pro-British members of the regime, and to prevent Iraq from supporting the Allies in the war. Of the three organisations that Haj Amin set up, the Secret Committee (or Committee of Seven) was the most prominent during the turbulent events in Baghdad in the spring of 1941.[8]

Haj Amin's arrival in Iraq ended the hesitancy that had characterised those who opposed the pro-British line pursued by Nuri al-Sa'id and the regent 'Abd al-'Illah. Haj Amin believed that a British victory would not serve Arab interests, and gradually instilled this belief in members of the opposition. As usual, having decided on a particular policy, Haj Amin stuck to it with consistency and determination. This attitude was one of the reasons why Nuri al-Sa'id failed to secure an understanding between Haj Amin and Colonel S.F. Newcombe, who had arrived in Baghdad in July 1940 on behalf of the British Propaganda Office in Cairo. Haj

Amin himself refused to participate in the talks, preferring instead to present his conditions – ones which the British could not accept – to them through his representatives, Jamal al-Husayni and Musa al-'Alami.[9]

That same month, the Justice Minister in Rashid 'Ali's government, Naji Shawkat, held secret talks with the German ambassador in Turkey, Franz von Papen. The Iraqis took advantage of Haj Amin's connections with the Germans, and Shawkat brought a recommendation from him to Turkey. A few weeks later, Haj Amin sent his personal secretary, 'Uthman Kama'al Hadda'ad, to continue the talks with the Germans in Turkey, and with the German Foreign Minister, Joachim von Ribbentrop, in Berlin.[10] Through Hadda'ad, Haj Amin requested that the Axis powers issue a declaration of support for the independence of the Arab states. He presented himself as head of a secret committee comprised of leaders of the Arab world, and sought to convince the Germans that he, more than any other leader, was authorised to negotiate in the name of the Arabs.[11]

In a letter dated 20 January 1941, which was passed on to Hitler by Hadda'ad, Haj Amin reiterated his central status in the Arab world, and described the suffering of the Arab states under British and French imperialism. He depicted how Palestine had been mistreated by the Jews, 'whose secret weapons – finance, corruption and intrigue – were aligned with British bayonets'. The letter ended, 'with best wishes for long life and happiness for His Excellence, and for a shining victory and prosperity for the great German people ...'[12] (see Appendix B).

The contacts with Germany in the autumn of 1940 and at the beginning of 1941 did not produce concrete results. Germany's allies (Italy, Spain and France) had interests of their own in the countries of North Africa and the Fertile Crescent, and Hitler was careful not to provoke them by issuing a declaration supporting the independence of these countries. Accordingly, Germany limited itself, at the beginning of April 1941, to issuing a general statement of support for the independence of certain Arab states – those under British influence – and undertook to extend military aid to the Arabs if the tensions with the British escalated into an uprising.[13]

The British were concerned about Haj Amin's contacts with the Germans and his anti-British stance in the Iraqi political arena. His behaviour particularly disturbed the India Office which, in October 1940, raised the idea of seizing Haj Amin and transporting him to Cyprus. The Colonial Office objected to the idea, not on principle, but rather for fear that such an act would have a detrimental influence on public opinion in the Arab world. The British army commanders in Iraq later considered the same idea, and came to the conclusion that Haj Amin should be killed. It was now the turn of the Foreign Ministry to veto the idea, for the same reason previously given by the Colonial Office.

After the military *coup d'état* in Iraq returned Rashid 'Ali to power on 1 April 1941 (he had resigned in favour of Taha al-Hashimi two months earlier), an attempt was indeed made to seize Haj Amin. General Archibald Wavell, head of the British Military Command in the Middle East, had ordered the release from prison of David Raziel and other members of the *Irgun Zeva'i Leumi*, with the intention of sending them to sabotage oil installations in Iraq. Raziel demanded that the group be allowed to kidnap Haj Amin and, in preparation for this mission, the group members were flown to the British air force base at Habbaniya. On 20 May 1941, Raziel was killed when his car was bombed by a German aircraft, and the idea of seizing Haj Amin was dropped.[14]

A month after the Golden Square officers returned Rashid 'Ali to power at the instigation of the Secret Committee, clashes broke out between British army forces, supported by the Arab Legion, and units of the Iraqi army. Rashid 'Ali's regime collapsed at the end of May,[15] and the Iraqi regent and Nuri al-Sa'id, who had escaped after the coup, hurried back to Baghdad.

In his memoirs, Haj Amin plays down his central role in the events that preceded the clashes of May 1941, events that led to the collapse of Rashid 'Ali's government and the conquest of Iraq by the British army.[16] The two principal factions within the Iraqi political leadership, one headed by Nuri al-Sa'id and the other by Rashid 'Ali, were not essentially divided over the question of whether to align with the British or the Axis powers. Although Nuri al-Sa'id and the regent inclined toward the British, Rashid 'Ali and his colleagues did not themselves adopt an unequivocally hostile position to the British. Rather, they favoured a neutral position, with Iraq in a state of abeyance. Indeed, immediately after forming his government, Rashid 'Ali publicly pledged to honour Iraq's international obligations, and sought to achieve British recognition of his regime.

In fact, the driving force behind the efforts to align Iraq with the Axis powers was Haj Amin, aided by officers of the Golden Square over whom he had great influence. The Secret Committee, headed by Haj Amin, planned the details of the coup that returned Rashid 'Ali to power. After the coup was successfully concluded, the committee's members continued to meet at Haj Amin's instigation, in order to pressure Rashid 'Ali not to accede to British demands to allow its army to pass through Iraq. Haj Amin's influence on Iraqi policy was also one of the factors that led to the failure of the Turkish attempts to mediate between Iraq and Britain. At the beginning of May 1941, Naji Shawkat (Minister of Defence in Rashid 'Ali's government) was sent to Ankara for talks with the Turkish Foreign Minister. It is a reasonable assumption that Shawkat's refusal to agree to Iraqi concessions regarding the movement of the British army through Iraq was largely due to his fear of Haj Amin and the Golden Square.[17]

When it became clear to the Iraqis that Britain had no intention of accepting limitations on the movement of its army, and after military aid was promised from Germany and Italy, Iraqi army units laid siege to the British Air Force base at Habbaniya. Iraq also concentrated a force to the north of Basra to prevent the British force stationed in the city from moving northward. In addition, the Iraqis sabotaged bridges and flooded certain areas, in an attempt to hamper the movement of the British army. Despite this military activity, the Iraqi opposition was wiped out within 26 days, and the military leaders joined the politicians who had already fled the country.

Haj Amin, who on 9 May declared a *jihad* (holy war) against Great Britain, 'the greatest foe of Islam', describes in his memoirs the part played by Palestinian Arabs in the clashes with the British. According to his account, Palestinian units under the command of 'Abd al-Qadir al-Husayni fought the British army at Sadir Abu-Gharib.[18] This account is in keeping with the general picture that Haj Amin wished to portray at the time, that is, that the 'al-Qailani revolt' had been a pan-Arab struggle.

The Iraqi defeat was the result of a shortage of combat means (for instance, the units bombarded at Habbaniya did not have anti-aircraft weapons), inferior fighting and technical standards, unreliable and confused intelligence, and, above all else, the fact that the German and Italian aid did not arrive in time.

Haj Amin, however, identified a further reason for the defeat – the Jews living in Iraq. Under the heading, 'The Fifth Column in Iraq', he wrote:

The Fifth Column had a great influence on the failure of the

Iraqi movement, and was comprised of many elements, most importantly, the Jews of Iraq. During the fighting, George Antonius told me that Jews employed in the telephone department were recording important and official telephone conversations and passing them on to the British embassy in Baghdad. Jewish workers in the post and telegram departments acted in a similar fashion, forwarding the messages and letters that they received to the embassy.[19]

On 1 June 1941, the Iraqis learned of the return to Baghdad of the regent 'Abd al-'Illah, and Nuri al-Sa'id. The crowd that turned out to welcome them included a group of Jews celebrating the end of the pro-Nazi regime and the return of the leaders of the old regime. Iraqi soldiers and civilians fell upon the Jews, and the attack rapidly developed into a pogrom that spread to other areas of Iraq. One hundred and seventy-nine Jews were killed, and 586 shops and warehouses looted. A committee of inquiry appointed by the Iraqi government noted Haj Amin as one of the figures who had incited the anti-Jewish riots.[20]

On 29 May, the Iraqi opposition in Baghdad was wiped out. On the same day, according to the evidence of one of the Palestinian leaders in Baghdad at the time, Haj Amin summoned members of the Arab National Party and Jamal al-Husayni,[21] and informed them of the failure of the revolt. In accordance with his instructions, 200 of them set out by train to Khaniqin, and from there they made their way via Turkey to Lebanon and Syria. Haj Amin himself, together with Rashid 'Ali, crossed the border into Iran.[22]

This brought to a close another stage in Haj Amin's turbulent political career. During his twenty months in Iraq, one of the critical periods of this country's annals, Haj Amin undoubtedly left his mark on its political history. With the outbreak of the Second World War and the succession of Axis victories, the latent resentment within the Arab world toward the British and French was given open expression. Not only in Iraq but in other Arab states, both politicians and the general public expressed their satisfaction at the British misfortune. Prominent figures in the Arab world made efforts to establish contacts with the Axis powers, and looked forward to their victory. However, some of these Arab states had contractual obligations of one kind or another with Britain, and British army units were stationed in their countries. During the course of the war, the British tried to ensure friendly regimes in the Arab world, an extreme example being their intervention in Egypt in February 1942 to force Farouk to form a pro-British government.

It is reasonable to assume that the British could have ensured the ascendancy of a sympathetic regime in Iraq, had it not been for the presence in Baghdad of Haj Amin. The organisational network that he established there, and the system of contacts that he cultivated with politicians and officers, gave him the power to influence Iraq in its decision to align itself with the Axis powers.

THE WAY TO EUROPE

When Haj Amin fled from Iraq, the German and Italian leaders already knew of his reputation. Apart from its failure in Iraq and defeats in Syria and Lebanon, the Axis continued to win victories in other areas. It thus seems quite likely that Haj Amin sought to reach Europe in order to ally himself with the victors. The Germans for their part welcomed Haj Amin's presence. On 13 June 1941, the deputy Secretary of State, Ernst Woermann, ordered his assistant, Dr Wilhelm Melchers, to invite Haj Amin and the other Arab leaders who had escaped from Iraq to come to Germany.[23] While those in Turkey were able to reach Germany with relative ease, Haj Amin and Rashid 'Ali, who had found refuge in Teheran, were in a more difficult position. Turkey initially refused to allow them to enter its territory, and only as a result of German pressure did it agree to change its decision in regard to Rashid 'Ali. He arrived on 22 July, but it was four months before the Germans succeeded in flying him to Germany – to the obvious displeasure of the British.

Haj Amin was refused an entrance permit to Turkey, apparently as a result of pressure from Britain. Britain, indeed, tried to seize him after he entered Iran on 25 August. Haj Amin's close assistants, including 'Uthman Kama'al Hadda'ad, Amin al-Tamimi, and Jamal al-Husayni, were caught and exiled to Rhodesia. Haj Amin himself managed to hide in the Japanese Legation in Teheran, although it was not until the beginning of October 1941 that he finally succeeded in evading the British. In disguise and with a false passport, he escaped, with Italian assistance, to Turkey. From there he made his way via Bulgaria, Romania, and Hungary to Italy, where he arrived on 11 October.[24] This was the fifth occasion on which Haj Amin had escaped; he had fled to Transjordan in 1920, to Lebanon in 1937, to Iraq in 1939, to

Teheran in June 1941, and to Europe five months later – each time with the British in pursuit.

Referring to this period, Haj Amin claimed that upon his arrival in Iran he had met the Iranian Foreign Minister, al-'Amari, and handed him precise figures concerning the secret invasion plan of the Allies for the conquest of Iran. Haj Amin had received these details from the Iraqi commander, Sala'ah al-Din al-Sabbagh, who in 1940 had participated in a meeting of commanders of the Allied forces in the Middle East. Although the Iranian Foreign Minister doubted the reliability of this information, Haj Amin's fears of a British invasion were not assuaged, and he continued the search for a safer refuge. He later tried to excuse his journey to Europe by claiming that his primary intention had been to reach Saudi Arabia, but that the British had already entered the southern areas of Iran, thus making the passage through there impossible. Haj Amin then requested permission to enter Afghanistan, and, despite the fact that a positive answer arrived from Kabul, he claimed to have discovered that the British were waiting in ambush on the border. When he finally arrived in Istanbul, he heard a radio broadcast of the British Foreign Minister's announcement to the House of Commons that a British army force had surrounded his hiding place in Teheran.[25]

Haj Amin described how the British harassed those members of his family who had remained in Teheran. According to him, the ten family members remaining in Teheran, mostly children, were transferred to southern Iran and held for fifty-two days in a prison in the town of Ahwaz. From here they were transported to Basra, finally arriving exhausted and sick in Baghdad, after a train journey of 600 km in a third-class carriage.[26]

AMONG THE NAZIS

What were Haj Amin's plans after the failure of the nationalist coup in Baghdad? Did he really seek to remain in one of the neighbouring countries under British influence, with his political activity limited? Although there are no clear answers to these questions, it is clear in the light of what occurred later that it was not for want of an alternative that Haj Amin acted as he did.

Almost thirty years after his escape from Teheran, Haj Amin still had to refute accusations that he had harmed the Arab interest in general, and the Palestinian cause in particular, by joining the war effort of the Axis powers. In his memoirs, in addition to claiming that he had nowhere else to go and that the British had put a price on his head to seize him 'dead or alive', Haj Amin also gave patriotic reasons for his actions. Explaining why he had gone to Germany, he wrote:

> Germany was considered friendly since it was not an imperialistic country, and since it had not harmed a single Arab or Muslim state in the past. It fought our imperialistic and Zionist enemies, and after all, your enemy's enemies are your friends. I was certain that a German victory would completely save our country from imperialism and Zionism ... I did not cooperate with Germany for the sake of Germany, nor because of a belief in Nazism. I do not accept its principles, and this never crossed my mind. None the less, I was, and continue to be, convinced that had Germany and the Axis been victorious, then no remnant of Zionism would have remained in Palestine or the Arab states.[27]

Haj Amin arrived in Rome on 11 October 1941, and remained in the Italian capital until 5 November. Immediately upon his arrival he presented himself as head of a secret organisation, the Arab National Party, with branches throughout the Arab states. Within two days he had already proposed cooperation with the Axis powers, on condition that Germany and Italy 'recognise in principle the unity, independence and sovereignty of an Arab state of a Fascist nature including Iraq, Syria, Palestine and Transjordan'.[28]

In Rome, as in Baghdad, Haj Amin wanted for nothing. He stayed in a luxury hotel, and, following a recommendation from the Foreign Ministry, Mussolini agreed to grant him the initial sum of one million Lire (an amount that was equal to approximately £10,000 sterling). On 27 October he met with Mussolini in the Venezia Palace. According to Haj Amin, Mussolini said to him:

> The number of Italian Jews is not more than 45,000 out of an Italian population of 45 million ... Each and every one of them is a spy and propagandist against us ... therefore, our position in regard to them is the same as theirs to us ... If the Jews want it [a Jewish State], they should establish Tel Aviv in America ... They are our enemies ... and there will be no place for them in Europe.[29]

After this meeting and a series of talks with the Italian Foreign Minister, Count Galleazo Ciano, the Italians proposed issuing a joint declaration with Germany that would contain a positive response to the Arab demands, with the exception of those which concerned the North African countries, such as Libya and Tunisia.

Haj Amin then travelled to Germany, arriving in Berlin on 6 November. The following day, he met with the Secretary of State in the German Foreign Office, Ernest von Weizsacker, to discuss the question of the declaration. Additional talks were held with the Foreign Minister, von Ribbentrop, and other officials in the German Foreign Office. The climax of these contacts came on 28 November, when Haj Amin was received by Hitler. Haj Amin described this meeting in detail, especially the agreement that prevailed between them. Hitler stressed that the Jewish problem should be solved 'step by step', and stated that Haj Amin would be 'the figure with the decisive opinion on Arab issues, and leader of the Arabs'. However, there was no progress concerning the claim for recognition of the independence of the Arab states. Hitler reiterated what Haj Amin had already heard from the Fuehrer's officials, that is, that such a declaration would not be published, even in secret, for fear of harming Germany's relations with its allies, at least not until the German army reached the southern Caucasus.[30]

In the meantime, Rashid 'Ali had also arrived in Berlin. Together with Haj Amin, he strove to persuade Germany and Italy, and later Japan as well, to publish a declaration in support of Arab aspirations. These efforts continued until the spring of 1942, when a decision was taken regarding an exchange of dispatches between the German and Italian governments and Rashid 'Ali and Haj Amin, which were to contain agreement to some of the Arab demands. Haj Amin then agreed to participate in the Nazi propaganda machine, and in May 1942 he began to broadcast propaganda speeches to the Arab world.

The basis for cooperation between Haj Amin and Rashid 'Ali was the demand that Germany and Italy support the independence of the Arab states after the war. However, the two continued to compete for recognition by the Axis leaders. Rashid 'Ali demanded recognition as Prime Minister, on the strength of having been Prime Minister of Iraq, and at the beginning of 1942 Rome, indeed, officially recognised his status. Haj Amin, who had no such official position, demanded to be recognised as the more senior of the two, and as the leader of the Arab world. In support of this demand, Haj Amin claimed to have played the central role in the coup of 1 April in Baghdad, and pointed to the fact that a clandestine pan-Arab organisation had been established there under his leadership. Since Rashid 'Ali denied both of these claims, Haj Amin appealed in writing to two of the organisation's founders (Sala'ah al-Din al-Sabbagh and Naji Shawkat) to confirm them, which they did.[31]

Of the three groups that Haj Amin founded in Iraq, the seven-man Secret Committee was the most substantial, having a date of constitution and designated members. The other two were less well defined, and apparently did not continue to function. In this writer's opinion, Haj Amin intentionally introduced an element of confusion between the three bodies in order to create the impression that he represented a pan-Arab organisation that included figures from throughout the Arab world. In order to refute Rashid 'Ali's denials, Haj Amin turned to the two members of the Secret Committee mentioned above. As far as can be ascertained, he made no attempt to obtain confirmation of his claims from senior figures from other Arab states who, according to him, were members of the Arab National Party. There was an obvious reason for this: although Haj Amin had indeed surrounded himself with a group of pan-Arab figures who had some influence on events in Baghdad, they by no means constituted a defined political body, and certainly not an institutionalised pan-Arab political party, as he sought to convince the Axis powers it was.

The Secret Committee that was founded at Haj Amin's home in February 1941 emerged against the background of the rivalry between Iraqi politicians. It had a very specific and concrete purpose – to overthrow the regime in Baghdad. The members of the committee also had pan-Arabic aspirations for the other Arab states, although they took no steps to realise them. Rashid 'Ali's claims, that a secret organisation had never been established in Baghdad, and that Haj Amin had taken no part in the April coup, were spurious. There was some truth, however, in his claim that no pan-Arab political organisation, in whose name Haj Amin now sought to speak, was active during this period. Although Haj Amin's hosts in Berlin and Rome were almost certainly aware of this, they estimated that he was a popular leader in the Arab world, and that, more than any other Arab leader, he remained attached to the idea of a partnership between the Arabs and the Axis powers.

The competition between Rashid 'Ali and Haj Amin continued without respite. Both apparently believed that an Axis victory was close, and that the question of who would be the leader of the Arab world would soon arise. This competition also had more immediate significance, since both leaders wished to be considered the senior of the two in their contacts with government heads in Berlin and Rome, and to receive budgets and other benefits. For their part, the Germans were not in a hurry to decide between the two, and meanwhile they preferred to adopt a cautious approach. In this context it is interesting to note the remark made by Dr Fritz Grobba, the German Minister in Iraq from 1932–41 and, later, liaison officer between the Reich government and Rashid 'Ali and Haj Amin. In a newspaper interview he said:

> When the deep split emerged in Berlin between Haj Amin and Rashid 'Ali, I found myself facing a serious dilemma. Both sought recognition from Hitler as leader of the Arab world, and both put pressure on me to influence the Fuehrer in this respect. Although Rashid 'Ali was the most prominent Arab politician who joined us against the democracies, we were aware that Haj Amin enjoyed tremendous prestige in the Arab and Muslim world, as being fearless in the revolt against the British. When I tried to raise the issue of recognition in my talks with Hitler, the Führer put me off, arguing that the time had not yet come to install an Arab leader, and that the subject would be discussed when we conquered the Arab region.[32]

Although they had recognised Rashid 'Ali as Prime Minister, the Italians were inclined to support Haj Amin's claim to leadership of the Arab world after the victory of Fascism, and his plan to set up in North Africa a centre for cooperation with the Axis powers. In July 1942, Haj Amin reached agreement with Count Ciano in Rome on this point. Rashid 'Ali, who was offended by this, left for Berlin, where he enjoyed greater support than in Italy.

The details of Haj Amin's plan were finalised after discussions with the Italian secret service. At the beginning of September, the head of military intelligence issued a document which received the backing of the Italian Foreign Ministry. This document confirmed the agreement that had been reached, by which Haj Amin would leave for North Africa to set up a propaganda and intelligence centre. There were also plans to establish Arab army units to carry out acts of sabotage behind the enemy's lines, and a military force that would fight under an Arab flag. Haj Amin was to be head of the centre, and commander of both the regular and irregular units.

At the end of 1942, the Axis powers' military situation along the

North African front worsened, and Haj Amin's design for the region was put in doubt. He himself continued to demand its implementation, and called on the Muslim leaders of Tunisia, Morocco, and Libya to fight the 'American–Jewish–English aggression'. By this time, such a call already sounded unrealistic. At the beginning of 1943, senior government and military representatives from Germany and Italy met in Rome, and a decision was taken to postpone for the time being the implementation of Haj Amin's programme.

After his North African plan was shelved, Haj Amin found a new area of activity – the Balkans.[33] As far back as July 1941, a unit called the 'Deutsch–Arabische Lehrabteilung' (DAL) had been established in Greece. Haj Amin later called for the transformation of the unit into an 'Arab liberation force', but his demand was not met. In the summer of 1942, the unit was transferred to the occupied area of the Soviet Union close to Stalino, where it was supposed to wait until the conquest of the Caucasus. The unit's members wore German uniforms with the inscription 'Free Arabia' on the sleeve. Even now, when it seemed that the war would turn against the Axis powers, Haj Amin continued in his efforts to recruit volunteers from the occupied European countries and from among the Muslim populations of Yugoslavia and Albania.

After the 'Jewish Brigade' was established within the framework of the British Army, Haj Amin announced the formation of an 'Arab Brigade' that would fight alongside Germany and Italy. At the beginning of 1944, he assembled a group of Palestinian paratroopers who were trained in Holland by the Germans. In the summer of 1944, two groups of paratroopers were parachuted into Palestine – one under the command of Shaikh Hasan Salamah and the other led by Jasim Kara'adi (both prominent commanders in the revolt of 1936–39).[34]

INVOLVEMENT IN THE DESTRUCTION OF THE JEWS

Since the end of the Second World War, a great deal has been written about Haj Amin's efforts to prevent the rescue of Jews, and his assistance in their destruction. For obvious reasons, this has been especially typical of those who saw him as an accessory to the Nazi crimes. As proof, these writers have pointed to Haj Amin's efforts to dissuade European governments from allowing Jews to leave their countries, as, for example, his involvement with the Bulgarian government, which resulted in preventing the emigration of 4,000 Jewish children to Palestine. It has been claimed that he requested that when the Germans reached the Middle East, they should allow the Arabs to 'solve the Jewish problem in Palestine and the other Arab states in accordance with the interests of the Arabs, by the same methods which were used to solve this problem in the Axis countries'.[35]

The historian Biyan al-Hut presents a very different view. It appears that al-Hut was influenced by conversations that she had with Haj Amin in Beirut, in an effort to clear the Arab leader of any suspicion of having assisted in the destruction of the Jews, or of even having supported such a plan. Al-Hut's comprehensive study of the Palestinian national movement is generally characterised by objectivity, and by an attempt to uncover the historical facts. Here, however, her objective judgement went astray, and she wrote as a propagandist rather than as a researcher. Al-Hut undoubtedly represents the new generation of Palestinian intelligentsia and leadership, and this adds a special interest to the way in which she portrays this less attractive chapter of Haj Amin's political career.

Under the heading 'Zionist Accusations', al-Hut claims that 'the struggle between Nazism and Zionism was in truth a struggle between two forms of racism, and two tyrannies'. She denies that Haj Amin was in any way involved in the Holocaust or that he assisted in it, and presents some astonishing arguments in support of this. For instance, she points to the fact that Haj Amin enjoyed high religious status, and that if he had indeed been involved in crimes such as these he would not have been so clearly supported by Arabs and Muslims. Al-Hut finds additional 'proof' of his non-involvement in the fact that the Zionists could not accumulate enough evidence with which to try him as a war criminal at Nuremberg.[36]

Haj Amin himself did not conceal the efforts that he made to prevent the departure of Jews to Palestine from the areas under Nazi occupation. Moreover, he later justified the Nazi final-solution plan. In a collection of his articles, he wrote:

> In return for a declaration [the Balfour Declaration], the Jews took it upon themselves to serve Britain and its policies, and to do their utmost to secure a British victory in the war. In pursuit of this aim, Jews played a central role in the acts of sabotage and destructive propaganda inside Germany at the

end of the [First World War] ... This is the principal reason
for Hitler's war against the Jews, and his hatred toward them.
They brought disaster on Germany, and caused its defeat in
the war – despite the fact that it had the advantage from a
military point of view.[37]

Twenty years after writing this, Haj Amin returned to the
subject in his memoirs. He claimed that Hitler was not initially
prejudiced against the Jews, and that he 'saw no difference between a Christian, a Jew, a German, and an Austrian', but that he
was 'surprised by the change that occurred in the attitudes of
German Jews after they received the undertaking (the Balfour
Declaration) from Britain'. They then began to take part, continues Haj Amin, in 'acts of corruption and damage in Germany,
and especially in the German army'. Haj Amin did not specify
what these acts were, although he claimed that the Jews had
conducted a propaganda campaign in favour of President Wilson's
peace plan, 'which treated victor and vanquished equally'. Haj
Amin noted other reasons for Hitler's anger at the Jews: he had
been wounded in the eye in the First World War, almost losing his
sight. According to Hitler, the cause of his injury was 'the inven-
tion of a poisonous gas by Haim Weizmann, which was handed
over to the British Foreign Office'. This gas was used by Britain
against the Germans during the war, and Hitler, who was injured
by it, never forgot this. He also believed that it was the Jews who
had brought about United States' involvement in the First World
War, that they had caused the German defeat and surrender, and
they were responsible for the degrading terms that the Allies had
dictated to Germany.[38]

Haj Amin also claimed to have studied the relations between
Germany and its Jewish citizens while at the 'Institute for Research
into the Israelite Problem' founded by the Germans in Frankfurt.
He claimed to be able to describe the destructive role played by the
Jews in Germany, their ingratitude toward Germany, and their
treason. According to Haj Amin, the exploitative capitalists and
usurers were Jews, and it was they who were responsible for the
economic crisis in Germany. The socialist thinkers were also Jews
('the Jew Mordechai who is none other than Karl Marx') who
sought to strengthen Germany's enemies and to bring about its
collapse.

Although Haj Amin continually insisted that he had not been
involved in the destruction of the Jews, he was afraid that he would

71

be brought to trial for crimes of which, according to him, he was falsely accused. At the same time, however, he gave details of his efforts to prevent Jewish immigration to Palestine. In 1968, he wrote the following in his memoirs:

> There were other serious occurrences during the war, such as the attempt by world Jewry in 1944 to bring about the immigration of Eastern European Jewry to Palestine ... just as today they are trying to prompt countries in the East, such as Russia, the Balkan states, and Eastern Europe, to allow Jewish immigration to occupied Palestine. I objected to this attempt, and wrote to Ribbentrop, to Himmler and to Hitler ... until I succeeded in frustrating the attempt.[39]

In a letter to the German Foreign Minister dated 25 July 1944, Haj Amin complained about the emigration of Jews from Europe. He reminded Ribbentrop of his declaration of November 1943 that, 'the destruction of what is known as the Jewish national home in Palestine is an inseparable part of the Great German Reich's policy'. Haj Amin added that, 'if there are reasons which make their removal necessary, it would be essential and infinitely preferable to send them to other countries where they would find themselves under active control, as for example Poland, thus avoiding danger and preventing damage'.[40] In letters that he sent to other European countries under German control, Haj Amin repeated his argument that if the Jews were allowed to leave, they would go to Palestine. In his memoirs, Haj Amin included photographs of the memoranda written in German, English and French.

In the answers which Haj Amin received, also quoted in his memoirs, these countries agreed to comply with his request, and expressed readiness to cooperate with him. None the less, in case some Jews might still manage to escape, Haj Amin appealed to Turkey not to allow them to pass through its territory, and requested that it prevent their entry even 'by air or sea'. He reminded those reading his memoirs that, 'during the war, Turkey was the only passage to Palestine'.[41]

It is impossible to estimate the extent of the consequences of Haj Amin's efforts to prevent the exit of Jews from countries under Nazi occupation, nor the number of those whose rescue was foiled and who consequently perished in the Holocaust.

Haj Amin adhered to a version of events that was aimed both at securing his rehabilitation and at demonstrating to Arab public opinion his success in preventing the strengthening of the Jewish Yishuv in Palestine during the Second World War. He described the accusations that were made against him as untruthful, fabricated and incendiary, and saw the results of his efforts as a success for the Palestinian cause. A year before his death Haj Amin wrote that:

> My letters [to the European countries, requesting them not to allow Jews to leave] had positive and useful results for the Palestinian problem ... That is the reason why a complaint was made against me to the UN in 1947, according to which my letters had prevented the immigration of hundreds of thousands of Jews to Palestine, thereby bringing about their destruction by the Nazis ... The claims of the Jews, and their lies, contradict what actually happened, since during the Nazi regime the Germans settled their account with the Jews well before my arrival in Germany, and they needed no prompting to do it. The Second World War broke out in September 1939, while I arrived in Europe in October 1941; in other words, more than two years later – a period of time that enabled the Germans to settle their accounts with the Jews.[42]

His explanation stands on very shaky ground, since the extermination of the Jews actually continued at an even greater pace during the second half of the war. In any case, there is no doubt that Haj Amin's hatred was not limited to Zionism, but extended to Jews as such. His frequent, close contacts with leaders of the Nazi regime cannot have left Haj Amin with any doubt as to the fate which awaited the Jews whose emigration was prevented by his efforts. His many comments show that he was not only delighted that Jews were prevented from emigrating to Palestine, but was very pleased by the Nazis' Final Solution.

FROM EUROPE TO THE MIDDLE EAST

During the last months of the war, Haj Amin's major preoccupation was the attempt to save his own life. Germany was being overrun by the Allied armies from both east and west, and Berlin suffered massive bombardment. During one of these barrages, the house in which Haj Amin lived was damaged. The house, owned by the German ambassador to Argentina, was a large one, and situated in Krumme Linker–Roter Strasse. Although the Germans quickly restored the ruined house, Haj Amin was transferred to safer accommodation, since it was clear that the region was dangerous; in the following days, his residence was changed frequently by Foreign Office officials. In his memoirs, Haj Amin speaks admiringly of the attention and concern which were accorded him despite the difficult circumstances then prevailing.[43] When the situation deteriorated seriously, the Germans offered to transfer Haj Amin to one of the Arab states by submarine. Despite the danger involved in such an operation, he was prepared to take the risk. However, in April 1945 he learned from a radio broadcast of the Swiss government's decision to grant asylum to political prisoners. The Germans proposed that he fly to Switzerland from a small air field as yet undamaged by the bombardments, but when Haj Amin discovered that he would only have a two-man light aircraft at his disposal, he decided not to take the risk. Instead, he chose to make the journey to Switzerland over land.

Haj Amin goes on to describe in detail[44] how he purchased a small car and tin of petrol for $100 and set out on 4 May 1945, from Badgastein in the direction of the Swiss border, heading for Berne. However the route was snowed in, and Haj Amin and his escort were forced to contact the German Foreign Ministry, which arranged to fly them to Berne in a military aircraft. When Haj Amin arrived, the authorities refused to grant him political asylum, since his name appeared on a list of thirty-two individuals whose entry into Switzerland was prohibited. He managed to make contact with Amir Shakib Arslan in Geneva and the Egyptian ambassador in Berne, 'Abd al-Fata'ah Assil, both of whom tried, unsuccessfully, to persuade the authorities to allow him to remain in Switzerland.

Having been refused permission to enter Switzerland, Haj Amin returned to the German border, and when he crossed into Germany he found himself in the town of Constance, already under French military occupation. After several transfers, he was taken to a prison in Paris, and from there approximately eight miles to la Varenne, where he was placed in isolation and under heavy guard. The French authorities took the trouble to send him a Tunisian cook and other luxuries.

Haj Amin's arrival in France elicited strong responses. Britain and other Western countries demanded his extradition so that he could be tried as a war criminal. Middle Eastern and North African rulers requested that he be released so that they could host him in their countries. In London, the Prime Minister and Foreign and Colonial Secretaries were under constant pressure from members of the House of Commons to do their utmost to ensure Haj Amin's extradition.[45] The Allied Forces Command in Europe and influential figures in the United States also demanded his extradition from France, but to no avail.

Haj Amin's house was guarded around the clock, but he was allowed to receive guests and establish contact with people both in France and abroad. Although obviously aware of the activity surrounding the demands for his extradition, Haj Amin was not overly concerned. In a moment of truth, he noted in his memoirs that from the moment of his arrival in Paris, on 19 May 1945, the French government had sought to protect him. According to him, General de Gaulle even intervened personally to allow him to remain politically active. Haj Amin emphasised that the French government rejected the demands of the British and Allied Commands to extradite him on the grounds that it supposedly had its own account to settle with him for having aided the Syrian revolt against France, and because he had cooperated with Germany during the war.[46] From Haj Amin's account it is clear that the French authorities did their best to prevent his capture by those who wished to put him on trial for war crimes.

This situation was in fact a repeat of an earlier one: at the end of the war, after his escape from Germany, the French treated Haj Amin just as they had in Lebanon between 1937–39, where he had been allowed freedom of political action and protected from the British. Now, as in Lebanon, he managed to escape from under the very noses of his guards. Shortly afterwards, he succeeded in leaving France. The French attitude toward Haj Amin is further revealed by a statement published by the French Foreign Ministry. This stated that Haj Amin had not been under house arrest, and that measures had simply been taken to ensure his safety. In a letter to the French Foreign Minister, which he left with a friend before leaving France, Haj Amin expressed his gratitude for his good treatment:

> I read with great pleasure the statement that was published in the press on 8 April 1946 on behalf of the spokesman for the French Foreign Minister ... which stated that the French government put no obstacle in the way of my journey to one of the Arab states that was prepared to accept me.[47]

The decision to leave Switzerland, where he was not permitted to remain, for a part of Germany under French occupation had apparently been thought out carefully. Haj Amin calculated that the French would treat him well and, as it turned out, he was not mistaken.

At the beginning of June 1946, there were rumours and counter-rumours throughout the Middle East that Haj Amin had left France and was now in the region. Different sources reported that he had left Paris on 29 May under the name and passport of Ma'ruf al-Dawalibi, a member of the Syrian embassy in Paris, and that on his way to Cairo he had stayed in a number of European and Middle Eastern countries. When the Husayni leadership in Palestine announced Haj Amin's escape, there was an outburst of joy among the Palestinian Arabs. Because of a prohibition by the censor against publishing his name, the announcement spoke of an 'important personality'. Three days of celebrations were declared, businesses were decorated and processions were organised in the Arab settlements.[48]

Haj Amin's escape astounded the world. The Paris Police Commander was in fact dismissed as a result of the omission, although this seems to have been only for show, in view of the statement issued by the French Foreign Ministry before the escape concerning the freedom of action that Haj Amin had enjoyed.[49] The behaviour of the French was heavily criticised in Europe and the United States, since it seemed to be have been aimed at securing an advantage in the Arab world at the expense of Britain, and at preventing anti-French agitation by the Arabs in Syria, Lebanon, and North Africa. In London, Churchill demanded in Parliament that Haj Amin be captured in Egypt, and the Prime Minister, Clement Atlee, announced that the British ambassador to Egypt had received instructions to examine what steps could be taken.[50]

Haj Amin justified both the very fact of his escape from France and the form that it took by his fear that enemies were plotting against him. He claimed that strangers had been watching his home at night, and that he had received information that members of the *Irgun* group had been planning to kidnap him. He also stressed that he had already decided to make his way to the Middle East, where 'the campaign for the future of Palestine' had begun.[51] Haj Amin indeed had good reason to fear that the Jews would seek revenge for the things he had done during his time with the Nazis, and he strove to reach a place of safety. He also wanted to participate in the events that were likely to decide the future of Palestine after the war. According to Haj Amin himself, however, his actions during this period were primarily motivated by the fear

76

that he would be brought before the Nuremberg court and tried as a war criminal. It is very clear from his writings that this fear increased when he learned of the written evidence given in Switzerland by Hermann Krumey, one of Eichmann's assistants, about the Palestinian leader's involvement in encouraging the destruction of the Jews.[52]

A few years before his death, Haj Amin described his escape from France to Egypt in his memoirs. According to this account, he had flown from Paris on 28 May, arriving in secret in Cairo the next day via Rome and Athens. After a short stay at the Metropolitan Hotel in the centre of the city, he had left for Heliopolis, where he had met his old friends, 'Ali Rushdi 'Ana'an, Muhammad Munif al-Husayni and 'Ali Rushdi Misri. Haj Amin claimed that he avoided appearing in public so as not to harm Egyptian government interests in the talks being held at the time between the British and Egyptian governments concerning the withdrawal of the British Army. According to his account, he preferred to wait until the talks had ended before disclosing his presence in Egypt. For this reason he left for Alexandria for a few days, and on his return rented an apartment in Heliopolis. From 11 June 1946, his account continues, Arab newspapers began to publish reports about his escape from France. News of his arrival in the Middle East spread quickly throughout Egypt, Palestine, Syria and Lebanon. According to Haj Amin, his friends were concerned for his safety, and made efforts to confirm the truth of the reports. In the meantime, he made contact with the royal family and received an invitation to meet King Farouk. On 19 June, he was received at the 'Abadin palace by the head of the palace court, 'Abd al-Latif Tala'at, and signed his name in the visitors' book. Immediately afterwards King Farouk received him for a half-hour conversation, in the course of which the king expressed his pleasure at his presence in Cairo. King Farouk told Haj Amin that he had been concerned for his safety during the twenty days that had passed after his escape from Paris until it became known that he was in Egypt, and that he had telephoned the Syrian and Lebanese presidents in order to clarify details of his whereabouts. At the end of the conversation, the king proposed that Haj Amin remain as his guest, and gave instructions to members of his entourage to accommodate him in the Inshas palace.

There is no reason to doubt the accuracy of this description, apart from Haj Amin's explanation that he wanted to prevent a crisis in British–Egyptian relations during the talks about the withdrawal of British troops from the Suez Canal area. The probable explanation for his hiding in Egypt for twenty days is that he was not certain that the Egyptians would prevent the British from capturing him. He believed that the British would try to arrest him, and indeed claimed that the British navy had carried out searches of naval craft aimed at preventing him from reaching the Middle East. He may also have feared that the Egyptian government would not be inclined to anger the British during their negotiations, and would be prepared if necessary to sacrifice him in order to maintain the momentum of the talks. It appears that he only disclosed his arrival in Egypt after ensuring that he could rely on the patronage of the king and government. On 20 June, Isma'il Sidki's government announced Haj Amin's arrival. In addition to greetings and words of praise, the statement also expressed the hope that he would help Egypt through 'the difficult period that it is experiencing'.[53]

In Cairo, Haj Amin learned of the excitement that his arrival had caused, and of the demands for his extradition from different parts of the world. However, the steps taken by the Egyptians to ensure his safety reassured him. He revealed that the Inshas palace was put under heavy guard, the entrance to the palace from the Nile was cut off by raising the bridge, and surveillance of the nearby airport was reinforced.

After spending nineteen days in the Inshas palace, Haj Amin was transferred to the al-Ma'amurah summer palace. Here he was visited by the king, and the two held a lengthy discussion about Egypt's problems. They discussed the need to defend Palestine and the al-Aqsa mosque, and the urgent necessity to unite the Arab world in view of the dangers facing it. Farouk ended the conversation by saying to Haj Amin, 'I am pleased that you are here and hope to benefit from your experience'.[54]

In actual fact, it is doubtful whether the leaders of the Egyptian regime were pleased at having the controversial figure of Haj Amin in their midst. As had been the case in Baghdad in 1939, however, the authorities were compelled to take into consideration his great popularity and the nationalist feeling among the masses.

Though the royal hospitality that he received from the Egyptians was very flattering, political events which touched on the question of Palestine were developing rapidly, and Haj Amin now sought to regain control of the Palestinian leadership. With this in mind, he left the palace and moved into an ordinary house in Alexandria which, for the time being, became the centre of activity for the Palestinian leadership.

RETURN TO THE HEAD OF THE PALESTINIAN LEADERSHIP

Haj Amin's political career, which had included confrontations with the British authorities, arrest warrants and sentences of imprisonment – which he always managed to evade – made him, in the eyes of many in the Arab world, a symbol of the nationalist struggle, and most Palestinian Arabs saw him as their unchallenged leader. Since his flight from Jerusalem in 1937, there had in fact been no organised Palestinian leadership in the country; those leaders who had remained had been subject to Haj Amin's authority and had acted only on his instructions. The Palestinian leadership thus became mobile: while Haj Amin was in Lebanon, the other Palestinian leaders would visit him in order to hold meetings of the Arab Higher Committee. (Although this committee had been disbanded by the Mandatory authorities in 1937, it continued to exist in practice.) When he moved to Baghdad, his home there became a meeting place for the Palestinian leadership. Even during the Second World War, several members of the Arab Higher Committee joined him in Europe, and although the conditions of the war made political activity difficult, they did their best to keep abreast of what was happening in Palestine and to maintain contacts with the Palestinian public. On his arrival in Egypt after the war, Haj Amin found three members of the committee there: 'Awni 'Abd al-Hadi, Ya'qub al-Ghusayn and 'Abd al-Latif Sala'ah.[55] The remaining members arrived shortly afterwards, and only two (Ahmad Hilmi 'Abd al-Baqi and Dr Husayn al-Khalidi) remained in Jerusalem. The Palestinian leadership had thus once again followed Haj Amin, this time to Egypt.

While Haj Amin was in Germany, the tension between the Jewish Yishuv in Palestine and the British authorities continued, characterised by the struggle against the White Paper. Meanwhile, the British encouraged the Palestinian leaders who had remained in the country, or who had returned, to reform the political leadership. Most of these leaders were identified with the al-Istiqlal party, which at the time inclined toward cooperation with the authorities. They sought to exploit the absence of the Husayni leadership from the country and to establish an alternative leadership in its place. On 19 February 1943, Rashid al-Haj Ibrahim organised a conference of political activists in Haifa, with the declared aim of founding a United Arab Front (*Jabhah 'Arabiyyah Muwahadah*). During the same period, a conference was held in Jerusalem with the aim of forming a new leadership. The initiators of this conference were leaders of the opposition and the Palestinian national movement, such as 'Awni 'Abd al-Hadi, Ya'qub al-Ghusayn, Dr Husayn al-Khalidi and Ahmad Hilmi 'Abd al-Baqi.

These attempts to create an alternative leadership were frustrated by Haj Amin's supporters. They undermined the opposition in the eyes of the authorities by claiming that the organisers of these conferences had no authority to represent the country's Arab population; and undermined them in the eyes of the Arab public by accusing them of cooperating with the government and of supporting the White Paper. Additional efforts to form a leadership were made during the course of 1944, all of which were undermined by supporters of Haj Amin, who acted in coordination with him. In the absence of their leader, the Husaynis were justifiably anxious about losing their position of seniority within the political leadership, despite the fact that the majority of the Palestinian Arabs revered both Haj Amin, whom they regarded as the leader who had fought for Palestine's independence while in Germany, and Jamal al-Husayni, who was in exile in Rhodesia.[56]

During this period, the Arab states discussed the possibility of establishing an Arab League. In September–October 1944, a preparatory conference was held in Alexandria, and the Arabs of Palestine were invited to send their representatives. The invitation led to renewed disagreement between the Husaynis and the various parts of the opposition concerning the composition of the delegation. No agreement was reached. An attempt was made to resolve the situation by the Egyptian Prime Minister, Mustafa al-Nahhas, who appealed to Haj Amin, still in Germany, to intervene. When this attempt failed, Nuri al-Sa'id travelled to Jerusalem, but his efforts to resolve the differences of opinion were also unsuccessful.[57]

By this time, a large number of Palestinian leaders had already returned to Jerusalem from exile. A few years earlier, they had all worked together. Despite this, and despite the fact that representation in the Arab League was very important for them, these same leaders were now unable to overcome their differences of opinion. Yet these differences derived from party and personal competition rather than from political incompatibility. The Palestinian Arabs were lacking the personality of Haj Amin. Had he been present in the country, a Palestinian representation to the Arab League would probably have been formed. Haj Amin, however, was still in Germany, broadcasting his call to the Arabs to revolt, as if the end of the Third Reich was not already in sight.

The Husaynis' Palestine Arab Party, which had renewed its activities in April 1944, demanded majority representation in the delegation to the Arab League. The demand was rejected by the opposition. In the absence of a consensus, it was finally decided that Musa al-'Alami, who was considered to be neutral, would be the single representative to the League. In Egypt, he contributed to the formulation of that part of the League's charter dealing with the status of Palestine in the Arab League. The document that was prepared for the founding of the League (the 'Protocol of Alexandria') in October 1944 stated that 'Palestine constitutes an important part of the Arab world'. The Arab League was officially constituted on 22 March 1945, and its founding document included an undertaking by the Arab states to strive to attain independence for Arab Palestine.[58]

In November 1945, a delegation of the Arab League arrived in Palestine. Headed by Jamal Mardam, who had chaired the League's second session in Cairo from 21 October until 14 December 1945, the delegation's mission was to try to settle the differences of opinion between the Husaynis and their rivals, and to establish a new committee for the Arabs of Palestine. For a time it seemed that it would succeed. A committee was set up, composed of representatives of the parties and non-party individuals, but it did not last very long. Haj Amin's followers reiterated their demand for majority representation, and the temporary bond disintegrated.[59] Following the failure of the attempts to create a unified leadership, two leaderships were created – that of the Husaynis, in the name of the Arab Higher Committee, and that of the opposition party, in the name of the Arab Higher Front (*al-Jabhah al-'Arabiyyah al-'Ulia*).

Haj Amin's absence from the country not only prevented the consolidation of a Palestinian representation to the Arab League, but also increased the Palestinian Arabs' dependence on the League. One immediate result of this situation was the resignation of Musa al-'Alami, after his failure to gain the support of the Palestinian leaders. Jamal al-Husayni, who returned to the country at the beginning of 1946 to an enthusiastic welcome,[60] led the Husaynis to adopt an even more hard-line position, thus preventing the possibility of any agreement over the issue of representation. The leaders of the League finally decided to act unilaterally, after giving up hope that the Palestinian Arabs would ever choose their representatives, and especially after despairing of the possibility of persuading Jamal al-Husayni to establish an Arab Higher Committee of the type that had existed in 1936. On 30 March 1946, the Arab League published a decision which stated that, in view of the special conditions prevailing in Palestine, it would assume authority for appointing the Palestinian representatives.[61]

At the same time, the Anglo-American Commission of Inquiry arrived in Palestine. In its report published at the end of April 1946, the Commission recommended that the provisions of the 1939 White Paper be abolished, and that 100,000 Jews who had survived the Holocaust be allowed to enter the country. In response to the Commission's report, leaders of the Arab states met at the end of May in Inshas (Egypt), and a decision was taken to oppose the recommendations and to extend aid to the Palestinian struggle.

As a continuation to the conference, the Arab League Council held a special session in Baludan, Syria, between 8–12 June 1946. Here too, a decision was taken to fight the recommendations of the Anglo-American Commission. Secret decisions were also taken at the conference regarding measures that would be taken against American and British interests in the region in the event that the Commission's recommendations were implemented.[62] It was also decided to establish two new committees: a committee for Palestinian affairs, comprised of representatives of Arab League members; and, on 12 June 1946, a new committee for the Arabs of Palestine. It seems that in order to differentiate between this committee and the Arab Higher Committee that had been founded in 1936, and between it and those committees that had been founded and disappeared in 1945 and 1946, the new committee was called the Arab Higher Executive (*al-Hyah al-Arabiyyah al-'Ulia*). This new body had four members: Ahmad Hilmi 'Abd al-Baqi and Dr Husayn al-Khalidi representing the Higher Arab Front, and Jamal al-Husayni and Emil al-Ghouri representing the Husayni faction. The Arab League Council also decided that the position of chairman would remain vacant until Haj Amin's return.[63] (In actual fact, by this time he was already in hiding in Egypt.)

Following the establishment of the Arab Higher Institute, mem-

bers of the Husaynis' Arab Higher Committee and the opposition's Arab Higher Front met in Jerusalem, and a decision was
taken to abolish both these bodies and to end the activities of the
political parties.[64] Henceforth, the Arab Higher Executive
operated as the supreme representative body of the Palestinian
Arabs, although this was neither the Arab Executive Committee
that had been active from 1920–34, nor the Arab Higher Committee that had been active from 1936, both of them founded by
the Palestinian Arabs themselves. At Baludan, the Arab League
assumed full guardianship for the Palestinian Arabs. They thus lost
custody of their own affairs and their dependence on the League
grew, a development which was to have a significant influence on
future events.

Shortly after the Arab League established the Arab Higher
Executive, Haj Amin took his place at the head of the new body.
This coincided with the London conference, which began on 10
September 1946, at which the Arabs rejected the Morrison–Grady
plan to partition the country into four cantons. Haj Amin and his
colleagues on the Arab Higher Executive also rejected the pan-
Arab proposal to establish a united state in Palestine. The Institute's members, who participated in the second part of the
conference, without Haj Amin, adopted a hard-line stance
throughout the discussions. It was the failure of these talks that
forced the British to raise the question of Palestine at the UN.[65]

The following days were marked by Haj Amin's struggle against
the Arab League's guardianship of the Palestinian issue, and his
efforts to ensure the place of the Arab Higher Executive at the
Arab League's conferences. In neither of these aims was Haj Amin
very successful. His rivals in the Arab world were not only powerful in themselves but were also in strong bargaining positions, and
in the following years the Arab League was to become the focus of
struggles surrounding the Palestinian issue.

3

The Struggle for an Independent Palestine

HAJ AMIN CONFRONTS ABDULLAH IN THE ARAB LEAGUE

Haj Amin had good reason to regret having delayed his return from Europe to Egypt in a period of such crisis. Although the Arab League had left his seat on the Arab Higher Institute vacant, it had assumed responsibility for the Palestinian issue at the expense of the Palestinian Arabs themselves. With hindsight, it appears that the Palestinian dependence on the Arab League was a consequence of its internal disputes, and, in particular, of its poor organisational and military situation. Nevertheless, Haj Amin still believed that if the Arab states honoured their guarantees to extend assistance to them, the Palestinian Arabs could meet the challenge. Haj Amin's aim was now to receive as much aid as possible while conceding the minimum of independence in return. In the event, this twofold aim proved impossible to achieve.

Haj Amin was opposed by King Abdullah, who was determined to exploit the opportunity presented by the end of the British Mandate in Palestine to extend the boundaries of his kingdom at the expense of the Palestinian Arabs. This was an old dream of Abdullah's, one that he had spoken of as far back as March 1921, when negotiating his appointment as Amir of Transjordan with Churchill. Abdullah had proposed at the time that the appointment also include Palestine.[1] The idea later crystallised into a comprehensive plan known as the 'Greater Syria' plan, and Abdullah continued to support it over the years, sometimes openly, and other times in secret.

Abdullah's intention was clear to Haj Amin, as it was to many others, and he thus had no alternative but to rely on the Arab League to try to block the king's plan. However, the League did not invite Haj Amin to the meeting of the Political Executive held in Sofar in September. The meeting was called at the instigation of the Iraqi Prime Minister, Salih Jabr, to discuss opposition to the partition plan. Despite appeals by the Arab Higher Institute, Jabr refused to allow Haj Amin to participate in the meeting. Haj Amin, who demanded to be recognised as representative of the Palestinian Arabs in the League, found himself blocked by Transjordan and Iraq. He decided to remove this obstacle at the seventh session of the Arab League Council that was held between 7–15 October in 'Aley (Lebanon). The participants at the session felt a special urgency to discuss the steps that should be taken following the publication of the report of the UN Committee of Investigation (UNSCOP) at the beginning of September. Also included in the session's agenda was the announcement by the British Colonial Secretary, Sir Arthur Creech Jones, of the British Government's decision to withdraw the British administration from Palestine.[2]

Although all of the subjects under discussion at the 'Aley conference concerned Palestine, Haj Amin was once again not invited to attend. Apart from Abdullah's opposition to his participation, Iraq's attitude to him was also extremely hostile. The Iraqis had not forgotten his subversive activities against the monarchical regime during the Second World War, nor his part in the revolt of Rashid 'Ali al-Qailani. This was one of a number of conferences that had been held since Haj Amin had returned to the region, and the Hashemite countries had prevented his participation in all of them. However, this time he surprised the leaders of the Arab states by entering the meeting in the middle of a discussion. Salih Jabr objected to his presence, and demanded that the chairman, Riyad al-Sulh, the Lebanese Prime Minister, refuse to allow him to participate. Al-Sulh claimed, however, that they were bound by the requirements of hospitality, and Haj Amin took his place in the discussions.[3] He later gave a speech demanding the establishment of an 'Arab government in Palestine',[4] to which Abdullah objected forcefully, as did Iraq. The other members of the League, who were aware of Abdullah's contacts with leaders of the Jewish Yishuv, rejected Haj Amin's demand, in order to avoid a breach with Abdullah and possibly even the dismantling of the League.

Haj Amin emerged from his struggle with the Arab League for Palestinian independence at a disadvantage. This episode clearly indicated that the Arab states' commitment to the issue of Palestine was devoid of any real value, and that all the decisions demanding the realisation of Palestine's independence remained worthless. The gap between words and deeds was repeated at

'Aley: while a decision was taken to safeguard the 'right of Palestine to become an independent state', Haj Amin's demand for even a symbolic move towards this independence was rejected.[5] Haj Amin demanded the correction of this affront to the Palestinian Arabs, and the League's Secretary General, 'Abd al-Rahman 'Azzam, left for Amman in an unsuccessful attempt to persuade Abdullah to change his mind.[6]

At the 'Aley conference, the League decided to set up a military committee under the leadership of General Isma'il Safwat, which would recruit volunteers from Arab countries for an Arab Liberation Army (*Jaysh al-Inqaz al-'Arabi*), and train them at an instruction base at Qatana, close to Damascus. Taha al-Hashimi of Iraq was appointed to supervise the recruiting and training. Haj Amin demanded that the Liberation Army be commanded by 'Abd al-Qadir al-Husayni, but the League appointed Fawzi al-Qawuqji. Haj Amin saw this appointment as an attempt by his rivals in the League to undermine his influence over the future of Palestine. He argued that al-Qawuqji was a British and Jordanian agent and, according to one version, he even dispatched emissaries to the camp at Qatana to encourage Palestinian Arabs training there to desert and join the *al-Jihad al-Muqaddas* militias which were being organised by the Arab Higher Institute. Not only the leaders of Iraq and Transjordan, but also the President of Syria, Shukri al-Quwwatli, and even Palestinian figures such as 'Izzat Darwaza, tried in vain to persuade him that al-Qawuqji was the only military figure who could reasonably be considered to command the Liberation Army. Taha al-Hashimi relates in his memoirs that a number of meetings were held with Haj Amin, during which it was stressed that the gravity of the situation left no room for disagreement. Haj Amin refused to concede, and continued to insist that he was better qualified than al-Qawuqji to be commander. The least he was prepared to accept was the appointment of 'Abd al-Qadir al-Husayni as commander under his supervision.[7]

When he realised that his opposition to the appointment of al-Qawuqji was futile, Haj Amin turned his attention to the re-organisation of those forces which did accept his authority, *al-Jihad al-Muqaddas*. It was planned that these forces would fight the implementation of the partition plan. However, no less importantly, they also constituted Haj Amin's answer to the challenge presented by the League which, having already appropriated political responsibility from the Palestinian leadership, had now deprived it of military responsibility too. Within a few weeks, Haj

Amin assembled a number of Palestinian commanders who had been active with him during the revolt of 1936–39, and who had followed him to Iraq and Europe. They were to head the *al-Jihad al-Muqaddas*. On 14 December 1947, the first official statement was issued, signed by the Supreme Palestine Command (*al-Qayadah al-'Ulia Li-Filastin*). In his memoirs, Haj Amin wrote the following about the establishment and objectives of this force:

> The Arab Higher Institute ... established the *Jaysh al-Jihad al-Muqaddas* under the command of the fallen 'Abd al-Qadir al-Husayni and his assistants, who were among the regional commanders known for their bravery and expertise. Some of them had previously held military positions in Germany and in Iraq ... Syrian, Egyptian, and Iraqi officers assisted the *al-Jihad al-Muqaddas* Command to prepare a precise plan and to select 3,600 targets ... against which the Jihad would operate. For every target a map was prepared, and the mode of operation and all that was needed in terms of manpower, weapons and expenses were detailed.
>
> In the Jerusalem area, some of these plans were indeed carried out, for instance the destruction of the Jewish Agency building and Ben-Yehuda and Montefiore streets, [as well as] the blocking of the Bab al-Wad pass ... and the siege of Jerusalem's 115,000 Jews. Their situation worsened ... and they asked to surrender in a column of white flags.[8]

Haj Amin goes on to list operations carried out by the *al-Jihad al-Muqaddas* against Jewish targets in the Jaffa and Haifa areas, and describes the supremacy that the Palestinian Arabs enjoyed over the Jews. He concludes by saying that:

> Had a number of Arab groups not been deceived by promises made by the imperialists, and had they not operated on their own initiative and placed obstacles in the way of the Palestinian Arabs' Jihad ... the Jews would not have established their aggressive entity in Palestine.

Although, with hindsight, this seems somewhat fanciful, it is possible that, after the 'Aley conference at the end of 1947, Haj Amin really believed that if his units were to receive aid from the Arab states in the form of money and arms, they could overcome the small Jewish Yishuv, unprepared as it was for war. It should be remembered that the excerpt quoted above was published more than twenty years after the period which it describes. The question remains whether he still believed then that the Palestinian Arabs could have succeeded where the Arab armies had failed.

Two months after the 'Aley conference, the leaders of the Arab states held consultations in Cairo. The background to this meeting was the decision of the UN, on 29 November 1947, to partition Palestine. The League's Secretary General, 'Abd al-Rahman 'Azzam, who, it will be recalled, had been unsuccessful in his earlier attempt to persuade Abdullah to remove his objection to the proposal raised at 'Aley to establish a Palestinian government, now put forward a different proposal, the constitution of a local administration in Palestine. Although the proposal was supported by Egypt, Syria, and Saudi Arabia, it was once again frustrated by Iraq and Transjordan.[9]

The situation at this stage was very clear: on one side stood Abdullah, who by now barely disguised his intention of taking over as much as possible of the territory of Palestine and annexing it to his kingdom; and on the other, Haj Amin, who strove to prevent Abdullah from realising this ambition. Abdullah had the advantage in this conflict: he enjoyed the unqualified support of Iraq. The other Arab states had no choice but to take him into account, since he had the longest border adjoining Palestine. His army was well-trained, and since the Second World War parts of it had been stationed to the west of the Jordan. The Arab League then numbered seven members, and should Abdullah have left, possibly taking Iraq along with him, the League would have been likely to disintegrate. All that Haj Amin had in his favour was the rather unstable support of Egypt, Syria, and Saudi Arabia, and even this support was motivated more by their opposition to Abdullah's expansionist intentions than by a desire to assist the Palestinian Arabs. Moreover, the opposition to Haj Amin within the Palestinian camp continued its campaign against his leadership, and this helped Abdullah to undermine his position. Haj Amin's uncompromising personality also contributed to the weakness of the Palestinian camp within the Arab League.[10]

It is true that Abdullah, who played a central role in the inter-Arab arena, was influenced by the British, and that his policy toward Palestine was coordinated with Britain; nevertheless it remained his own policy, one that derived from personal ambition and from his conception of the interests of his kingdom and of the Hashemite family. Although the situation was clear to everyone, Haj Amin was inclined to portray it differently. Looking back many years after these events, he chose to place the blame on

Britain, whose welfare, according to him, was all that the leaders of the Arab states pursued. He claimed, in a collection of his articles, that the Arab League conference at 'Aley was, in practice, run by British agents. According to him, it was Britain which prevented the Palestinian Arabs from overcoming the Jews.

Haj Amin claimed that when the Jews and the British had recognised 'the seriousness, the decisiveness, and the self-sacrifice of the Palestinian Arabs', they had resorted to tricks to put an end to 'the guerrilla war' and to remove the Palestinian fighters from the battlefield. According to him, the 'Aley conference had decided that 'the war over Palestine would be borne by its inhabitants', but that the British worked to change the plan of the Arab states. This incessant outside pressure on the leaders of some of these states reached such a pitch that it put an end to any objections to the invasion.[11]

Haj Amin's arguments were groundless. The 'Aley conference was no more than the continuation of those at Inshas, Baludan, and Sofar. A decision was taken at this conference to implement the secret decisions that were taken at Baludan (sanctions against Britain and the United States) 'in the event of the U.N. taking any decision that harms the right of Palestine to turn into an independent Arab state'. In an open decision, it was stated that 'material and moral assistance [should be extended] to those fighting in Palestine', although the secret decisions provided, as in previous conferences, for the adoption of 'military measures along the whole length of the borders of Palestine', and instructed the Arab states to 'begin their preparations ...'.[12]

It is worth noting here Haj Amin's attempt to rewrite history: he makes no mention of the fact that he was not invited to the conference at 'Aley, nor that Iraq demanded that he not be allowed to participate in the discussions after his dramatic arrival, and he conceals the opposition of Transjordan and Iraq to any decision recognising the right of Palestinian independence. Rather than discussing the conflict with Abdullah and the Transjordanian-British coordination of policy toward Palestine, he chooses to fabricate a British–Jewish conspiracy which aimed to bring about the Arab invasion of Palestine and thus to prevent a Palestinian victory in the campaign for the future of Palestine.[13]

The only explanation for Haj Amin's selective approach to the historical facts is that during his stay in Egypt in the 1950s he was anxious to avoid confrontation with the Arab states. Writing the truth would have involved burning his bridges as far as countries such as Jordan and Iraq were concerned; and he apparently preferred to keep his options open.

Haj Amin was not defeated by the 'Aley conference. He refused to accept the decisions taken at the conference which, to all intents and purposes, deprived him, and the institution that he headed, of any authority over the management of the affairs of Palestine. His response was to establish a Palestinian military force, and to increase the activities of the Arab Higher Institute. He opened new offices in Syria, Lebanon and London. At the same time, the Arab Home Treasury (*Bayt al-Mal al-'Arabi*) in Jerusalem was consolidated. To demonstrate his determination to preserve the independence of the Palestinian decision, the Institute's office in Jerusalem declared a three day general strike from 1 December in protest of the partition plan.[14]

The next stage in Haj Amin's struggle with Abdullah was the conference of the Arab League Council which was held in Cairo between 7–16 February 1948. In the months preceding the conference, Abdullah was active in two areas. He pressured his colleagues in the Arab League in an effort to prevent Haj Amin from operating independently in Palestine; and he strengthened his ties with the Palestinian opposition to Haj Amin. Many of those who opposed the Husayni leadership preferred a solution that involved annexation to Transjordan rather than the establishment of a Palestinian entity under the leadership of Haj Amin. Delegations visited Amman, and Abdullah's representatives – and even Abdullah himself – visited towns such as Nablus and Hebron for talks with local leaders.[15]

The conference of the League's Council in Cairo failed to reach agreement regarding the implementation of economic sanctions (an economic boycott and the abolition of oil concessions) against Britain and the US which had been decided upon at the Baludan and 'Aley conferences. Decisions were taken, however, concerning the preparation of the Arab armies for invasion – something which was demanded by Transjordan and Iraq. Haj Amin, who felt that time was working against him and in favour of Abdullah, raised the following demands at the conference:

1. The establishment of a provisional Palestinian Government which would assume responsibility when the British withdrew, or even before.
2. The appointment of a Palestinian representative to the General Command for Palestinian affairs.

3. The transfer of the government of Arab areas evacuated by the British to the local National Committees.

4. A monetary loan to cover the management of Palestinian affairs and aid to those injured in the riots.[16]

The League's rejection of all of these demands was a clear indication of its continuing adherence to the policy dictated by Abdullah, namely, to divest the Arab Higher Institute, an institution which the League itself had established at the Baludan conference, of all significance. Nevertheless, Haj Amin continued to behave, probably with the encouragement of Egypt and Saudi Arabia, as if the institute that he headed constituted a government in the making.

In the period preceding the withdrawal of the British, Palestinian Arabs began to flee to the Arab states, and this concerned members of the Arab Higher Institute. On 8 March 1948, Haj Amin sent a memorandum to the Arab heads of government requesting that they refuse to allow Palestinian Arabs to enter their countries, and that they instruct their representatives in Jerusalem to issue visas only in accordance with authorisations from the Arab Higher Institute and its local branches, the National Committees.[17] It is reasonable to assume that had the Arab governments responded to his appeal, Haj Amin would have included it in his collection of articles. He does not mention it, and it later became clear that the stream of Palestinian Arabs leaving the country only increased.

Haj Amin was especially concerned to refute claims made after 1948, both by the Arab states and Israel, that at the beginning of 1948 he and the Arab Higher Institute had called on the Palestinian Arabs to flee to the neighbouring countries. In addition to these memoranda, Haj Amin included in his memoirs photographs of telegrams that he sent from Cairo to Palestinian figures on the subject of the Palestinian exodus.

In March 1948, the head of the Catholic Church in Galilee, Bishop Haqim, put forward a proposal to evacuate Palestinian women and children to Lebanon and Syria. On 13 March, Haj Amin sent a telegram to Rashid al-Haj Ibrahim, the chairman of the National Committee in Haifa, protesting that the evacuation would harm the interests and morale of the Palestinian Arabs. Instead of evacuating them to neighbouring countries, he proposed that women and children should be transferred from areas involved in the fighting to less dangerous Arab towns and villages.

On the same day, he sent a telegram to Kama'al Hadda'ad, head of the office of the Arab Higher Institute in Beirut, instructing him to demand that the Syrian and Lebanese authorities prevent the entry of Palestinian Arabs into their countries.[18]

TOWARD THE ARAB ARMIES' INVASION

In his collection of articles, Haj Amin writes that at the 'Aley conference the Arab states had supposedly decided to rely on the Palestinian Arabs themselves in the 'war over Palestine', and that it was only 'foreign pressure' that altered the plan and led to the invasion of the Arab armies. Twenty years later, he still adhered to this version of events. In his memoirs, he accused the British of having expelled the Palestinian Arabs from the battlefield and of having 'imposed on a number of Arab states the task of sending their armies into Palestine', after it had become clear that the Palestinian Arabs had the advantage.[19] In actual fact, all the Arab states hoped to bring about the non-implementation of the partition plan and to prevent the establishment of the Jewish state. Abdullah sought to achieve this result by enticing the Jews to participate in a political arrangement under his aegis, although he intended to invade the country in the event that such an arrangement was not reached. The last attempt to arrive at such an arrangement took place a few days before the British withdrawal. At a meeting with Abdullah, the Jewish representatives, Golda Meir (Meirson) and Ezra Danin, attempted to persuade him not to invade, and instead to be content with sending a governor to rule the part allocated to the Arab state. 'I am no longer alone, but one of five, and I have to join the battle', was Abdullah's reply.[20] Abdullah really longed for a situation that would facilitate an invasion by his army, possibly with Iraqi assistance, and without his partners from the Arab League. This was revealed not only in his discussions with representatives of the Jewish Agency, but also in his contacts with Iraqi representatives at the Arab League.

At the meeting of the Arab League's Political Committee in Cairo at the beginning of December 1947, following the UN partition decision, the Iraqi Prime Minister, Salih Jabr, demanded that a decision be taken regarding immediate 'armed intervention', as required by the report submitted by the head of the Military Committee, the Iraqi General Isma'il Safwat. He also demanded that sanctions be imposed on Britain and the United States, and expressed Iraq's readiness to halt the operations of the oil companies in his country immediately. The representatives on the League did not greet Salih Jabr's suggestions enthusiastically, and the Iraqi delegation left for Amman to report to Abdullah about the hesitancy of its colleagues in the League. Abdullah calmed them, and told them that if Iraq supported his efforts, the two countries could implement the Safwat report (the invasion of Palestine) unaided.[21] One can easily imagine how pleased Abdullah was to waive such 'aid' from his rivals in the League.

Egypt was clearly unwilling to be dragged into an invasion by Abdullah and Iraq. It supported the League's decisions threatening sanctions and the intervention of Arab military forces in the hope that these measures would deter the superpowers from carrying out the partition plan. The Arabs almost managed to achieve this: as a result of the acts of violence (which increased with the arrival from Syria of thousands of members of the Liberation Army), the US representative at the UN declared, in March 1948, that his government was of the opinion that the partition plan should be abandoned, and that the assembly should discuss imposing a provisional UN trusteeship in Palestine.[22]

The United States' proposal was seen throughout the world as marking the success of the Arab attempt to prove that the UN's partition decision could not be carried out, or at least that its implementation would involve ever-increasing bloodshed. Most of the Arab states were satisfied with the steps taken by the US representative. Haj Amin, however, saw their position as a grave mistake, and expressed his reservations in a memorandum that he sent to the Arab League's Political Committee on 4 May in the name of the Arab Higher Institute. He argued that a trusteeship would be just another form of the Mandatory regime, and that the only beneficiaries would be the Zionists. He rejected the opinion of those Arab leaders who held that the Arabs had in fact only two options, partition or trusteeship, and argued that the Arabs also had a military option, and that they should fight in order to preserve the Arab character of the country. Attempts by the Egyptian Prime Minister and Foreign Minister to convince Haj Amin to accept the US proposal failed.[23]

In addition to Saudi Arabia and Egypt, Syria and Lebanon also had their doubts about the invasion plan. Although they were inclined not to participate in the operation, they feared leaving the stage free for Abdullah and Iraq. Egypt, which was the backbone of the League, also set the tone among those who opposed the Hashemites, and as the time for the British withdrawal approached, the number of leaders in Cairo who supported an invasion grew. The protocol from the secret meeting of the Egyptian Upper House with government representatives provides interesting documentation of this issue. With the exception of Isma'il Sidki, who reiterated the danger involved in an invasion and called for a peaceful solution of the problem, the representatives expressed enthusiastic support for the position of the Prime Minister, Mahmud al-Nuqrashi, who demanded authorisation for the sending of an Egyptian army to fight in Palestine.[24]

Doubts concerning the invasion also characterised the discussions of the League's Political Committee which met on 10 April in Cairo. The meeting took place against the background of Isma'il Safwat's gloomy report of the Liberation Army's difficulties, and the confusion in the Palestinian camp following the death of al-Qadir al-Husayni two days earlier at Kastel. General Safwat demanded an immediate decision to involve the regular armies. After the Transjordanian delegation made it clear to those at the meeting that Abdullah's decision to invade, with or without other Arab states, was final, those states which opposed the invasion felt obliged to re-examine their positions.[25]

Abdullah wasted no time. On 26 April 1948, the Transjordanian Parliament ratified the decision to dispatch the Arab Legion to Palestine. At the same opportunity, Abdullah declared that his efforts to solve the dispute peacefully had failed, and added, 'To me has fallen the honour to save Palestine'.[26]

The political considerations dividing the League between the countries which supported the Hashemites and those which supported their rivals were not the only issues in the background of the discussions about the invasion. Another factor which concerned the leaders of the Arab states was the growing public support in favour of intervention on behalf of the Palestinian Arabs, and against the implementation of the partition plan. A number of Arab states, notably Syria and Lebanon, hoped that the Liberation Army would be able to win the war without them having to involve their own armies.[27] When this failed, they reluctantly joined the invasion in the hope that the 'liberation of Palestine' would not prove too difficult. On 30 April 1948, the League's Political Committee met in Amman and decided that every Arab state must prepare its army for the invasion, which was to take place on 15 May. Following pressure from Transjordan and Iraq, the League appointed Abdullah as general commander of the invading armies.[28]

On the day that the Arab armies crossed the border into Israel, the League's secretariat delivered a memorandum to the UN announcing the invasion and listing the reasons as follows: Palestine was a holy trust of the Arab states, which aimed to put an end to the anarchy prevailing there; the disturbances in Palestine had to be prevented from spreading to the neighbouring countries; the vacuum created by the withdrawal of the British and the absence of any legal order had to be filled. The memorandum concluded that the only solution was the establishment of a Palestinian state on democratic principles, whose residents would enjoy equality before the law. This state would guarantee minority rights and safeguard free access to the holy sites.[29]

AFTER THE INVASION

The confrontation between Haj Amin and Abdullah intensified after the invasion on 15 May. Units of the Arab Legion had remained in various parts of the country, and had fought in the war that preceded the British withdrawal. Now, when the Trans-jordanian Army crossed the border, the Legion quickly gained control of most of the Arab territories to the west of the Jordan. At the same time, efforts were made to organise a Transjordanian military administration to assume the authority of the British administration. Four days after the Legion crossed the Jordan westwards, Abdullah appointed Ibrahim Hashim as general military governor over those parts of the country in the hands of the Arab Legion. Shortly afterwards, he appointed Ahmad Hilmi 'Abd al-Baqi as military governor of Jerusalem.[30] Transjordanian officers were also appointed in other districts as military governors, and they issued orders prohibiting residents from following orders given by the local National Committees that were subordinate to the Arab Higher Institute.[31] On 24 May 1948, Abdullah published a manifesto announcing that the laws which had been in force during the British Mandatory regime were to be retained, 'provided that they do not contradict the Jordanian defence laws and emergency regulations'.[32] During the following months, the Transjordanians continued their efforts, on both the constitutional and executive levels, to nullify the independent status of the territories occupied by the Legion, and to turn them into the 'West Bank' of the Hashemite Kingdom.

Haj Amin's status had deteriorated in the period preceding the invasion. The *al-Jihad al-Muqaddas* units were rife with disorder and internal quarrelling, and suffered from a shortage of weapons and ammunition. Even before the death of 'Abd al-Qadir al-Husayni, the units in each area operated autonomously; following his death, this situation worsened. Each local commander was in direct contact with the Arab Higher Institute in Cairo and with the League's Military Committee in Damascus, and did his utmost to mobilise money and weapons for his own unit.[33]

The hopes of the Palestinian Arabs, which had been raised by the entry of the Liberation Army, were soon disappointed. The two attacks launched by al-Qawuqji, on Tirat Zvi and Mishmar Ha-Emeq, failed, and in the course of the following days his men dispersed among the Arab settlements.[34] According to Muhammad Nimr al-Hawari, commander of the *Najadah*, they were involved in skirmishes, extortion and weapons trading. Haj Amin also describes the corruption and cruelty of the Liberation Army units toward the Palestinian population, and claims that in Jaffa their acts of robbery and killing led to a mass exit from the town[35] (see Appendix C). Throughout the period preceding the invasion and immediately after it, the relationship between Haj Amin and al-Qawuqji was extremely tense. This tension, together with the propaganda campaigns conducted among the Palestinian Arabs by the Arab Higher Institute, led to fights between soldiers of the Liberation Army and *al-Jihad al-Muqaddas*, and a sense of helplessness among the population.[36] The Palestinian camp was further weakened by the fact that the members of the Arab Higher Institute, especially Haj Amin, were so far away. Their absence was made more conspicuous by the fact that Abdullah was not content with his army taking control of the population, but also visited the Arab territories to the west of the Jordan and participated in demonstrations of support organised by his supporters.[37]

The Palestinian Arabs were like a shepherdless flock. Prior to the British withdrawal, a prohibition issued by the Mandatory Government had prevented Haj Amin from entering the country. Now that the British had left, what was it that kept him away? What prevented him from taking his place at the head of his people during the most critical period in their history? And why did most of the members of the Arab Higher Institute remain outside the country?

Haj Amin flatly denied accusations against him that he had avoided returning to Palestine in order to go on enjoying the 'good life' in Egypt. He added, 'My greatest desire is to return to this beloved country to which my soul is bound'. He also described the attempts that he had made to return, together with members of the Institute, both before and after the British withdrawal. In one of these attempts, at the end of September 1948, he had managed to get to Gaza in secret. He remained there for a few days, until the Egyptians returned him forcibly to Cairo.[38]

In keeping with his usual approach, Haj Amin blamed the British for his failure to return. They had supposedly applied pressure on the Arab states when he attempted to enter the country on other occasions, once from Egypt, and once from Syria and Lebanon. It is true that until 15 May 1948 he was prevented from returning by the British. After that date, the fact that he did not return was primarily the result of Abdullah's opposition, for he saw Haj Amin's presence as a threat to his efforts to gain control of Palestine.[39] Abdullah had an obvious interest in keeping Haj Amin out of the country, and it was he who put pressure on members of the League not to allow the Palestinian leader to cross their borders into Palestine.

Haj Amin and the members of the Arab Higher Institute could probably have entered the country had they been really determined to do so. Haj Amin's depiction of their attempts to return was designed to cover up the tensions within the Institute (two of the ten members had resigned), and the arguments surrounding their return to the country.[40] The members of the Institute were aware of the strong criticism being levelled at them by the Palestinian public. A few months before the British withdrawal, Dr Husayn al-Khalidi proposed, at a conference of Palestinian leaders in Damascus, 'to save the honour of the Arab Higher Institute' by having all of its members return to Jerusalem.[41] The members did not accept al-Khalidi's suggestion, preferring to remain in Cairo, which was then the centre of inter-Arab political activity. Concern for their personal security and comfort undoubtedly constituted an additional consideration.[42]

Shortly after the invasion, and disregarding the Arab League's decisions, Haj Amin gave orders from Cairo that the National Committees do their best to reinstate those Palestinian officials who had been employed in the Mandatory administration. The Arab Higher Institute also appointed department directors in place of the British directors who had left, and announced a state of emergency throughout the country.[43] In response, Abdullah sent a communique to Haj Amin with a demand that he stop publishing 'announcements causing confusion', and thanking him for his past services[44] – in effect, attempting to prevent Haj Amin from 'providing such services' in the future, and demonstrating Abdullah's guardianship of Palestinian affairs. As proof of his intentions, Abdullah announced, on 20 December 1948, the appointment of Shaikh Husam al-Din Jarallah (who had been a candidate for the office of Mufti in 1921) as Mufti of Jerusalem in place of Haj Amin. Abdullah later appointed this same shaikh as President of the Supreme Muslim Council.[45]

Although Haj Amin continued his correspondence with the Arab Higher Institute office in Jerusalem, as well as his attempts to rally the Palestinian Arabs under his leadership, he did not present much of an obstacle to Abdullah, and the Palestinian Arabs generally accepted the authority of the Transjordanian officers. The willingness of Ahmad Hilmi, one of the leaders of the Institute, to accept the position of military governor of Jerusalem, probably also contributed to the Palestinian residents' acceptance of the Transjordanian regime. The Iraqi army, which controlled northern Samaria and the 'small triangle' area, also cooperated with the Transjordanian authorities. Problems arose only in Jerusalem and the Hebron hills.

The units of the *al-Jihad al-Muqaddas* which were stationed behind the lines of the Arab Legion were a thorn in the side of both the League's Political Committee and the Transjordanian officers. The Legion's commanders were of the opinion that these units did nothing to help reinforce the line, and that they spent their time in exercises and show training. When the establishment of a Palestinian Government was declared in Gaza, the hostility of these units to the Transjordanian soldiers increased, and Abdullah decided to disarm the units and disperse their members around the areas under his control. The disagreements between Egyptian and Transjordanian officers surrounding the authority to govern was temporarily settled by simultaneously appointing governors from both sides.[46] This arrangement did not interfere with the increasing control of the Arab Legion, and Haj Amin looked on helplessly at the decline of *al-Jihad al-Muqaddas*, one of the last remaining expressions of the idea of Palestinian independence.

In practice, the Transjordanians now had complete control of the Arab areas to the west of the Jordan, and Haj Amin's struggle for the control of Palestine was hopeless. His single source of hope was the Arab League, where Abdullah's activities were noted by his rivals with anxiety. There, Haj Amin and his colleagues found willing listeners for their continued demands for the establishment of a Palestinian Government.

THE EMERGENCE AND DEMISE OF THE 'ALL-PALESTINE GOVERNMENT'

It seems that by July 1948 those Arab states who were opposed to the Hashemites, and who for months had been hesitating about whether or not to accede to Haj Amin's demands to establish a Palestinian Government, had finally made up their minds to do so. The immediate reason for this decision was probably the publication, on 4 July 1948, of the recommendations of the mediator appointed by the UN Security Council, Count Folke Bernadotte. These recommendations included the annexation by Transjordan, with UN approval, of the Arab territories in Palestine to the west of the Jordan and of the Negev region. The British influence in these recommendations was clear, and Abdullah's rivals in the League felt that they had to act.[47] Shortly after the publication of the report, the League's Political Committee met to discuss the proposals, and a decision was taken to set up a provisional Palestinian civil administration. On 10 July, the League's Secretary General publicly announced the decision (see Appendix D).

It might appear that the Arab League had thus acceded to the demands of Haj Amin and the Arab Higher Institute, but this was not the case, since the latter also demanded a government and independence. However, it did mark a thaw in relations and the beginning of a process that was to continue thereafter.[48] The decision did not refer to the establishment of a government, but rather to a provisional civil administration which was to include nine departments headed by Palestinian Arabs, almost all from the Husayni faction. Nevertheless, despite this decision, Abdullah's rivals on the League continued to have their doubts about the project,[49] and this probably explains why no steps were taken to put the new administration into operation.

The Bernadotte plan was never carried out, since it met with opposition from Jews and Arabs alike, with the exception of Abdullah, who alone wished to see it implemented. When reports about the provisional civil administration reached Palestine, the Palestinian Arabs living in areas under the control of the Egyptian army welcomed it with undisguised joy. In the Arab towns to the west of the Jordan, demonstrations broke out against the annexation measures. Abdullah held Haj Amin responsible for organising the demonstrations, and in a secret conversation with the US representative in Transjordan, Wells Stabler, he revealed his opinion of Haj Amin, comparing him to a 'devil straight from hell', and claimed that he operated with 'active material and financial assistance from the League'.[50] At the same opportunity, Abdullah also disclosed that he had been 'obliged ... to call on the League in strong terms to cease its support to the Mufti', and added that he was considering 'quitting the Arab League and withdrawing his army from Palestine'. Abdullah repeated this threat on numerous occasions, and it became clear that this was an efficient way to dictate his wishes to members of the Arab League.

Abdullah took further measures against the League's plan by condemning Haj Amin, and by an appeal to the Palestinian Arabs under Transjordanian control to oppose having their political future determined by others, arguing that they should decide their own fate.[51] At this stage, however, the move within the League to prevent Abdullah from completing his take-over strengthened. Arab states which until then had supported the Transjordanian position, or which had at least avoided taking a stand in the conflict between Abdullah and Haj Amin, now began to move toward the Palestinian side.

During the meeting of the League's Political Committee held between 6–15 September 1948, the League took a further step in this direction by resolving to establish a Palestinian Government, and on 20 September it published an official announcement to this effect. To avoid giving the impression that the decision constituted acquiescence with the partition plan, and to head off such accusations from Transjordan and Iraq, the government was named the All-Palestine Government (*Huqumat 'Ummum Filastin*). This time, Haj Amin and the Arab Higher Institute had a major role in the task of forming the government. Ahmad Hilmi, who had left the Institute to join Abdullah's camp when the latter appointed him governor of Jerusalem, was 'recalled' by the Egyptians, while Haj Amin was placed at the head of the All-Palestine Government.[52] Jamal al-Husayni was appointed Foreign Minister, Raja'i al-Husayni Defence Minister, and Anwar Nusseibeh Government Secretary.

There were signs that this radical step, the establishment of a government, was designed to thwart Abdullah while trying to prevent a complete break with him. Accordingly, the League's Secretary General initially tried to deny the existence of a process aimed at establishing a government.[53] In any case, the opinion prevalent in the League was that Haj Amin should not be included in the government.[54] Abdullah was not satisfied by these attempts to assuage his fears, and responded angrily. He sent telegrams to the League's Secretary General and to Ahmad Hilmi, in which he stated that 'we cannot allow any other hand to interfere in responsibilities or our military government, especially by those who are keen to rule Palestine'.[55] Abdullah proscribed all activity in the 'security zone of the Transjordan Government which extends from the Egyptian kingdom's frontier to Syria and Lebanon'.[56]

On 22 September 1948, the Arab Higher Institute published a statement concerning the establishment of the government.[57] In contrast to the carefully worded formulation of the League's announcement, which spoke of a decision to turn the Palestinian administration into a Palestinian Government, the Institute's announcement was unequivocal: 'The residents of Palestine, by virtue of their right to self-determination, and in accordance with the decisions of the Arab League, have decided to declare the whole of Palestine ... an independent state.'[58] Haj Amin and Ahmad Hilmi, who were acting in unison, were concerned by the efforts of the League's Secretary General to appease Abdullah by obscuring the situation, beginning with a denial of the very intention to establish a government, and followed by declarations that the All-Palestine Government had no connections with the Arab Higher Committee and Haj Amin, and that the government was a 'temporary measure in the present situation'.[59] Abdullah dismissed all of these explanations, stating that 'the Transjordanian army which is presently fighting in Palestine will not allow anyone to interfere with the military authorities there', and that the government 'was established against the wishes of the Arabs of Palestine'.[60] Most of Abdullah's anger was directed at Ahmad Hilmi. Apparently, he was especially angered by the fact that this central figure in the Palestinian leadership (Ahmad Hilmi was the only Palestinian leader of the period who had received the title 'Pasha' from the Ottoman regime) had returned to the fold of his enemy. In a telegram to Hilmi, Abdullah wrote that the establishment of the government was harmful to the Arab cause, and expressed his anger that, of all people, Hilmi had been chosen 'to be the spearhead in this conflict'.[61] At the same time, there were reports that Abdullah was organising the Palestinian Arabs under his control to oppose the All-Palestine Government, and that he intended to hold a conference in Nablus with the aim of establishing a rival government.[62]

Haj Amin knew the figures active in the League very well, and for a number of months had been aware of Abdullah's ability to influence changes in the policies of the Arab states. It was therefore not surprising that both he and the Arab Higher Institute saw the League as too weak a base from which to draw legitimacy for the existence of the All-Palestine Government. Accordingly, and in view of Abdullah's repeated claim that the government had not been elected by the Palestinian Arabs, they decided to hold a founding conference in Gaza (later known as the 'Palestine National Council') and to invite Palestinian representatives from throughout the country to attend.

The League's Secretary General met with ministers of the All-Palestine Government and learned of the preparations for the conference. The preparations themselves were made during meetings of the ministers that were held alternately in Haj Amin's home in the al-Zaitun neighbourhood, and at the Continental Hotel where Ahmad Hilmi was staying.[63]

In accordance with the plan formulated by the Palestinian Arabs in Cairo, Haj Amin was designated to head the planned conference in Gaza. There were those on the League's Secretariat who feared that this would widen the breach with Abdullah unnecessarily, and they tried, unsuccessfully, to convince Haj Amin to remain behind the scenes.

In his collection of articles, Haj Amin describes how he left Cairo secretly on the evening of 27 September, arriving in Gaza on the following day 'with the aid of some free officers and others committed to the cause'.[64] Despite his illegal entry, the Egyptian military authorities in Gaza made no attempt to arrest him. He received an enthusiastic welcome from the local residents and refugees, and Haj Musa al-Surani, one of Gaza's notables and a local representative of the Supreme Muslim Council, hosted him in his home. Ahmad Hilmi stayed at the home of Fa'iq Bsaisso, and the ministers of the All-Palestine Government, who had arrived previously, stayed at the Dia'afat al-Walid hotel owned by Kama'al Mahmud Hassaniyyah on 'Umar al-Mukhtar street.[65] Hassunah describes the period in which the All-Palestine Government ministers stayed at his hotel as follows:

> They arrived at the hotel during the second half of September by taxis from Cairo. Their lodging cost twenty piastres per person per day, and this was paid by Raja'i al-Husayni (the Defence Minister). The members of the government in the

hotel were joined by Husayn al-Husayni, who was responsible for security, and Fa'id al-Idrasi, their intelligence officer. Since the hotel was only designed for overnight stay, the
All-Palestine Government hired a cook and waiter who
looked after their meals. The meals were served in the hotel
entrance room, where the government meetings were also
held. Haj Amin generally participated in the discussions, as
did Hasan Abu al-Sa'ud and Musa al-Surani. In the middle of
October the ministers left and returned by taxi to Egypt.[66]

Haj Amin's stay in Gaza lasted only eight days. In his collection of
articles he describes at length how the Prime Minister, al-Nuqrashi, sent the commander of the Egyptian frontier force to bring
him back to Egypt, and how, when he refused, he was taken back
by force.[67]

During his stay in Gaza, Haj Amin was very busy meeting with
local Palestinian figures and representatives who had arrived from
other areas. Although the Arab Higher Institute invited nearly 150
people to attend the conference, only seventy-five arrived (according to other sources, 83–87). Those who participated included
heads of local municipalities, members of the National Committees, religious and community leaders, tribe leaders, and important professional figures. The Palestinian National Council met
at the *Madrasat al-Falah al-Islamiyyah,* at the entrance to Gaza.
The modest hall was decorated with the flags of the Arab states and
with pictures of Arab rulers, and the representatives who had
arrived took their places on school benches which had been set out
in rows facing the presidential table.[68]

Many of those who did not arrive lived in areas under the control
of the Transjordanian and Iraqi armies, and those who had requested permission to travel to Gaza had been informed by the
military governors that they would not be allowed to return.[69]
Some of those who were thus prevented from attending the
conference sent telegrams expressing their support and identification.[70]

The Palestine National Council was opened on 30 September
1948 by Haj Amin, who said that a Palestinian Government should
have been set up when the British Mandate came to an end in May.
He stated that the Arab Higher Institute had fought for this, but
that 'political desires and obstacles had delayed it, as a result of
which the establishment of a government had been put off until
now'. Although Abdullah's name was not mentioned, it was clear

to those present to whom Haj Amin was referring. Next was the turn of Ahmad Hilmi, who spoke of plans for the future, and called on the representatives to express confidence in the government. The conference unanimously chose Haj Amin as President of the Palestine National Council, and approved the composition of the All-Palestine Government by a majority of sixty-four to eleven.[71] The following day, the Sharif flag of the 1916 Arab revolution was adopted as Palestine's flag, and Jerusalem was declared its capital. Decisions were also taken concerning a general mobilisation to 'save Palestine', the organisation of refugee life, aid for injured families, and the collection of money to finance the government's activities.[72] Finally, the representatives signed the declaration of Palestine's independence, which stated, among other things, that the Arab–Palestinian people had the right to declare the independence of Palestine and found a free, democratic, and sovereign state. The northern borders of the new state were Syria and Lebanon; the eastern, Syria and Transjordan; the western, the Mediterranean sea; and in the south, Egypt[73] (see Appendix E).

The provisional basic law of the All-Palestine Government was passed during two additional meetings of the Palestine National Council, held on 2–3 October. This law provided for the constitution of a three-man Supreme Council in addition to the Palestine National Council and its subordinate Council of Ministers. Arrangements about representation and the authority of the legislative and executive branches were also decided on (see Appendix F).

The Palestinian leaders in Gaza operated under rather miserable conditions. The Egyptian administration was situated in the former British police building, and the offices of the general military governor were in one of the elegant buildings that had been appropriated for the needs of the Egyptian army. In contrast, not one member of the Palestinian leadership was allocated any space in the buildings of the Egyptian authorities. The members of the Palestinian Government were forced to find their own solution. The school building in which the Council met was itself a wretched structure, lacking even electricity. Everything seemed to point to the fact that, while the Egyptians wished to set up the government, they also wanted to conceal it, or at least to give the impression that they were not assisting the Palestinian Arabs, and that the latter were acting on their own initiative.

Notwithstanding these problems, this was a moment of jubilation for the Palestinian Arabs. They finally had a government,

Palestinian ministers and a Palestinian Council, with Haj Amin as President, and a declaration of independence and announcements to the UN and foreign states. Yet in all this enthusiasm, everyone had forgotten that the Palestinian struggle for independence was not at an end. Even those Arab states which had initiated the establishment of the All-Palestine Government avoided giving their outspoken support. Meanwhile, from the east, came the threatening tones of Abdullah, who was not at all inclined to see the Gaza conference as an established fact.

While the Palestine National Council discussions were being held in Gaza, a Palestinian congress was being organised in Amman. This took place on 1 October, at the instigation of the Hashemite regime. The participants included Palestinian municipal heads and notables, and the Transjordanian military governor, Dthuqan al-Husayn. The congress was headed by Suleman Ta'aji al-Faruqi from Ramallah, and the secretary was 'Ajaj Nuwyhed. The conference passed a declaration that the establishment of the All-Palestine Government in Gaza contradicted the wishes and interests of the Palestinian Arabs, that Transjordan and Palestine constituted a territorial unity, and that a Palestinian Government would only be established after the liberation of Palestine and in a democratic fashion.[74]

An additional conference was held in Ramallah on 18 November, at the instigation of the Hashemite Propaganda Society. The participants again included Palestinian notables, and decisions were taken similar to those taken at the Amman congress. At this conference, special emphasis was laid on the desire of those assembled to see Abdullah as 'liberator of Palestine', and to hand over to him the responsibility for finding a solution to the problem, 'either through war or through peace'. The conference also called on the Palestinian youth to enlist in the Arab Legion.[75]

Abdullah's efforts to delegitimise the All-Palestine Government were not limited to organising conferences in Amman and Ramallah. He also arrested Jamal al-Husayni, who had apparently travelled to the Palestinian centres of population in order to promote the All-Palestine Government, and prevented him from reaching the Palestine National Council conference in Gaza.[76] Further, he made efforts to persuade ministers in the All-Palestine Government to desert Haj Amin's camp, and even before the government was ratified in Gaza it was reported that Suleman Tuqan, the mayor of Nablus, had refused to be included in the government as Minister of Transport.[77] Similarly, 'Awni 'Abd al-

Hadi, one of the leaders of the *al-Istiqlal* party, who had been appointed a minister, later resigned his position.[78] On the other hand, both the latter agreed to be included in the Palestinian Government that Abdullah tried to set up in Nablus.[79] Dr Husayn al-Khalidi, who was also a candidate to become a minister, wrote to Ahmad Hilmi that 'we should wait and employ wisdom and deliberation'.[80] As mentioned above, Abdullah also appointed Husam al-Din Jarallah as Mufti of Jerusalem and President of the Supreme Muslim Council, in an attempt further to reduce Haj Amin's prestige.[81]

At this stage of the struggle, it seemed that the political future of Palestine depended on whether or not there would be an All-Palestine Government. Apart from the fact that the Trans-jordanian army was in control of most of the territory that was to constitute the new state, Abdullah was doing his utmost to undermine the All-Palestine Government by organising conferences in competition with the Palestine National Council conference in Gaza, and by persuading members of Haj Amin's camp to withdraw their support from him. However, the real struggle was fought over the position of the Arab states. The immediate question was whether those member states of the League which had instigated the establishment of the All-Palestine Government would now officially recognise it.

Ahmad Hilmi initially declared that 'Egypt, Iraq, Syria, Lebanon, Yemen and Saudi Arabia will grant the new government immediate recognition', and additional reports suggested that a further ten states would follow suit.[82] These forecasts were made on the basis of undertakings that had been given to the All-Palestine Government by members of the League on the eve of the Palestine National Council's conference in Gaza. Shortly after the opening of the conference, the Saudi Foreign Minister, Muhsen al-Barazi, who was in Cairo at the time, met with the Egyptian Prime Minister and Secretary General of the League to discuss the All-Palestine Government and Abdullah's opposition to it. After the talks, al-Barazi announced that 'matters are progressing from good to better and that there is no doubt that the All-Palestine Government will be recognised by the Arab states'.[83] When asked why a Palestinian Government had not been established on 17 May 1948, al-Barazi replied that the current breakdown in relations with Abdullah was less serious than it had been then, because public opinion throughout the Arab world was now rapidly turning against Abdullah.[84] It seems that the All-Palestine Prime Minister was optimistic that his government would be recognised, and he even appealed to the US ambassador to Egypt on the matter. After describing to him the process that had led to the constitution of the All-Palestine Government, he expressed his government's eagerness to establish ties of friendship and cooperation with the US.[85]

This optimism waned and finally disappeared when it became clear that Abdullah's pressure on the League was taking its toll. Meanwhile, consultations continued in Cairo in an attempt to reach an agreement that would enable Egypt to recognise the All-Palestine Government while avoiding an extreme response from Abdullah. Britain also pressured Egypt not to recognise the new government, although al-Nuqrashi announced that he was not prepared to give the British an undertaking that Egypt would not do so. The League's Secretary General was of the opinion that the Arabs were united, and that Abdullah would eventually add his voice to Arab unity.[86]

Ahmad Hilmi continued to urge the Arab states and the League's Secretary General to speed up recognition of his government. The Egyptian Government met for a special discussion on the subject, but the Prime Minister, al-Nuqrashi, could only say that, 'the question of granting recognition has almost reached a positive solution'.[87] On the other hand, in his meeting with the League's Secretary General on 10 October, Jamal al-Husayni was given the impression that there had been no real progress on the issue. On leaving the meeting, al-Husayni said that 'his government would continue tirelessly to organise its work, despite the League's decision to postpone recognition of it for the time being'.[88]

Members of the League blamed Haj Amin for the situation that had arisen, claiming that were it not for him, it would have been easier to reach agreement regarding the recognition of the All-Palestine Government. Mahsan al-Bawarzi claimed that all the Arab states had tried to convince Haj Amin not to participate in the government because of the negative attitude of the foreign countries to him, and added that the Arab states had been disappointed when Haj Amin rejected their advice.[89] One may assume that even had Haj Amin taken their advice, Abdullah would still not have conceded his annexation plans. But al-Bawarzi's argument was designed more to conceal the reluctance to provoke a confrontation with Abdullah than it was to explain the hesitancy in granting the All-Palestine Government recognition.

In any case, Haj Amin was not at all inclined to concede his position at the head of the Palestinian leadership, and, to the obvious displeasure of the Arab states, continued to operate the All-Palestine Government from Cairo. The offices of the Higher Arab Executive had not been closed after the establishment of the government, and its activities continued as before. Bearing in mind the changing situation in the inter-Arab arena, Haj Amin was clever enough to create a political structure that prevented his status from being undermined: at the bottom of this structure stood the Council of Ministers of the All-Palestine Government; above this the Palestine National Council; and above that the Supreme Council. In practice if not in theory, Haj Amin placed the Higher Arab Executive at the very top of this pyramid. Haj Amin was officially President of the National Council, the Supreme Council, and the Executive. As such, he demanded the central authority in the Palestinian issue, and fought the plans of the Arab League members to reduce him to a marginal figure. In the eyes of many of his countrymen, Haj Amin remained the spokesman and representative of the Palestinian Arabs, a status that he guarded jealously.[90]

After being brought back to Cairo at the beginning October 1948 by the Egyptian army at the conclusion of the Palestine National Council's discussions, Haj Amin sent telegrams to all the Arab kings and presidents. He thanked them, along with their people and armies, for their 'help in saving Palestine and preserving its Arab character'. On 24 October 1948, he sent a telegram to the chairman of the Transjordanian Parliament with a proposal for 'cooperation to further the interests of the Arab nation in all its lands'.[91] His government, which remained in Gaza for only a few days, was primarily occupied with securing recruits to turn the *al-Jihad al-Muqaddas* units into a Palestinian army; Ahmad Hilmi announced that this army would be one of the active Arab armies. The preparations which the recruiting of a Palestinian army involved generated the feeling that the All-Palestine Government really was occupied in building the new state, a feeling that was boosted by reports that the Foreign Minister, Jamal al-Husayni, had decided to send representatives of the All-Palestine Government, among them Ahmad al-Shuqairy and Henry Qatan, to the UN.[92] The government also decided to issue passports to anyone recognised as a member of the Palestinian people, and within a short period of time approximately 14,000 passports were distributed, mostly to notables and businessmen in the Gaza Strip[93] (see Appendix H). While the All-Palestine Government was in

Gaza, the Prime Minister, and Defence and Interior Ministers had plenty to do: the Prime Minister worked to secure recognition of his government, the Defence Minister was busy recruiting for the army, and the Interior Minister was busy with the preparation and issuing of passports. The other ministers, however, could not carry out the functions of their colleagues in other countries, for the simple reason that these were within the jurisdiction of the Egyptian military authority.

A year after the Palestine National Council conference in Gaza, the idea arose of renewing the composition of the All-Palestine Government. In response, one of the important Egyptian newspapers wrote that such a government would be meaningless, 'because it would lack financial resources and territory to govern, as the Gaza Strip is managed by the Egyptian authorities and the rest of Palestine is under the control of the Transjordanian army'. The newspaper noted that the proposal to renew the government in the Gaza Strip, with its mainly refugee population, was unreasonable, 'since Egypt is not prepared to hand over to anyone its southern border'.[94] Indeed, apart from the months of Israeli rule following the Sinai campaign, Gaza remained under Egyptian military administration from May 1948 until 1967, and before the signing of the Rhodes agreement in February 1949 the Gaza Strip was known as 'the Palestinian areas subordinate to the supervision of the Egyptian forces'. The civilian Governor General, who was always an Egyptian general, and the regional governors controlled every aspect of life. They remained the only ruling authority even during the period in which a Legislative Council (al-Majlis al-Tashri'i) operated in the area in the 1950s and 1960s. Referring to this subject in his collection of articles, Haj Amin describes how the Egyptian authorities prevented him from returning to the Gaza area after the Rhodes agreement. He claims that the authorities even refused to allow him and a few other members of the Higher Arab Executive to visit residents of the refugee camps, for reasons connected with the maintenance of law and order.[95]

There was indeed something grotesque in the existence of a Palestinian population which had its own government, but which was governed by an Egyptian regime and had its affairs managed by the Egyptian army. The situation, in fact, illustrates very clearly that the whole idea of the All-Palestine government was conceived in the League as a function of inter-Arab disputes rather than in order to honour any undertaking given to the Palestinian Arabs by the Arab states.

While contacts continued in Cairo regarding the recognition of the All-Palestine Government, expectation centred on the results of Iraq's efforts to persuade Abdullah to accept the establishment of the government. A few days after the end of the Palestine National Conference, it was reported that Iraq was about to recognise the government, and that 'it is already possible to see the beginning of a split between Iraq and Transjordan'. A short time later, however, Iraq was still hesitating about whether to join Abdullah or Farouk.[96] In his memoirs, Taha al-Hashimi describes a conversation that he had at this time with the Iraqi Prime Minister, Muzahim al-Pachachi. The Prime Minister told al-Hashimi that he had failed to win Abdullah over, and advised the Iraqi regent not to grant the All-Palestine Government recognition should Abdullah remain adamant in his refusal, 'because the matter bears on the continued existence of the League and he does not want it to collapse'. Finally, however, the Egyptians persuaded the Prime Minister to change his mind, and on his return to Baghdad he passed a decision in the government recognising the All-Palestine Government.[97] Toward the middle of October, Egypt announced its recognition of the government,[98] after which Syria, Lebanon, Iraq, Saudi Arabia and Yemen followed suit.[99]

The recognition of the Palestinian Government was unaccompanied by formal or ceremonial measures; no official documents were exchanged, nor were diplomatic representatives appointed. In fact, it was only in media announcements that this event was given expression. It was clear that the Arab governments' recognition of the government was half-hearted, the reason being that between the League's decision to establish the Palestinian administration in July, following the Bernadotte plan, and the recognition of the Palestinian Government in October, the situation of the Arabs in their war in Palestine had changed for the worse.

At the very same time that the government was being recognised by those Arab states which had decided on its establishment, IDF (Israel Defence Forces) troops were preparing to attack the Egyptian army, with the aim of cutting off its supply lines and conquering the Negev. 'Operation Yoav' (or the 'Ten Plagues') began on 15 October 1948, and within a few days a large part of the Negev had been captured, along with the town of Beersheba.[100]

The Egyptian army was routed; part had retreated and the remainder was under siege. This development, coming as it did in the second half of October, had an immediate influence on the status of the All-Palestine Government. The Egyptians had entered the war confident that they would soon be marching on Tel Aviv, but now saw their army convincingly defeated and trapped by the IDF forces. In contrast to the Egyptians, the Arab Legion was still at its full strength, and in fact remained the only real Arab force left on the battlefield. The Egyptians no longer had the heart for political conflict with Abdullah. As a result, Egypt's relations with the All-Palestine Government fluctuated between disinterest and viewing this body as a nuisance and source of trouble.

On the eve of 'Operation Yoav', there were reports of a British warning that 'the Gaza Government is likely to be captured by the Jews', thus supposedly justifying Abdullah's demand to position the government in the old city of Jerusalem, which was 'safer, and guarded by elite soldiers of the Legion'.[101] The condition of those in Gaza deteriorated daily, both as a result of reports that Egyptian army units were retreating in the south and east, and because of the bombing and shelling of the city by the IDF.[102] After just two weeks of activity, and a few days after the All-Palestine Government secured recognition from six Arab states, its ministers left Gaza. They evacuated the hotel in which they had been staying and, before the way to Egypt was totally cut off, left despondently for Cairo.[103]

In Cairo they met Haj Amin, who had been updated on recent events, and held a number of consultations with him. It seems that what Haj Amin had to say was not very optimistic, since a few days later it was reported that the Foreign Minister in the All-Palestine Government, Jamal al-Husayni, had declared: 'The Palestine Government is prepared to hand over its territories to Transjordan, if Abdullah will cooperate with the other Arab states to remove the Zionists from Palestine'.[104] A further report (from Paris) stated that Jamal al-Husayni had announced that 'he does not object to the annexation of Palestine to Transjordan, or to any other Arab state, on condition that this be decided by the Arab League'.[105] The League took no such decision, although a different source reported that at the end of October 1948 the Secretary General, 'Abd al-Rahman Azzam, had requested that the Arab states cease their contacts with the All-Palestine Government.[106] Whether or not this source was accurate, the general trend at the time was clearly to appease Abdullah. This seems to have been successful, since, in a speech to the Transjordanian Parliament on 1 November, Abdullah said that, 'there are no disagreements between the Arab states', and added: 'If we did not agree to the

111

establishment of the All-Palestine Government, this was not because of disagreements of principle, but rather because we did not believe that the time was right for it'.[107]

In order to ensure that the 'right time' for the establishment of an independent Palestine never would arise, Abdullah now authorised preparations for a Palestinian conference to be held in Jericho. The aim of this conference, which was held on 1 December and known as the 'Jericho Congress' or the 'Second Palestinian Conference', was to give the annexation process the appearance of a democratic proceeding. With the Gaza Strip isolated from Egypt and the All-Palestine Government absent from the region, it was not difficult for the Transjordanian military governors and Abdullah's Palestinian supporters to gather a few hundred people in Jericho, including delegations from the different Arab towns. Apart from the Palestinian representatives, participants in the congress included the military governors, representatives from various organisations, religious and educational figures, and a large number of representatives of the media.[108] 'Ajaj Nuwyhed, who had been secretary of the First Palestinian Congress held in Amman two months previously, now served as secretary of the Jericho Congress. As President of the Congress, Abdullah chose Muhammad 'Ali al-Ja'abri, who had deserted Haj Amin's camp to join the king in the wake of the recent changes.[109] In his speech to the congress, al-Ja'abri denied the legitimacy of the All-Palestine Government, and called for annexation as a move toward the unity of the Arab states. He proposed that the task of solving the problem of Palestine be imposed on Abdullah.[110]

Proposals adopted by the Jericho Congress included an expression of thanks to the Arab states for their efforts to liberate the country, opposition to the partitioning of the country, the unification of Transjordan and Palestine as the first step toward the unification of the Arab states, a campaign to return the refugees, and an oath of allegiance (*Bayah*) to Abdullah as King of Palestine.[111] This was the first version of the decisions taken at the Jericho Congress, and it included a reservation that the regime would be handed over to Abdullah in return for his undertaking to liberate the whole of Palestine. Abdullah was furious with this text, which had already been broadcast on Radio Ramallah, and its authors were forced to make changes to it after the close of the Congress. The amended decisions called for the unification of Palestine and Transjordan into one political entity to be called the 'Hashemite Arab Kingdom', and authorised Abdullah to solve the

112

problem of Palestine *as he saw fit*.[112] Shortly after Abdullah received the decisions from a delegation that came to his palace at Shuna, they were approved by the Transjordanian Government.[113] Not surprisingly, this caused a wave of protests throughout the Arab world. The League's Secretary General condemned the annexation, Radio Damascus expressed displeasure, and in Egypt the heads of the *'ulama* met to give religious content to the objection to the measures taken by Transjordan.[114] Abdullah was apparently unimpressed by these protests, and sent a message to the Egyptian Prime Minister, al-Nuqrashi, requesting Egypt's support for the decisions taken at the Jericho Congress. The Egyptian Prime Minister's only comment was that, in adopting a separatist policy and abandoning the consensus set by the League, Transjordan had taken an 'unsuccessful step'.[115] Despite the helplessness of both the Arab states and the Palestinian leadership in the face of the measures taken by Abdullah, Haj Amin managed to cause disturbances in those areas under the control of the Transjordanian army. He was involved in the incitement and organisation of acts of terror against Abdullah, which even spread to the Palestinian refugees on the east of the Jordan. Abdullah responded with a wave of arrests among Haj Amin's colleagues and supporters.[116]

Law and order was eventually restored, and Haj Amin was unable to halt the rapid development of events. On 6 January 1949, Israel and Egypt announced a mutual cease-fire and their readiness to enter negotiations immediately.[117] On 1 February 1949, the acting UN mediator, Ralph J. Bunche, announced that invitations had been sent to the other six members of the League to conduct armistice negotiations with Israel.[118] Although the call of the League's Secretary General in Cairo to concentrate efforts for a war with the Zionists and their supporters still resounded,[119] the League was no longer a body capable of uniting the Arab states for any kind of effort. Each of its states was now occupied with its own problems, and particularly with the effort to end its involvement in the war.

In December 1948 and January 1949, Abdullah organised additional conferences in Nablus and Ramallah, with the participation of Palestinian leaders, during which support was expressed for the annexation plan. Although in private they criticised the measures taken by Abdullah, in public the dignitaries of the Palestinian towns competed among themselves to demonstrate loyalty to the king, and fought for the offices that he had to distribute.[120] Without waiting for the formal annexation, which was to take place in April 1950, Abdullah began to distribute state offices – in the interior administration, foreign service, and Upper House of the Transjordanian Parliament – to Palestinian Arabs who were at the centre of the conferences organised by the Hashemites.[121] The process of integrating the Palestinian political public into the Transjordanian kingdom was at its height.

Parallel to this integration, the Palestinian leadership in Cairo began to disintegrate. In the first years after its establishment, the All-Palestine Government was inactive and lacked even the means to pay the salaries of its ministers. As a result, they began to return to their previous occupations. Dr. Futi Freij, the Minister of Economic Affairs, opened a private clinic, as did the Minister of Health, Dr Husayn al-Khalidi. The Minister of Agriculture, Amin Aqil, received a position in the League. Michel Abaqarius, the Minister of Finance, went to Beirut where he was appointed a lecturer in the university. Raja'i al-Husayni, the Minister of Defence, found a position as advisor in the Ministry of Transport of the Saudi Arabian Government. 'Awni 'Abd al-Hadi (Minister for Social Affairs), 'Ali Hassnah (Minister of Justice), and Anwar Nusseibeh (Secretary of State), left for Amman. In the Transjordanian capital, Nusseibeh was given a seat in parliament, Hassnah was appointed deputy Minister of the Interior, and 'Abd al-Hadi was made Transjordan's ambassador to Egypt. Yusaf Sahiyun (Minister of Propaganda) found a position as manager of a medicine warehouse in Amman.[122]

In spite of this, the All-Palestine Government continued to function in a limited way in Gaza, where its small staff was primarily occupied with recruiting volunteers for the *al-Jihad al-Muqaddas* units that still existed in the region. The Prime Minister, Ahmad Hilmi, remained in a modest office in the al-Zaitun district of Cairo from which, with a few assistants, he managed what was left of his government. This now mainly consisted of issuing passports to those who still wanted them. The office also continued to manage the affairs of the Arab National Bank which was headed by Hilmi. Raja'i al-Husayni, who retained his position as Minister of Defence in the All-Palestine Government until the signing of the armistice agreement between Egypt and Israel,[123] sent an appeal to the League's finance committee on 30 January 1949 concerning the financial distress that was paralysing the activities of the *al-Jihad al-Muqaddas* units in the Gaza area.[124] On 15 February, the League's Secretary General sent a reply to Raja'i al-

114

Husayni, and later to the Prime Minister, Ahmad Hilmi. The Secretary General wrote that the Arab League could no longer continue to fund Palestinian activity in Gaza, since the Arab states had stopped sending their promised payments.[125] In a separate letter, Raja'i al-Husayni informed the League of the decision to dismantle the 'Palestinian Brigade' in Gaza, and demanded that the League cover those debts still remaining. This letter was dated 21 February 1949 – three days before the signing of the armistice agreement at Rhodes between Israel and Egypt.[126]

The two Palestinian leaders who remained in Cairo during the following years – Haj Amin and Ahmad Hilmi – continued to struggle to ensure that the Palestinian issue remained on the Arab League's political agenda. Egypt's attitude to the issue was ambivalent: it had faced a serious crisis as a result of its involvement in the war, and now suffered from both a budgetary deficit and from the growing strength of militant organisations. The most prominent of these was the 'Muslim Brotherhood', whose members murdered the Prime Minister, al-Nuqrashi, at the end of December 1948.[127] Leaders of the regime in Cairo were not pleased by the cooperation between the Palestinian Arabs and the Muslim Brotherhood, and showed singular impatience at the repeated appeals of the All-Palestine Government and the Arab Higher Institute for political and financial support from the Arab League.[128] However, Egypt still wished to preserve its image as defender of Palestinian interests against the scheming of its rival, Transjordan. Cairo thus spoke with two voices – one rejecting the All-Palestine Government and the other supporting it.

In August 1949, Ahmad Hilmi reminded the League's Political Committee that the All-Palestine Government was 'the legal government' of Palestine and demanded that it be invited to meetings of the committee.[129] On 17 October 1949, the day that the Arab League Council met for its eleventh session, the All-Palestine Government protested at not having been invited to participate. It also threatened that if it were not invited to future sessions, it would not consider itself bound by any decisions taken on the Palestinian issue. Transjordan objected vehemently to the idea of the participation of the All-Palestine Government, and even rejected two compromise proposals put forward by Egypt: one, that the League appoint a Palestinian representative, as had been the custom in the past; and, two, that two Palestinian representatives appear, one appointed by Transjordan, and the other by Egypt.[130] The Transjordanian delegation argued that conditions had changed, and that by this time, the end of 1949, the delegation also included Palestinian representatives. After the Transjordanian representative threatened to leave the session, the Lebanese Prime Minister decided that, 'the damage caused by the absence of a small Palestinian representation is less than that caused by the absence of the Transjordanian representation', and the League decided not to invite Palestinian representatives, even if they were not part of a delegation from the All-Palestine Government.[131] The League went on to remove the issue from its agenda. Despite the disinclination of the Egyptian press to show any favour to Abdullah, in its coverage of the dispute within the League it had expressed criticism of the All-Palestine Government ever since its establishment. The newspaper *al-Ahram* wrote that, 'the establishment of a Palestinian state is a very difficult matter', and added that, 'the problem is already not a state, but rather to which neighbouring country the remaining territories of Palestine should be annexed'.[132] A different Egyptian newspaper declared: 'It is clear that what remains of Palestine will not be able to exist independently, either economically, or politically'.[133]

Haj Amin and Ahmad Hilmi did not give up, and they renewed their efforts to ensure the participation of a Palestinian delegation in the forthcoming twelfth session of the League, to be held in April 1950. It is 'not honourable', began one of the All-Palestine Government's letters, 'for these states that a government they have recognised is not invited to a session at which its case is to be examined and discussed ... This government appeals to the conscience of the Arab League and abjures the Arab Nations ...'[134]

This time the members of the League ignored Transjordan's objections and decided to invite a Palestinian observer. Both sides were furious, Abdullah because a representative had been invited, and the All-Palestine Government because the representative was not from its ranks.[135] Abdullah's preparations for formal annexation apparently angered the Egyptians. At their behest the League's Secretariat decided, at the end of March 1950, to take a further step and to request the All-Palestine Government to send a representative to the session, despite Abdullah's protests.[136]

Nonetheless, it became clear in the following days that this invitation did not signify a change in the League's approach to the government. Now, as always, the stand taken by the Arab states in regard to the Palestinian problem was a result of their respective policies toward each other. Although Ahmad Hilmi continued to write memoranda and demand that the League and its members make amends for the affront to the All-Palestine Government, the government was fated to decline. After its first conference in Gaza, the Palestine National Council never met again, and the government ceased to be a factor in the complicated web of inter-Arab rivalry. On 23 September 1952, the League Council took the following decision:

> In view of the cessation of the activities of the All-Palestine Government as a result of the prevailing conditions, the Head of the Government [Ahmad Hilmi] shall represent Palestine on the Council of the League of Arab states, and the sum of 1,500 Egyptian pounds, out of the funds under the control of the financial experts, shall be allocated to him to cover the expenses of his office for the year 1952.[137]

The decision was passed unanimously, and thus the thirty-year drama of Haj Amin's efforts to achieve independence for Palestine came to an end. The curtain had fallen, but not completely: the All-Palestine Government continued to exist, even if only symbolically, until Ahmad Hilmi's death on 29 June 1963, and the establishment of the PLO at the beginning of 1964.

During the last years of his life, Ahmad Hilmi tried to demonstrate some kind of activity by publishing statements and representing the government at the Arab League – efforts which Jordan never stopped trying to sabotage. In July 1958, he sent a telegram to those responsible for the coup in Iraq, in his capacity as Prime Minister of Palestine, wishing them success 'in the name of the Palestinian people'.[138] Haj Amin was quick to demonstrate his superiority over the All-Palestine Government, and a few days later sent a delegation to Baghdad on behalf of the Arab Higher Committee. The delegation presented the Foreign Minister of the new regime, 'Abd al-Jaba'ar Jumrad, with a map of Palestine with the inscription, 'We are returning'. The delegation also expressed the support of the Palestinian people for the Iraqi revolution.[139]

As far as Ahmad Hilmi was concerned, this seems simply to have been another of his attempts to demonstrate that the All-Palestine Government was still active, as well, perhaps, as an attempt to find a patron for his neglected government. Qassem's regime did indeed adopt the Palestinian issue, although it turned to Haj Amin, the enemy of the previous monarchical regime. The Iraqis preferred him to Ahmad Hilmi because, given the background of the decline of the All-Palestine Government, Haj Amin had once again became prominent as a leader who enjoyed the trust of the

Palestinian Arabs. For its part, the League did not shut down the government's office, and continued to allocate small amounts of money to Ahmad Hilmi for the next few years.[140] Possibly this was an attempt by Egypt to preserve a rival body that would serve as a substitute to Haj Amin's Arab Higher Institute, possibly a gesture to the aged Pasha who had defected from Abdullah's camp to throw his lot in with Egypt. In contrast to his colleagues in the All-Palestine Government, Hilmi had not gone to Amman after the government's escape from Gaza.

The news of Ahmad Hilmi's death in Beirut at the age of eighty received only modest coverage in the Arab press. Those who published death notices included 'The Organisation of Palestinian Pupils' in Egypt, 'The Palestinian Women's Society', employees of the 'Arab Egypt Bank', 'The Arab National Bank' in Gaza, and a number of figures in the Arab world. Haj Amin also published a notice in the name of the Arab Higher Institute, and praised Ahmad Hilmi, who had died 'grasping the flag of Jihad'.[141] Nothing was heard from Jordan, although the authorities permitted Ahmad Hilmi's burial close to the al-Aqsa mosque. After his death it was reported that the League's Secretary General, 'Abd al-Khaliq Hassunah, was in contact with various figures with the aim of choosing a new Prime Minister.[142] Jordan, however, frustrated the attempt, since Husayn objected to the existence of a body that would contradict the legitimacy of his continued rule of the West Bank, even if such a body was no more than a symbol.

In his collection of articles published in 1954, Haj Amin makes no reference to the conflict between the All-Palestine Government and Abdullah, nor to the fact that the Arab states preferred to preserve the unity of the League rather than honour their commitment to the Palestinian cause. Of this whole period, it is his arrival in Gaza to participate in the conference of the Palestine National Council, and his forced expulsion from it after eight days, that he chooses to write about.[143] In their campaign for independence, during the most critical period in their history, the Palestinian Arabs had suffered a defeat at the hands of their Arab brothers, and on this matter Haj Amin remains silent. The explanation for this would appear to be Haj Amin's hope that he still had a role to play, and that he would need these 'brothers' in the future.

118

4

From the Defeat of 1948 to the Establishment of the PLO

FAILURE OF THE EFFORTS TO PREVENT THE ANNEXATION OF THE WEST BANK TO JORDAN

As mentioned above, Haj Amin did not abolish the Arab Higher Institute or close its offices after the meeting of the Palestine National Council in Gaza and the establishment of the All-Palestine Government. In fact, there was no longer any justification, at least in theory, for the existence of a pre-state body such as the Arab Higher Institute, since institutions of state had now been established: a government, a National Council under Haj Amin's Presidency, and even a Supreme Council with him at its head. There were two apparent reasons for Haj Amin's policy. First, his fear that the members of the League would not recognise him as president of the Palestine National Council; and second, his fear that the All-Palestine Government would be abolished or simply decline. These fears were supported by the fact that the members of the League who had decided on the establishment of the government were careful not to place Haj Amin at its head and continued in their refusal to grant him any position, in an attempt to reduce the opposition of the Hashemite regime to a minimum. Haj Amin, refusing to accept such dictates, organised and headed the conference in Gaza. In effect, this move amounted to a challenge not only to Transjordan and Iraq, but also to the block of League members who opposed the Hashemites. Haj Amin was well aware of the fact that the very establishment of the All-Palestine Government was merely part of the ongoing conflict between Abdullah and his rivals, and therefore took into account the possibility that those who had initiated the establishment of the government would give in to Abdullah at a later stage, as they had in the past. Thus he kept the Arab Higher Institute in existence, for this was a body which, over the years, had gained recognition and a reputation within the Arab world. In retrospect, his fears were justified by the events of the following months: the capitulation of the Arab League to Abdullah, and Egypt's refusal to transfer any governing authority in Gaza to the All-Palestine Government.

Among those Palestinian leaders who had scattered at the end of 1948 and the beginning of 1949 were some of Haj Amin's personal assistants and members of the Arab Higher Institute. Assisted by the handful of supporters who remained with him, Haj Amin continued his activities from his house in Cairo, warning against the actions of Transjordan, and claiming that the Arab Higher Institute was the sole legitimate representative of the Palestinian Arabs. However, the 1920s and 1930s, the years in which Haj Amin had been able to enlist support and funds from the Muslim and Arab world with ease, were past. So too was the period when he had controlled the resources of the *waqf* himself, by means of the Supreme Muslim Council, without Egypt's involvement. The Institute now had financial problems, and Haj Amin could not cover the expenses of the office staff which operated from his home in the al-Zaitun neighbourhood of Cairo. In January 1949, he was forced to dismiss fifteen of the Institute's employees, leaving only ten.[1] In addition, Haj Amin's support for the Muslim Brotherhood, a serious rival to the Egypt regime, led to increased tension between him and the Egyptian authorities. The police suspected his supporters of cooperating with the Brotherhood in their violent activities, and from time to time searches were conducted in the homes of some of the members of the Husayni family in the al-Zaitun district.[2]

It was a mere two and a half years since Haj Amin had been welcomed in Farouk's palace as an honoured guest, and less time still since he had organised the conference of the Palestine National Council in Gaza. Egypt had then granted him refuge and given him both political backing and material help in his struggle against Abdullah over the future of Palestine. But now the tables had turned. Egypt, which had once been a source of great support, could no longer be relied upon. Haj Amin eventually came to fear that should he leave Egypt, he would not be allowed to return.[3] According to Munir Abu Fadil, a Lebanese Christian appointed by Haj Amin as commander of one of the *al-Jihad al-Muqqadas* units, Haj Amin had begun to think in uncharacteristic ways.

He admitted to Abu Fadil that he had pursued the wrong policy, and that it would have been preferable had Palestine turned into a British colony rather than end up in its present condition. He also expressed a desire to return to Jerusalem in a private capacity.[4] Whether or not this description by Abu Fadil is accurate, it is clear that Haj Amin's situation in Egypt was difficult and that he had begun to search for ways to extricate himself from it.

One option was to enlist the support of Saudi Arabia, whose relations with Transjordan were marked by cooperation accompanied by a mutual suspicion that had existed since the 1920s.[5] Saudi Arabia was less sensitive than Egypt to Abdullah's threats to the unity of the Arab League, and was therefore more willing to oppose the annexation of areas of Palestine to Transjordan, and to support Haj Amin's efforts to achieve an 'independent Palestine'.

In July 1949, there were reports that Ibn Sa'ud was planning to hold a World Islamic Congress in Mecca in October of that year. The Congress was to discuss the question of annexation, and Haj Amin was to be the guest of honour. The Saudis considered passing a resolution at the Congress to make Haj Amin ruler of Palestine, or, alternatively, to offer the post to Farouk and make Haj Amin second-in-command to the king.[6]

There is no question that in the collection of articles and memoirs which he wrote in Lebanon, Haj Amin greatly exaggerates in attributing responsibility for all that had occurred in the Arab states concerning the Palestinian issue to the pressure put on those countries by the Western superpowers. On occasions, however, there was some truth to his claims, as when the United States and Britain intervened in his activities in Saudi Arabia.

In September, there were reports of discussions among the Palestinian Arabs in Cairo about the possibility of establishing a new Palestinian government or reorganising the All-Palestine Government. The reports added that Haj Amin had assembled his supporters to discuss this subject, since a number of ministers in the Palestinian Government had resigned or returned to their previous occupations, and 'the government could not function'.[7] In the meantime, Haj Amin arrived in Mecca, and it was reported that he was there as a guest of King Ibn Sa'ud.[8]

This activity did not go unnoticed in Amman. The British representative there, Sir Alec S. Kirkbride, sent a telegram to the Foreign Office in London, saying that the Prime Minister, Tawfiq Abu al-Huda, had informed him of Haj Amin's activities, which were designed, according to him, to 'prevent [the] formal union of eastern Arab Palestine with Jordan'. The Prime Minister verified

121

that Syria and Lebanon would oppose this activity and requested that it be made clear to Saudi Arabia that Haj Amin's plan contradicted the wishes of Britain, and that the United States would use its influence on Ibn Sa'ud. Kirkbride added in his telegram that he had no doubt that the 'continued delay in union [i.e. of Jordan and Palestine] under reference is permitting [the Mufti] and other anti-Hashemite elements to regain ground in Palestine'.[9] Kirkbride contacted London on 4 October, and only four days later the British Foreign Office instructed its ambassador in Jedda to make clear to the Saudi Government 'the undesirability of giving any encouragement to the political activities of Haj Amin el-Husseini', and noted that 'we are suggesting to the U.S. Embassy [in London] that similar instructions should be sent to your U.S. colleague' (the US ambassador in Jedda).[10] Four days later, the ambassador to Saudi Arabia, Scott Fox, reported to the Foreign Ministry that he had already spoken with Shaikh Yusuf Yasin (of Syrian origin, who served as advisor on foreign affairs to the king), who had told him that Haj Amin was staying in Mecca as a pilgrim, and that it had been made clear to him that as such he was prohibited from taking part in any political activity. He added that Haj Amin was complying with this prohibition, and that guards were accompanying him to supervise his behaviour.[11]

Haj Amin's hope for a Saudi initiative against the annexation of Palestine proved false. Although the intervention of Britain and the United States was not the only factor in halting the initiative, it was certainly an important one. Another was the impossibility of forming a common front of those member states in the League who opposed the annexation and were displeased by the continuation of Abdullah's steps to implement it. Although Haj Amin returned to Egypt from Mecca highly frustrated and aware that his influence had suffered a further decline, he was not prepared to accept what was happening to the Arab territories to the west of the Jordan.

In these territories, the new reality very quickly took shape. As early as the middle of 1949, Abdullah had included four Palestinian Arabs in the government of Tawfiq Abu al-Huda,[12] as well as having appointed a number of Palestinian Arabs to positions in the various departments of the Transjordanian administration. Haj Amin's great rival, Raghib al-Nashashibi, became Minister for Palestinian Refugees, and was later appointed deputy Governor General for the Arab territories to the west of the Jordan.[13] All this took place while preparations for the elections to the Jordanian Parliament, which were to take place in April 1950, were at their height. There were also rumours at the time about negotiations for a non-aggression treaty between Abdullah and Israel, which caused agitation among the 700,000 Palestinian Arabs (400,000 indigenous residents and 300,000 refugees) on both sides of the Jordan.[14] These events provided Haj Amin with great scope for his activities.

The decision taken by the Arab League between 1946–48, to leave the responsibility for determining the political future of Palestine in the hands of its residents, had never been altered. This decision became central to Haj Amin's struggle. Applying to the heads of all the Arab states in the name of the Arab Higher Institute, he demanded that they honour their promises, since Abdullah's decision to annex parts of Palestine 'contravenes the obligations that all the Arab rulers and the Arab League Council took upon themselves'.[15] An appeal signed by the Arab Higher Institute called on the Palestinian Arabs to boycott the elections to the Jordanian parliament, and included threats against those taking part.[16] In a further appeal very shortly before the elections, Haj Amin accused Abdullah of using the elections as 'a means to return what remains of Palestine to the British regime, since Jordan is an ally of Britain'.[17]

The elections were held as planned on 11 April 1950, and the Palestinian Arabs flocked to the polls. Jordanian officers and governors again used 'persuasion' on those Palestinian Arabs who were caught conducting propaganda for Haj Amin to boycott the elections,[18] just as they had done at the time of the Jericho Congress. Immediately following the elections, Abdullah issued a royal decree appointing twenty members to the Upper House (*Majlis al-A'ayan*), including seven Palestinian Arabs. In addition, 50 per cent of the seats in the Lower House (*Majlis al-Nuwab*) were allocated to Palestinian Arabs.[19] Jordan responded to the protests of the Arab League and Arab states with an announcement that the annexation 'was irrevocable and not open to further discussion'.[20] The new parliament convened on 24 April, and after Abdullah had delivered the Crown's speech, it voted in favour of unification, and ratified Abdullah's sovereignty over both the West and East Banks of the Jordan.[21] When the vote was taken to rename the Arab territories to the west of the Jordan as 'the West Bank of the Hashemite Kingdom of Jordan', instead of 'Palestine', the new Palestinian representatives raised their hands in support.

The League's Political Committee met shortly after the elections in Jordan and, by threatening sanctions, tried to influence Abdullah to reconsider his annexation.[22] Haj Amin added his efforts to the pressure being put on Jordan by announcing the establishment of a 'Military Organisation for the Liberation of Palestine', and a manifesto was circulated in Cairo calling on Palestinian youngsters to enlist in the new organisation.[23] After prolonged argument, however, the Political Committee agreed to the demand of Iraq and Yemen to reject the motion to expel Jordan from the Arab League. It is doubtful, in fact, if Egypt, which had initiated the discussion, was prepared to follow the proposal through to its conclusion, thereby endangering the existence of the League, especially since those countries which supported Egypt were not convinced that it was possible to take a decision which was not acceptable to all members of the League.[24] During its discussions in May and June, the League found a somewhat tenuous solution to the problem. It adopted the compromise proposal put forward by Iraq and Lebanon, according to which Jordan would be considered as 'trustee' of Palestine. Representatives of the Arab Higher Institute, and not the All-Palestine Government, attended the discussions and tried, unsuccessfully, to prevent the decision from being passed.[25]

ATTEMPTS TO PREVENT THE CONSOLIDATION OF THE NEW SITUATION

Haj Amin's disappointment with the policy of the Arab states toward Abdullah gave him the impetus to turn to Muslim groups in the Arab world. The Muslim Brotherhood in Egypt, which had gone underground since the murder of the Prime Minister, al-Nuqrashi, began to increase its subversion against the regime. Haj Amin, known to be connected to the group since the 1948 war, stood by some of its members who were put on trial in Cairo on charges of smuggling weapons into Egypt, and at the end of 1950 he gave evidence on their behalf.[26] Shortly afterwards, thirty-two of its members were accused of a series of political murders and of an attempt to overthrow the regime. Haj Amin again gave evidence on their behalf, singing their praises and describing the part that they had played in the war in Palestine.[27]

During this period, Haj Amin also dedicated a great deal of time to preparations for the World Islamic Congress (*Mu'tamar al-'Alam al-Islami*) which was to be held in Karachi. Pakistan was then striving to be at the centre of a group of Muslim states, and

124

Haj Amin seemed an appropriate personality to assist it in achieving this aim. The congress opened on 10 February 1951 with the participation of Muslim representatives from approximately thirty countries, and Haj Amin was elected president. In his opening speech he called on Muslims to sign a mutual defence agreement, and to strengthen their unity. He declared that 'the whole Muslim world has an obligation to liberate Palestine. If the enemies of Islam remain the rulers of Palestine, the day will come when they will try to conquer other Muslim countries'[28]. In February and May 1952, Haj Amin attended two other Islamic Congresses in Karachi, and his popularity soared in Pakistan. The local *'Ulama* Society offered him the position of *Shaikh al-Islam* in Pakistan, but his concerns remained in Cairo, the focus of political activity, and he decided to return there.[29] While in Karachi, Haj Amin apparently came to the conclusion that the pretensions of the Pakistani rulers to establish a block of Muslim states had no chance of succeeding, and that Karachi was not destined to become a centre for political decision making.

The League's institutions, which met alternately in Cairo and Damascus, continued to discuss the Palestinian issue, in particular the question of the refugees. Although Ahmad Hilmi was based in Cairo and continued to hold the title of Prime Minister of the All-Palestine Government,[30] it was Haj Amin who represented the government at the discussions of the League's Political Committee held in Damascus in May 1951. At this meeting, he demanded that every Palestinian capable of bearing arms should be recruited for the war for the liberation of Palestine.[31] He then participated in a conference of refugees in Beirut, and delivered a speech calling on the League to set up a 'Palestinian Brigade' in each of the Arab armies.[32]

Two months later, Abdullah was murdered in the Old City of Jerusalem. He was shot by a Palestinian while on his way to take part in the Friday prayers at the al-Aqsa mosque, on 20 July 1951. The assassin was Mustafa 'Ashu, a twenty-three-year-old apprentice tailor from Jerusalem, who was himself shot dead by Abdullah's bodyguards.[33] Following the murder, soldiers of the Arab Legion conducted searches among Palestinians in an attempt to find those responsible. A large number of Palestinians were arrested and interrogated, and many were injured and suffered damage to their property. Haj Amin denied having any connection with the assassination, despite the fact that responsibility for the murder was traced to his associates, and the suspects included

125

members of his family.[34] His response was to call on the Arab states
to halt the 'cruel campaign of terror' being conducted by Jordan
against the Palestinian people.[35]

When the trial of those involved in the assassination opened in
August, Haj Amin appealed to the Arab states to force Jordan to
halt the proceedings and appoint a commission of enquiry to
investigate the 'campaign of terror, corruption, and harassment
being conducted by the army of Glubb Pasha'.[36] Four of the
accused were found guilty and sentenced to death. Abdullah al-
Tal, who was also accused of participating in the organisation of
the assassination, was sentenced to death *in absentia*.[37]

Although no official accusations were made against Haj Amin,
it was widely believed that he had known of the planning of the
murder. When the death sentences were carried out, he called for
'the death of the tyrants'. It is reasonable to assume that, had the
Jordanian authorities possessed any proof of Haj Amin's com-
plicity in the assassination, whether direct or indirect, they would
have made good use of it against him. No such proof existed,
although members of Haj Amin's family were among the defen-
dants: Dr Musa Abdullah al-Husayni, who was one of those
sentenced to death; and Tawfiq Salih al-Husayni and Dr Da'ud al-
Husayni, who were released due to lack of evidence. In any case,
even if Haj Amin was not directly involved in the murder itself,
there is no doubt that he influenced those who planned and
perpetrated it. From 1948 onwards, especially after the annexation
in April 1950, Abdullah had been the target of an aggressive
propaganda campaign by Haj Amin. The latter had portrayed the
king as the plunderer of Palestine's independence, and accused
him of handing over Arab lands to the Jews under the terms of the
Rhodes agreement. He also attributed to Abdullah the responsibility for the fate of the hundreds of thousands of refugees.[38]

Although Abdullah's assassination was condemned in the Arab
media, he was not deeply mourned by the many people who had
been in conflict with him. The Palestinian camp greeted the event
with satisfaction, and joyful demonstrations were held in those
Arab villages that had been annexed to Israel. However, the hopes
entertained by some that the death of this figure, who had prevented the Palestinians from attaining any form of political independence would bring the process of the West Bank's integration
into the Jordanian Kingdom to an end, were mistaken. The
process had already become an important element in Jordanian
policy, and many of the Palestinian elite had a vested interest in its

continuation, since public figures and heads of the Palestinian *hamulahs* (clans) derived personal benefit from the new situation.

Haj Amin, though, apparently continued to believe that the course of history could be altered if the Palestinians would only refuse to accept the existing situation. His aim during the following years was to establish contact with the refugees living in camps in the Arab states, and to prevent any solution that would involve their remaining in these countries. To this end, he conducted a propaganda campaign throughout the Arab world, and sought the help of Arab rulers. In August 1951, he met with Dr Sala'ah al-Din, the Egyptian Foreign Minister, to discuss the representation of the All-Palestine Government in the forthcoming session of the League's Political Committee which was to consider the refugee question.[39] On 12 February, he arrived in Beirut and met with the Lebanese President, Bashir al-Huri. The aim of this visit to Lebanon was to persuade the refugees to reject the UN plan to settle them permanently in the places where they were now resident.[40] Shortly afterwards, he organised a conference of representatives of the refugees in Beirut with the same aim in mind.[41]

Since Haj Amin was prohibited from entering Jordan, and Egypt prevented him from operating in the refugee camps in the Gaza Strip, his main area of activity concerning the refugee question was Syria and Lebanon. However, on 31 July, a few days after the officers' revolution and the overthrow of the Farouk regime, he held talks with the leader of the revolutionary regime, Muhammad Neguib. After their meeting, Haj Amin declared that he had 'discussed with the Supreme Commander the questions of Palestine, the Gaza Strip, and the refugee problem'.[42]

Haj Amin's relations with the monarchical regime had deteriorated on the eve of the coup by the Free Officers in Egypt. At the time, he was heading a Palestinian delegation in Pakistan that was involved in preparing an Islamic Congress, and reports circulated that 'Ali Mahir's government preferred that he did not return to Egypt because of his negative influence on the radical Muslims.[43] The change of the regime in Egypt brought an improvement in relations, especially with 'Abd al-Nasser, with whom he had been friendly since before the 1948 war.

In his collection of articles, Haj Amin describes how some of the Free Officers visited him at his home in the al-Zaitun district and offered assistance in the Palestinian struggle:

I remember that the hon. Lt. Col. (al-Beqbashi), a staff

officer, and Jamal 'Abd al-Nasser, visited me on more than one occasion at the beginning of 1948, together with the late Major Mahmud Labib. He expressed his willingness, and that of his brothers among the Free Officers, to take part in the war over Palestine and also to command the *Jihad* movement.

Haj Amin accepted the offer, but, according to him, the authorities objected.[44]

Two years after the revolution in Egypt, Haj Amin's relations with 'Abd al-Nasser and his colleagues deteriorated. The reason for this was Haj Amin's support for Saudi Arabia, with which the Officers' regime in Egypt did not sympathise, and because he stood by the Muslim Brotherhood in its struggle against the regime – a struggle that reached its peak with the attempt by a member of the Brotherhood to assassinate 'Abd al-Nasser on 26 October 1954, while the Egyptian leader was delivering a speech in Alexandria. Following the attempt, a state of emergency was declared in the country, 400 members of the organisation were arrested, and the headquarters of the Muslim Brotherhood in Cairo were set on fire by demonstrating students.[45]

However, it transpired that the regime in Cairo was not inclined to expel Haj Amin from Egypt, despite their differences of opinion. Apart from the fact that the presence of the Arab Higher Institute and the All-Palestine Government in Cairo was consonant with the pan-Arabism that the Egyptian regime represented, the Palestinian issue continued to be one issue that Egypt could use against Jordan.[46] Egypt and Haj Amin thus shared both pan-Arabism and an antagonism toward Jordan.

In most of the Arab countries, a propaganda campaign was carried out in the media against Jordan's policy on the Palestinian issue and its contacts with Israel. Unperturbed, Jordan continued to integrate the West Bank residents into its kingdom, and all that Haj Amin could do was to continue to denounce the Hashemite regime and to ensure a continued awareness in the Arab states that the Palestinian problem had not yet been solved. To this end, he utilised various opportunities. For instance, he was quick to express support for the officers who, one after the other, seized power in Syria. After a speech by Adib Shishaqli at Homs in August 1952, he sent a telegram to the Syrian ruler thanking him for his declarations which 'encouraged and gave hope to all Palestinians', and added that 'the Palestinians bless Shishaqli, and wish much success to Syria and its courageous army'.[47]

Haj Amin periodically visited Saudi Arabia, Lebanon, and Syria

1. Haj Amin as an officer in the Ottoman Army.

2. (above) Haj Amin
riding in the Nabi
Musa procession in
Jerusalem at the
beginning of April
1920.

3. (right) 'Arif al-
'Arif. Together with
Haj Amin he incited
the masses during the
Nabi Musa cele-
brations. Both were
sentenced *in absentia*
to ten years'
imprisonment.

4. (above) Members of the Arab Higher Committee in Jerusalem, April 1936. Haj Amin is in the centre.
5. (bottom, left) 'Arif 'Abd al-Raziq, one of the commanders of the 1936–39 revolt.
6. (bottom, right) Fakhri 'Abd al-Hadi (right) and Fawzi al-Qawuqji, August 1936, during the 1936–39 revolt.

7. (above) Haj Amin and Rashid 'Ali al-Qailani during the crisis in Iraq.

8. (below) Palestinian volunteers to the Iraqi Army, Baghdad, May 1941.

9. Haj Amin reviews Muslim units recruited by him for the Nazi regime.

10. (above) The meeting with Hitler, Berlin, 28 November 1941.
11. (below) Haj Amin with a group of Arabs in Germany during the Second World War.

12. Haj Amin with a German officer, during a meeting in Berlin.

13. Leaving the 'Abadin Palace, after receiving political asylum from Farouk. Haj Amin escaped from France to Egypt in the summer of 1946. Standing next to him is a member of the palace staff.

opposite page
14. (above) With members of the Arab Higher Institute and other Palestinian figures, Cairo, December 1946.
15. (below) Receiving guests in Cairo, 1946.

16. (above) The Arab League Council conference in Baludan (Syria), June 1946, which discussed ways to prevent partition.

17. (below) Unit of the 'Holy Jihad', 1948. In the centre (wearing boots) is Kama'al Araqat, assistant to the General Commander, 'Abd al-Qadir al-Husayni.

18. 'Abd al-Qadir al-Husayni, Commander of the 'Holy Jihad', 1948. He was killed at Kastel in April 1948.

19. (above) The Palestine National Council conference in Gaza, in the *al-Fala'ah al-Islamiyyah* school, 1 October 1948. Haj Amin is seated at the presidential table; to his right, the Vice-Chairman of the Palestine National Council, Hasan Abu al-Sa'ud; to his left, the two secretaries of the Council, Emil al-Ghouri and Mahmud al-Nijim. Making a speech, standing, is the Defence Minister, Raja'i al-Husayni. The hall is decorated with flags and with pictures of Arab heads of state. The picture emphasises the squalid conditions in which the Palestine National Council conference was held.
20. (below) Delegates of the Palestine National Council conference in Gaza.

21. (above) The ceremony marking the signing of the declaration of independence at the Gaza conference. The Prime Minister of the All-Palestine Government, Ahmad Hilmi 'Abd al-Baqi, is signing.
22. (below) The All-Palestine Government. The Prime Minister (front row, middle) and government ministers.

24. (right) Haj Amin shortly
before his death.
25. (below) The PLO
leadership, at the home of the
deceased, visiting the
mourners. From left to right:
Yasser Arafat, Abu Iyad, Abu
al-Za'im.

26. Haj Amin's funeral. Giving the eulogy is the Mufti of Lebanon. To his left is Yasser Arafat.

from his base in Cairo. In Saudi Arabia, he sought to enlist political support and raise money, while in Lebanon and Syria he held intensive contacts with the leaders of the refugee camps. He also tried to ensure the support of these countries' governments in his struggle against Jordan. At the end of 1953, on his way back from Saudi Arabia, he visited Beirut and assembled the refugee leaders. After discussing their situation with them, he called on the refugees to unite in anticipation of the campaign for the liberation of Palestine. In a speech to the leaders, Haj Amin said: 'Israel, which is surrounded by 70 million Arabs, will not last very long. The land which was robbed from the Arabs will be returned to them. The Arabs will expel not only the Zionists, but also the imperialists.'[48] During this period he met the Syrian ruler and Lebanese president again, and implored them to extend assistance to the Palestinians in their struggle.[49] Before returning to Cairo, Haj Amin told an American journalist that he rejected direct negotiations between Jordan and the 'Tel Aviv Government', and called on the US and British Governments to adopt a neutral policy toward the Israeli–Arab dispute. At a press conference held in Damascus, Haj Amin thanked the Syrian authorities for their help to the refugees.[50] It was during this period that the Israeli raid on the Jordanian village of Qibya was carried out, and Haj Amin declared that 'the Zionists plotted the massacre at Qibya in order to terrorise the residents of Arab Jerusalem, and to compel the Arabs to make peace with Israel'.[51]

The raid on Qibya was, in fact, an Israeli reprisal action for acts of terror and murder that had been carried out within Israel by infiltrators. Although Haj Amin's accusations concerning Israel's intentions in carrying out the raid were groundless, he had good reason for his fears, in light of the recently initiated contacts between Israel and Jordan and Israel and Egypt, which aimed at turning the armistice agreements into permanent peace settlements. Haj Amin was not content with his efforts to influence Arab leaders and public opinion to end these contacts. He also initiated acts of terror that were carried out by Palestinians within Israel's territory, with the aim of increasing tension on the borders and bringing further difficulties in relations between Israel and the Arab states.[52] At the beginning of the 1950s, he dispatched groups of infiltrators to carry out attacks within Israel. Until July 1954, he cooperated with Jamal al-Husayni (who had gone to Saudi Arabia and now worked in its government service) on these infiltrations into Israel. Tensions later emerged between the two, and Jamal

129

al-Husayni organised groups of his own, which he operated from Riyadh with Saudi funding.[53] Haj Amin was helped in the attacks which he organised by commanders of the *al-Jihad al-Muqaddas* and by activists of the revolt of 1936–39. Paid by the Arab Higher Institute, they carried out a series of killings and acts of sabotage within Israel. Among the infiltrators, who generally set out from the Gaza Strip, were those sent by merchants from Gaza to steal property. The IDF retaliated with raids and reprisal actions in the Gaza Strip and in the Palestinian centres of population in Jordan.

Haj Amin's activities increased the antipathy of the Egyptian authorities toward him, since the Egyptian regime was then concerned to prevent incidents along its border with Israel which might lead to military confrontations. Accordingly, the military governors in Gaza imposed curfews and restrictions on movement, and prohibited anyone from approaching the border. On 4 February 1950, for example, General Mahmud Fahmi 'Aqashah, the commander of the Egyptian frontier force, issued an order prohibiting entry to 'Jewish areas', and laid down punishments for those acting in breach of the order. Between 1948–56, the Egyptian authorities in the Gaza Strip issued seventeen curfew orders. Although some were for internal security purposes, most of these orders were directed at preventing anyone from getting too close to the major roads and to the areas adjacent to the armistice lines, from the early hours of the evening until dawn.[54]

Especially interesting in this context is the study by Ehud Ya'ari, based on documents of the Egyptian security services that were captured by the IDF in 1956. He states that, 'without exception, the Egyptian documents that were at my disposal pointed to a consistent policy of halting the infiltrations'. Just one month before the IDF's raid into Gaza (February 1955), the Egyptian Governor General, General 'Ajrudi, held a discussion on the infiltrations into Israel with the participation of senior officers, including an intelligence officer, Mustafa Hafez. At this meeting, it was decided to prohibit movement to the east of the Gaza–Rafiah road during the hours of darkness, to open fire on any infiltrator crossing the armistice lines, to organise ambushes against infiltrators, and to bring infiltrators to trial quickly and to publish their sentences.[55]

The acts of murder and sabotage were among the factors that further undermined relations between Israel and Egypt, and led to the IDF's raid into Gaza on 28 February 1955. This operation left many dead, and caused a storm in the region itself and throughout the world.[56] Following the raid, violent demonstrations broke out in the towns of the Gaza Strip, in the course of which the new Governor General, General Abdullah Rifa'at, was injured, and Egyptian troops opened fire on the demonstrators, killing four.[57]

The Israeli raid on Gaza represented another turning point in the region. It was one of the factors that led to the first arms deal between Egypt and Czechoslovakia, and the aligning of the revolutionary Egyptian regime with the group of Third World non-aligned states. During this period, Egypt also changed its attitude to the infiltrations into Israel: henceforth, it gave these actions its support and encouragement. In place of 'infiltrators' (*mutasalilun*), a term with negative connotations, they were now called 'suicide-fighters' (*fedayeen*), and Egypt treated them as heroes. The Egyptian security forces organised the operations of the *fedayeen* and made use of the National Guard (*al-Haras al-Watani*) and the Civil Guard (*al-Haras al-Ahali*) to this end.[58]

The Egyptian regime no longer considered Haj Amin a burden. Both were now fighting the same battle, and both enjoyed prestige within the Arab world, against the background of the growing tension with Israel. Haj Amin's star was again rising, and as the Afro-Asian Conference, which was to be held in Bandung in April 1955, approached, he sought to ensure his participation. With this in mind he appealed to a number of Arab states, and eventually succeeded in receiving an invitation from Yemen to join its delegation, with the status of observer.[59]

The All-Palestine Government continued to exist during this period, although in a very limited format, and Ahmad Hilmi still held the title of Prime Minister and continued to issue passports in Cairo. Nevertheless, Haj Amin behaved as if the government no longer existed, and did not demand its participation in the Bandung Conference. He wrote in his memoirs that the Arab Higher Institute 'saw in the decision to hold the Bandung Conference a golden opportunity to strengthen the ties of Palestine with the Eastern Muslim countries'. Haj Amin arrived in Bandung accompanied by two assistants, Muhammad Ishaq Darwish and Emil al-Ghouri, and, according to his account, his arrival surprised the other participants. He described Israel's efforts, supported by the Prime Ministers of Burma and Ceylon, to be allowed to participate in the Conference; the hesitancy of the chairman, Nehru; and the eventual success of Amir Faisal of Saudi Arabia in frustrating the

131

Israeli attempt to participate. 'In spite of the many obstacles set up by those countries supporting Zionism at the Bandung Conference, the Palestinian problem aroused a great deal of interest at that historic conference, and took up three out of the six days of discussions.'[60]

Although Haj Amin's description was somewhat exaggerated, his achievement at the Bandung Conference was not insignificant. Among its decisions, the Conference expressed its support for the rights of the Palestinian Arabs, and called for the implementation of the UN resolutions concerning Palestine.[61] Haj Amin was present at a reception held by the Saudi Arabian delegation at the end of the Conference, where he met the Chinese Prime Minister, Chou En-lai, and thanked him for his support of the Palestinian cause. The Prime Minister replied that China supported all oppressed peoples in their struggle for independence.[62]

Relations between Haj Amin and leaders of the Egyptian regime continued to improve after his return to Egypt.[63] In Cairo his popularity rose, and he was once again invited to appear at various national events and conferences. At the end of 1955, the government announced an 'armament week', with the aim of collecting donations to fund the large arms deal with Czechoslovakia, and Haj Amin appeared on different platforms encouraging the public to donate to the fund. Having denounced him until 1955 because of his support for the Muslim Brotherhood and for his part in the infiltrations from the Gaza Strip into Israel, the Egyptian press now praised his appearances and gave prominent coverage to his speeches.[64]

These good relations continued for the next three years. In his collection of articles and memoirs, Haj Amin describes how 'Abd al-Nasser showered praise on the Palestinian Arabs in a speech which he delivered in Gaza to units of the *fedayeen* during '*Eid al-Fitr* (a festival marking the end of Ramadan), a short time before the 1956 Suez War, and again in December 1957, a few months after the IDF withdrawal from the Gaza Strip.

The joint action of Israel, Britain, and France in the Suez Canal region at the end of 1956 presented Haj Amin with an opportunity to emphasise the need for Arab solidarity in face of the 'Zionist enemy'. He pointed to the three-fold attack on Egypt in the Suez Canal area as proof of his claims about a joint imperialist and Jewish conspiracy against the Arab nation, and claimed that the Palestinian fighters had fought together with the Egyptian army to repel the attack on Egypt and the Gaza Strip.

After the withdrawal of the IDF and the transfer of the territories to a UN emergency force on 7 March 1957, the Egyptians
presented the Sinai War as a heroic campaign and erected monu-
ments to commemorate the 'victory'. Haj Amin did the same,
writing of a 'glorious chapter in the history' of the Palestinian
Arabs, and claiming that the Egyptians and Palestinian Arabs had
inflicted heavy losses on their common enemy.[65]

In reality, the Egyptian army had retreated after brief battles in
the Sinai desert and Gaza Strip, and thousands of its soldiers had
been taken captive. Moreover, the decision of the Israeli Government to withdraw the IDF was a result of pressure from the
superpowers and the UN. In fact, throughout the campaign there
was little evidence of Palestinian opposition, except during a short
battle at Khan Yunis.

The Sinai campaign did not constitute a 'glorious chapter' in the
history of the Palestinian Arabs. Nevertheless, Haj Amin could
enjoy the satisfaction of having contributed to the increase in
tension between Israel and Egypt, which was one of the causes of
the war.

It is possible that the events of this period prevented a process of
dialogue between Egypt and Israel which would have replaced the
temporary Rhodes agreement with a permanent settlement. On
the other hand, the process by which the Palestinian character of
the territories controlled by Jordan was being effaced continued,
while the Egyptians for their part showed no indication that they
would allow political independence for the Palestinian Arabs
living in the Gaza Strip. One might sum up by saying that the Arab
heads of state ceased to feel any urgency regarding the Palestinian
issue, and that Haj Amin now needed a political situation that
would enable him to return the issue to the top of the inter-Arab
agenda. Such a situation was evolving at that very moment in Iraq.

BETWEEN NASSER AND QASSEM

Some months later, the good relations between the Egyptian
regime and Haj Amin came to an end. The principal cause of the
renewed tension was the Palestinian leader's contacts with the new
regime in Baghdad headed by 'Abd al-Karim Qassem, who had
been put into power after the Iraqi monarchy had been overthrown
in a coup on 14 July 1958. Initially, relations between the officers
led by Brigadier Qassem, who seized power in Iraq in July 1958,
and their colleagues in Egypt who had seized power six years

previously were cordial. However, at the end of 1958, relations began to deteriorate, and after Qassem decided to oppose the efforts to subordinate Iraq to the authority of the UAR, they became characterised by outright hostility.[66] The Palestinian issue, which had traditionally served Arab rulers as a tool for mutual criticism, was exploited by Qassem for the same purpose. For his part, Haj Amin tried to gain the support of the Iraqi regime for the Palestinian struggle for national independence.

Exploiting the inter-Arab rivalry, in November 1959 Haj Amin sent a memorandum to every Arab government in the name of the Arab Higher Institute. Its central subject was the continued adherence of most of these governments to the UN's partition plan of November 1947 and to its December 1948 resolution that refugees either be allowed to return to Palestine or receive compensation. Haj Amin condemned this position as 'soft and conciliatory', and declared that 'the Arabs of Palestine request the Arab states to handle the Palestinian question with a view to realising one aspiration ... stamping out Jewish aggression against Palestine and purging it of Zionism and imperialism ... A Palestinian army must be created, trained and armed to be the vanguard of the Arab forces which will march to regain Palestine'.

In previous years, such memoranda sent by Haj Amin had received little attention; now, with the increasing conflict between 'Abd al-Nasser and other Arab leaders, the memorandum received an immediate reply. At the end of 1959, on Iraq's Military Day, Qassem delivered a speech. Determined to exploit the Palestinian issue against his rivals in Cairo, he coined the term 'Palestinian entity', and called for the establishment of a 'Palestinian Republic'. In his speech he said:

> No one can at present find a map or an area bearing the name Palestine. I have enquired of the Minister of Education, I have looked at several maps. Is there at present a map which has on it the name of Palestine? Undoubtedly, you will reply that there is not such a map. But a map exists in our hearts, and we will bring it into being.[67]

In accordance with orders from Qassem, Palestinian youngsters among the 5,000 refugees living in Iraq were recruited, armed, and trained by the Iraqi army. At the ceremony marking the end of the training, in August 1960, Qassem promised those completing the course that the *Jihad* would begin in the near future, and looked forward to the 'birth of the eternal Palestinian Republic'.

No Arab Prime Minister had ever championed the Palestinian issue to such an extent. Haj Amin welcomed Qassem's declarations enthusiastically, and devoted himself to showing his loyalty to the regime in Baghdad. As a result he became a target for condemnation and attacks in the Egyptian media. He was accused of having caused the 'Palestinian catastrophe', of exploiting Palestinian money for a life of luxury, of retaining a bureaucracy of more than '25,000 people under his control dispersed throughout the world'(!), and of attempting to establish a 'Palestinian Government with the aid of a foreign superpower'.[68] The Egyptian press tried to arouse the suspicion that the 'foreign superpower' with which Haj Amin was cooperating was Israel, which was operating through the Iraqi Government. Meanwhile, in Beirut and Tunisia, the press wrote that Egypt was angered by Haj Amin's intention to establish a Palestinian Government independently, and claimed that the Egyptian regime would respond by setting up a Palestinian Government of its own, headed by Abdullah al-Tal or Ahmad al-Shuqairy, and a Palestinian army under the command of 'Ali Abu Nuwa'ar. Shortly afterwards, 'Abd al-Nasser decided to take up the challenge presented by Qassem and Haj Amin, by establishing Palestinian military units in two areas of the UAR and in Gaza. Also established in Gaza was the Palestine National Union, as an extension of a similar body in Egypt.[69]

A gulf of hostility was created between Haj Amin and the officers' regime in Egypt, and in August 1959 he was forced to transfer the offices of the Arab Higher Institute to the Suk al-Ghab neighbourhood in Beirut.[70] At the end of the year, he travelled from Beirut to Baghdad, where Qassem received him for an interview. He also met with other Iraqi figures to discuss the questions of a republic and of a Palestinian army.[71] Like Egypt, Jordan took a grave view of the activity aimed at 'the establishment of a Palestinian state on the West Bank which, in the opinion of Jordan, is an inseparable part of the Hashemite kingdom of Jordan', and demanded that the Lebanese Government prevent Haj Amin from continuing his operations. The government in Beirut acceded to the demand, and passed on a warning to Haj Amin that he could no longer take part in any political activity.[72] Attempts were also made on Haj Amin's life, and in Beirut it was reported that four people had been arrested for trying to murder him.[73] He was, apparently, not impressed by the Lebanese warning, nor by the attempts on his life, and continued his activities. Beirut served him as an operational headquarters, and from

135

here he travelled to Baghdad on a number of occasions, in order to keep abreast of the military training of the Palestinian Arabs who were to constitute the Palestinian Liberation Army.[74]

Throughout his political career, Haj Amin remained faithful to the idea of pan-Arabism, calling for Arab unity in order to face the challenge posed by western imperialism and Zionism. However, reality had proved unkind to him: the greater the emphasis placed on the need for unity between the Arab states (for instance after the founding of the Arab League in the mid-1940s), the more inclined these states were to compromise among themselves at the expense of their commitment to the Palestinian issue. The opposite was also true: the greater the conflicts and differences of opinion between the Arab states, the easier it was for Haj Amin to manoeuvre between them and gain the support of one or another. This was true of the situation in the 1950s and 1960s, although the states that supported him during this period, such as Iraq and Saudi Arabia, and later Algeria and Morocco, were distant and did not control Palestinian territories. Naturally, their ability to assist the Palestinian cause was limited accordingly.

Against the background of the tensions with Qassem in 1959, 'Abd al-Nasser altered his policy toward the conservative regimes in the Arab world. He renewed relations with Jordan, and made an effort to improve relations with Saudi Arabia and Tunisia. Haj Amin viewed this turnabout with anxiety, and expressed his concern that the growing closeness between the UAR and Jordan 'would lead to a coordination of their policies regarding the question of Palestine'.[75] For Haj Amin, the destruction of the State of Israel was the only possible solution, and he was concerned by the efforts directed toward solving the problem of the Palestinian refugees within the Arab states. The UN Secretary General, Dag Hammarskjold, and the UN Conciliatory Committee that was established in December 1948, held talks with the states in the region in an attempt to resettle the refugees in those countries.

At that time, the Arab Higher Institute's delegation to the UN, whose major concern was to conduct propaganda against the settlement of refugees in whichever countries they were now resident, was headed by Emil al-Ghouri. On a number of occasions at the beginning of the 1960s, Haj Amin demanded that this delegation be recognised as the official representative of the Palestinian people.[76] In the spring of 1962, shortly before the Conciliatory Committee's discussions on the subject of the settlement of refugees, Haj Amin wrote to every Arab government of 'the unswerving adherence of the Palestinian people to its right to return to its homeland, and its refusal to accept any other plan to settle the Palestinians in the Arab states outside Palestine'.[77]

At the beginning of May 1962, Haj Amin visited Baghdad for talks with Qassem and the Foreign Minister, Hashim Jawad. In the course of these talks, Qassem stressed that the Palestinians would have to act independently and imitate the Algerian model.[78] After a few days of discussions in Baghdad, Haj Amin left for Mecca. Before parting from Hashim Jawad at the airport, he requested that the Foreign Minister pass on to Qassem the gratitude of the Palestinian people for his efforts on their behalf.[79]

Haj Amin arrived in Mecca for the Muslim Society Conference (*Mu'tamar al-Ra'abitah al-Islamiyyah*). Although on this occasion he did not play a central role in the conference, he did ensure that a decision was taken rejecting the attempts to settle the refugees in the Arab states. At the end of May, Haj Amin returned to Baghdad to head the World Islamic Congress, and in the opening speech he issued a call to fight Zionism, which 'aspires to establish a homeland from the Nile to the Euphrates'.[80]

Toward the end of 1962, Haj Amin's enthusiasm about the alliance with Qassem, which had continued since 1959, began to wane. Qassem might make impassioned speeches and speak of a Palestine Liberation Army and an 'eternal Palestinian Republic', but Iraq was far from the borders of Palestine and could do nothing of any real consequence. More significant was the growing hatred toward Haj Amin which was felt in Egypt, the centre of inter-Arab activity, as a result of this very alliance.

Haj Amin now began to lay less emphasis on his contacts with Baghdad. In a move seemingly aimed at achieving rapprochement with the bloc of states headed by Egypt, he arrived in Algeria in October 1962 at the head of a Palestinian delegation to participate in the local independence celebrations. However, like the Iraqis after 1941, the Egyptians were not willing to forgive Haj Amin. At the end of November 1962, a huge protest rally was held in Cairo to mark the fifteenth anniversary of the UN partition decision. Not only was Haj Amin not invited to attend, but the Egyptians saw to it that the spokesman for Palestine at the rally would be none other than a member of the Nashashibi family – Nasr al-Din al-Nashashibi.

At the beginning of February 1963, the Ba'ath party seized power in Iraq. Asked at a press conference about the relations of the new regime with Haj Amin, Hashim Jawad, who had been

137

appointed Minister of State for Presidential Affairs, replied that the revolutionary regime would end its special ties with him. The new Iraqi regime's negative attitude to Haj Amin was not only a result of the relationship which he had enjoyed with Qassem. It was also influenced by the desire of the new ruler, al-Sala'am 'Arif, to remove any obstacles in the way of reaching an understanding with 'Abd al-Nasser. Haj Amin, who was seen as such an obstacle, thus lost the advantage that had been occasioned by the split between Cairo and Baghdad before 'Arif's rise to power. When the breach was healed and an understanding reached between the Arab rulers, Haj Amin did his best not to be excluded. Two months after the Ba'athist coup, the heads of Egypt, Iraq, and Syria met in Cairo to discuss the establishment of a federation. Haj Amin sent a telegram to the conference in the name of the Arab Higher Institute, with the message that 'the Palestinian Arab people views this union as the realisation of the objectives for which it is struggling'.[81] This hopefulness had not been borne out by Haj Amin's past experience, and in fact it is doubtful that he believed what he had written.

Despite the fact that during the years of deep animosity between these Arab rulers each had tried to prove that he was more devoted to the idea of Palestinian independence than the others, not one of them was prepared to allow independent Palestinian activity in his regime. But the slogans about Palestinian independence bandied about by these rulers had a significant influence on the emergence of militant Palestinian groups (especially of students in the Arab states) who supported a policy of armed struggle against Israel and adopted the idea of imitating the Algerian FLN. The appearance of these Palestinian groups in the Arab states,[82] either under the aegis of various Arab regimes or independent of them, was one of the factors that led to the establishment of the Palestine Liberation Organisation (*Munazamat al-Tahrir al-Filastiniyyah* – PLO) at the beginning of 1964. Haj Amin, whose untiring propaganda had greatly influenced this process, was excluded from its ranks.

CONFRONTATION WITH SHUQAIRY AND *RAPPROCHEMENT* WITH JORDAN

It is difficult to know how events would have developed had Qassem not been assassinated at the beginning of 1963. In his absence, it was easy for 'Abd al-Nasser to ignore Haj Amin when he conceived the idea of setting up the PLO at the end of 1963. In

Haj Amin's place, Nasser proposed that the head of the new organisation be Ahmad Shuqairy. As mentioned above, Ahmad Hilmi had died in June 1963 and the Egyptians proposed to Shuqairy that he become the representative of Palestine at the Arab League. Shuqairy, who had been dismissed by Saudi Arabia in August 1963 from his position as its representative at the UN, was indeed appointed to this office in September, in accordance with a decision of the League's Political Committee. This decision was preceded by an Iraqi proposal to establish a 'Palestinian Government in exile', which was rejected following opposition from Jordan. The Egyptians assigned Shuqairy the task of preparing for the establishment of the PLO and of organising the Palestine Liberation Army. In January 1964, an Arab summit conference was held in Cairo at the instigation of 'Abd al-Nasser, and a decision was taken to establish the PLO.[83]

Haj Amin was not invited to participate in the event marking the foundation of the PLO, despite the fact (or perhaps because of the fact) that this event symbolised his long struggle to return to the Palestinians the right that had been taken away from them by the Arab League on the eve of the 1948 war – the right to be masters of their own fate, or at least to participate in the determination of that fate.

In fact, neither Haj Amin nor the other organisations, particularly Fatah, believed in the sincerity of 'Abd al-Nasser's initiative or in the intentions of the other Arab rulers who had gathered in Cairo. They assumed that the Arab governments feared an increase in the strength of independent Palestinian organisations, and that the recent decisions were aimed at making these organisations dependent on them and putting them under the supervision of the League.[84]

The proverb which says that in politics there are no eternal friends or enemies, only interests, proved true as far as the relations between Haj Amin and the Arab states were concerned. After having transferred his loyalty from one Arab state to another, with the sole criterion being the readiness of each to recognise him as leader of the Palestinians and assist him in his opposition to Jordan, the time eventually came when Haj Amin saw the Hashemite state itself as a potential ally. A few months after he was forced to leave Cairo, and a few years before Egypt initiated the formation of the PLO, Haj Amin's keen senses warned him that at some future time 'Abd al-Nasser would not renew his confidence in him, and would choose a different Palestinian personality in his place. As a result, Haj Amin decided to make a conciliatory gesture toward his long-standing enemy, and in March 1960 he conveyed good wishes to King Husayn on the occasion of the Muslim festival of *'Eid al-Fitr*. Behind this gesture lay the hostility to the king by the rulers of the UAR. Husayn was in need of demonstrations of support from every possible quarter, and Haj Amin's telegram was received gratefully, and was even broadcast on state radio in Amman.[85] The following year, a delegation from the Arab Higher Institute arrived in the Jordanian capital to discuss the 'unification of the Arab struggle concerning the question of Palestine'.[86]

Both Haj Amin and Husayn viewed the establishment of the PLO as a threat, and both therefore tried to put the bad feeling of the past behind them, in order to concentrate on their immediate interests. Husayn continued to do his best to maintain his improved relations with Egypt, and was careful not to allow his growing cordiality with Haj Amin to damage them. Two years before the establishment of the PLO, the king officially invited representatives of the Arab Higher Institute (although not Haj Amin himself) to Amman, and, on 25 April 1962, Munif al-Husayni, Emil al-Ghouri and Issah Nahlah arrived in the Jordanian capital to discuss plans for the solution of the Palestinian problem. The Jordanian press gave prominent coverage to the arrival of the Arab Higher Institute representatives, and reported that for the time being Haj Amin himself would not be participating in the discussions. His arrival in Jordan was reported to depend on future developments.[87]

Shuqairy, who was still Saudi Arabia's representative at the UN, was also in Jordan at the time. He toured the towns of the West Bank accompanied by senior officials of the Jordanian administration, and met for talks with King Husayn and the Prime Minister, Wasfi al-Tal. To journalists, he voiced his opposition to the establishment of a Palestinian government before its time,[88] possibly because he feared that some kind of an agreement would be reached between Husayn and Haj Amin and the Arab Higher Institute. In any case, he preferred to gamble on 'Abd al-Nasser rather than on Husayn.

For the time being Haj Amin did not visit Jordan. Although the murder of the Prime Minister, Haza'a al-Maja'ali, in August 1960 had been attributed to Egypt and to Syrian intelligence,[89] the atmosphere prevailing in Jordan as a result of the assassination was not conducive to such a visit. Moreover, the idea of a 'Palestinian entity', which meant detaching the West Bank from Jordan, continued to be an issue. During the first half of the 1960s, Haj Amin campaigned for this idea during his visits to North African countries and at Islamic conferences that he organised in Saudi Arabia and Somalia.[90] The climate was not yet suitable for a full reconciliation with Husayn, but there was, nevertheless, a definite move in that direction. Shortly after the summit conference in Cairo in January 1964, members of the Arab Higher Institute – Emil al-Ghouri, Issah Nahlah and Ziad al-Khatib – returned to Amman to discuss the new situation, and to demand Jordanian support for the right of the Arab Higher Institute to 'represent the Palestinian people' in the Arab League.[91] Haj Amin's anger was directed especially at Shuqairy who, with Egyptian assistance, had secured recognition from the Arab League as leader of the Palestinians. At this stage, Husayn was careful not to criticise Shuqairy, who enjoyed the support of 'Abd al-Nasser, nor the summit's decision to set up the PLO, for after being isolated and denounced for so many years, he was concerned not to lose the legitimacy that he had acquired at the summit conference in Cairo. But the Jordanian authorities still permitted Haj Amin and members of the Arab Higher Institute to conduct a propaganda campaign against Shuqairy among the Palestinian population.[92]

At the end of March 1964, Shuqairy announced his decision to set up a preparatory committee in anticipation of the Palestinian Conference to be held in Jerusalem in May. The committee was to be made up of representatives of all the various Palestinian factions, including the Arab Higher Institute. Haj Amin appealed by telegram to Palestinian figures, including Anwar Nusseibeh, Sa'id 'Ala' al-Din and Ruhi al-Khatib,[93] whom Shuqairy had invited to take part in the conference, and demanded that they reject the invitation. It was reported in the press that the Arab Higher Institute would be participating in the Palestinian conference in May, and that it would even be bringing a plan of its own concerning the 'Palestinian entity'.[94] Haj Amin dismissed such a possibility. A statement published on behalf of the Institute declared that Shuqairy had no authority to call such a conference, and that by giving in to his pressure the League had lent a hand to the establishment of 'a Palestinian entity' that would deny sovereignty to the Palestinian people[95] – as if this sovereignty had not already been taken away from the Palestinians by the League in 1946 when, during its discussions on the Palestinian problem, it had ignored the Palestinian leadership.

141

Haj Amin considered this move by the Arab League and Shuqairy a challenge to his leadership. He also saw in it a continuation of the Arab states' policy of usurping the Palestinians' responsibility for their own affairs, and he sought to defend their independence in decision-making. But was he himself independent? Had he not sought to be dependent on Saudi Arabia, 'Abd al-Nasser, and finally on Qassem's Iraq? What in fact really worried Haj Amin was that the role that the Arab rulers had imposed on Shuqairy constituted, for the first time since the 1920s, a real threat to his status as the acknowledged leader of the Palestinians. This was the first time that Haj Amin had lost his position as the acknowledged leader, a position that in the past no one had dared to assume, even when it had remained vacant for years because of his absence from the region.

In an effort to deny the legitimacy of the Jerusalem Conference, Haj Amin reiterated that those representatives taking part must be elected and not appointed. He also appealed in the name of the Arab Higher Institute to those Palestinian figures holding senior positions in Jordan whom Shuqairy wished to include in the list of representatives at the Conference, and demanded that they refuse to accept the appointments.[96]

As the Palestinian Conference in Jerusalem approached, visits by Haj Amin's emissaries to Amman became more frequent, as efforts were made to prevent the Conference being held. For the same purpose, in April 1964, Munif al-Husayni and Emil al-Ghouri met with the Jordanian Prime Minister, Shrif Husayn Ibn Nasser. Had Haj Amin been allowed to enter Jordan, he would almost certainly have conducted the campaign against Shuqairy himself. In his absence, it was al-Ghouri who strove to make Haj Amin's position known to the heads of the Jordanian regime and in the Palestinian refugee camps. Throughout this period, the efforts to prevent the Conference in Jerusalem taking place continued incessantly.[97]

At this time, the Egyptian press reported that during Shuqairy's visit to Lebanon he had received letters containing threats to his life, and that leaflets had been distributed in the refugee camps calling for opposition to the decisions taken by the Arab rulers at the Cairo summit. In the opinion of observers, Haj Amin had been involved in these acts.[98] In the middle of May, Haj Amin assembled 300 Palestinians in Lebanon for a conference aimed at enlisting Palestinian public opinion against Shuqairy's organisation. It was decided at this conference that 'the Palestinian Arab people will

142

continue its struggle to reclaim its homeland and will object to the proposal [of the League and Shuqairy] to put an end to the Palestinian problem'. In a statement attacking their inability to do anything about the operation of the national water carrier by Israel, Haj Amin expressed his anger at those Arab states who preferred Shuqairy to himself: 'The Palestinian Arab people will express its protest at the theft of Arab water and ... at the helplessness displayed by the Arab states in this matter.'[99]

Tension increased, and Shuqairy began to fight back. He told a journalist in Beirut that 'there is an invisible hand operating at work'. He added that Haj Amin was paying Palestinian refugees 100 lire for signing petitions and was distributing propaganda leaflets in the refugee camps, but that the 'Palestinian people had trodden them underfoot'. Shuqairy's assistant, Hamid Abu al-Sita, declared that, while on a trip to the Palestinian centres of population, 'we discovered that the Arab Higher Institute is operating energetically in every Arab country that we visited to frustrate the mission of the representative of Palestine [Shuqairy] by cooperating with foreign embassies'.[100]

Despite the efforts of Haj Amin, the Palestinian Conference was held as planned on 28 May 1964, at the Intercontinental Hotel in Jerusalem. The Arab Higher Institute obviously did not participate, and Haj Amin vilified Shuqairy. The Conference was also boycotted by Fatah, an organisation under the leadership of Yasser Arafat, which had been launched in Egypt in the mid-1950s as an organisation of Palestinian students. Other, smaller, Palestinian groups, such as the that under the leadership of Suhi Yassin followed suit. They set up a political office in opposition to Shuqairy, and joined Haj Amin in claiming that the new organisation was an instrument under the control of 'Abd al-Nasser, and that the Arab governments had established it in order to prevent the strengthening of independent Palestinian groups.[101]

The conference in Jerusalem was attended by official representatives of the Arab states and by the Arab League's Secretary General, 'Abd al-Khaliq Hassunah. King Husayn opened the Conference, and played down his concern at the establishment of the PLO and the activities of Shuqairy, declaring 'I am one of you, and a soldier in your army, the army of Palestine, to which I have dedicated my life'. Shuqairy was elected president of the Conference and chairman of the executive, and in a long and ardent speech he spelled out the principles of the 'Palestinian entity'. The Conference ratified both the Palestinian National Covenant (*al-*

143

Mithaq al-Qaumi al-Filastini) and the PLO's founding articles of association, and decided to appoint itself, with the same composition, as the first Palestine National Council (*al-Majlis al-Watani al-Filastini* – PNC), thus displacing the body of the same name that had met in Gaza. The decision taken at the summit meeting to establish the PLO had thus been carried out.[102]

Those Palestinian organisations which did not participate in the Conference continued to operate separately from, and in rivalry with, Shuqairy's PLO, until his resignation following the Six Day War, and the takeover of the organisation by Fatah and Arafat in 1968.[103]

5

Decline

In effect, the establishment of the PLO in 1964 marked the end of
Haj Amin's 44-year-long political career. The dominating voice
now heard in the institutions of the Arab League, at meetings of
Arab ministers, in the Palestinian centres of population and in the
media, was that of the new leader, Shuqairy. Haj Amin was to live
for another ten years, but in the course of these years his name
gradually disappeared from the Arab press, and he was almost
never seen on the platform of Arab or Islamic conferences.
Nevertheless, until his death Haj Amin maintained that the Arab
Higher Institute existed and that he remained its president.[1] At this
stage he turned to writing the memoirs of his turbulent life in the
quarterly *Filastin* which he published in Beirut.[2]

Even during his political decline, Haj Amin continued his efforts
to be active in shaping the course of events, claiming that the Arab
Higher Institute – of which only he and a handful of assistants
remained – was the representative of the Palestinians.[3] A year and
a half after the establishment of the PLO, Haj Amin was interviewed by a journalist from the *al-Hayat* newspaper. He was asked
to comment on Shuqairy's statement that he was holding contacts
with all Palestinian organisations in an effort to bring about mutual
cooperation. His reply was to express contempt for Shuqairy and
to declare that the Arab Higher Institute was always prepared to
cooperate with him, as it was 'with every Arab and Palestinian
citizen'.[4] In light of his situation, such a statement was no more
than vainglory. But despite his predicament, Haj Amin did not
despair.

Had the Arab states agreed between themselves that the PLO
was the sole representative of the Palestinians, it is doubtful

whether Haj Amin's pretensions would have had any significance. However, Jordan, Saudi Arabia, Iraq and Syria each considered that the existence of the PLO conflicted with its own interests, and Haj Amin exploited this to secure an advantage, in a last attempt to prevent his complete disappearance from the political scene.

In September 1964, the second summit meeting of Arab heads of state met in Alexandria, where it was decided to set up a Palestine Liberation Army. Jordan had its reservations about implementing the decision in its territory, and King Husayn declared that Jordan was the last country in which Palestinian divisions should be set up, since 65 per cent of the Jordanian army and 90 per cent of its national guard were Palestinians. As far as declarations were concerned, the leaders of the regime in Amman were careful to abide by the inter-Arab decisions, but in practice they allowed members of the Arab Higher Institute to work to undermine Shuqairy's status, and even extended them aid. Rumours were rife in Jordan that Haj Amin intended to set up a rival military organisation to the PLO, the Veteran Fighters Society (*Jamiyyat al-Munadilin al-Qudamah*). In response to a question on this point, the Jordanian Prime Minister, Bahajat al-Talhuni, replied that Jordan would not allow any such organisation to be established, and that it 'adhered to all of the decisions of the kings and presidents'.[5] Such declarations failed to conceal the encouragement that the Jordanian regime extended to Haj Amin. His two almost permanent emissaries, Emil al-Ghouri and Munif al-Husayni, travelled back and forth between Beirut and Amman. Husayn did not meet the two himself, but they were frequently received by other senior figures in the Jordanian administration. When asked in June 1965 about the nature of the connections between the Arab Higher Institute and the Jordanian Government, Haj Amin replied that the Institute's constituent manifesto laid down that 'good relations should be maintained with all Arab states'. He added:

> It is no secret that the great majority of the Palestinian people are situated in Jordan, and that what remains of Palestine is under Jordanian control. From this it follows that the connection with it, and the strengthening of ties with it, are natural and necessary for the Palestinian cause. The enemies' ambitions are directed primarily against Jordan ... and there is thus a national obligation to cooperate with it.[6]

The ambivalent attitude of the Jordanian Government

146

perplexed a number of Palestinian figures who had deserted Haj Amin in the past and sought refuge with the regime in Amman. Some of them concluded from the *rapprochement* between Jordan and the Arab Higher Institute that Haj Amin had regained his political strength, and that it was therefore worthwhile to leave Shuqairy's organisation to rejoin Haj Amin. One such figure was Dr 'Izzat Tannus, who decided to resign from his position in the PLO and to cooperate instead with the Arab Higher Institute. He travelled to Amman, and there met with colleagues of Haj Amin – Emil al-Ghouri and Munif al-Husayni.[7]

The Egyptians, who had initiated the move to establish the PLO, viewed Husayn's manoeuvres with displeasure. One Egyptian newspaper wrote that Jordan's declaration that it adhered to the decisions taken at the Arab summit conferences ran counter to its policy of non-cooperation with the PLO. The newspaper hinted that the strengthening of ties between Husayn and Haj Amin was the fruit of a Saudi-Jordanian agreement to hamper the progress of the PLO.[8] According to this same source, Husayn, despite enjoying a budget of 65 million Egyptian lire from the Arab states, was operating in opposition to their decisions regarding the PLO. The newspaper stated that Haj Amin was serving the interests of the Saudi king, Faisal, and that he was a candidate for the position of head of the Arab Higher Institute office which was to be opened in Amman in accordance with the understanding that had been reached between Husayn and Faisal. In Egypt, allegations were made that Haj Amin was plotting with the Muslim Brotherhood in Jordan, the enemy of the Egyptian regime, under the aegis of the Jordanian authorities. It was also reported that a representative of the Arab Higher Institute in New York, Issah Nahlah, was visiting West Bank towns in order to set up a Palestinian front, with the aid of the Jordanian authorities, which would serve as a counterbalance to Shuqairy's organisation.[9]

In Fatah, Haj Amin found an ally for his struggle against the PLO. The understanding between them was based on agreement that the PLO did not represent the Palestinians on a democratic basis; that it had been founded in order to neutralise the activities of the existing Palestinian organisations and to serve the interests of certain Arab states; and that the Palestinians must preserve their independence, especially in decision-making. Both Haj Amin and Fatah were of the opinion that terrorist activity beyond the armistice lines with Israel should be encouraged, in order to elicit reprisal action and thus push the Arab states into an all-out

147

war against Israel. This was, in short, Haj Amin's doctrine at this time. It was adopted by Fatah and appeared in the pages of *Filastinina*, the organisation's first official mouthpiece.[10] Fatah also adopted 'Abd al-Qadir al-Husayni, who had been Haj Amin's right-hand man and commander of the *al-Jihad al-Muqaddas*, as the symbol of Palestinian national heroism.[11]

Husayn had lent his support to the establishment of the PLO in 1964, following the waves of messianic nationalism that had spread from Cairo throughout the Arab states. The move was designed to relieve the pressure that Husayn faced from this movement, but he was forced to pay an increasingly high price for this opportunity to gain a degree of legitimacy for his regime. Shuqairy's impassioned speeches, and his activities among the Palestinians, who formed the overwhelming majority of the Jordanian population, constituted a danger to the unity of the two banks of the Jordan, a unity which the Hashemite kingdom had taken great pains to preserve since the time of Abdullah. As Shuqairy's activities gathered momentum, Husayn had to choose between two risks: exposure to attacks and to accusations that he was a traitor to the Arab cause if he came out against the PLO; or the threat to the unity of the kingdom and to the Hashemite regime, if he continued to support it. Husayn chose the former.

This decision was expressed in a speech made by Husayn on 14 June 1966, at the graduation ceremony of a teacher training institute at Ajlun. He spoke of the 'long arm' that Jordan had extended in helping to establish the PLO at the Cairo summit in 1964, and pointed to the organisation's ingratitude and its subversion against the unification of the two banks of the Jordan. Husayn threatened that 'any hand which dares infringe the unity of the country will be cut off'. Shortly after this speech, he had the 'Voice of Palestine' on Radio Amman shut down. Shuqairy responded by demanding that the Palestinian ministers in the Jordanian cabinet resign immediately.[12] From this time on, the close relations between Jordan and the Arab Higher Institute began to take on a more formal character.

The breakdown in relations between Husayn and Shuqairy became increasingly serious, and, at the beginning of February 1967, Jordan delivered a memorandum to the secretariat of the Arab League concerning its decision not to recognise the PLO or participate in conferences to which Shuqairy was invited. At the same time, tension also increased between Jordan and Egypt. After Husayn was severely criticised by 'Abd al-Nasser, Jordan decided to recall its ambassador to Cairo, 'Abd al-Mun'im al-Rifa'ai. At this stage, Husayn also decided to extend an official invitation to Haj Amin to visit Amman, and Jordan's chief *qadi* was sent to Beirut to meet him. During their talks, the *qadi* passed the king's invitation on to Haj Amin, and expressed Jordan's readiness to see the Arab Higher Institute and Haj Amin as substitutes for the PLO and Shuqairy. As well as constituting an attack on Shuqairy, this move was also designed to increase the popularity of the Jordanian regime among the Palestinians, in anticipation of the forthcoming elections.[13]

During this period, there was also an exchange of letters between Haj Amin and Husayn, in the course of which Haj Amin denounced the 'dangerous machinations aimed at causing the disintegration of Jordan and division within the nation'. Haj Amin further conveyed the Arab Higher Institute's support for Jordan's efforts to prevent the 'conspiracy to destroy Palestine'. He praised Husayn and declared that the king 'can be absolutely certain of the support of the sincere, of the believers, and of those fighting the forces of evil from without and within'.[14] The letters received prominent coverage in the Jordanian press, and an immediate response from the king, who thanked Haj Amin and promised that 'Jordan will stand firm in the face of the conspiracies being hatched against the Palestinian cause and against the peace and stability of this country by the enemies of the Arabs and Islam'.[15]

Haj Amin apparently felt the need to explain his new alignment with the Hashemite regime. In a long and apologetic manifesto published at the end of February, he concealed his real motive, namely opposition to Shuqairy's appointment as head of the PLO by the Arab League. The document explained the need for co-operation with Jordan in order to repel the conspiracy faced jointly by Jordan and the Palestinians. According to Haj Amin, apart from imperialism and Zionism, those taking part in this plot included 'Palestinian elements [Shuqairy], appointed and dictated' by Egypt.

> The enemies' and agents' plans are designed to detach the West Bank from Jordan and turn it into a weak and flimsy republic, disarmed, and under international supervision, until the time should come to merge it completely with the occupied Jewish state. These plans are also directed at internationalising the Arab part of Jerusalem in preparation for making the whole city Jewish.

According to Haj Amin's manifesto, the realisation of the PLO's plans, under Shuqairy's leadership and with the support of Egypt, would have additional results: international recognition of the results of the Zionist aggression, and the conquest of the West Bank by the Jews in their own good time. Haj Amin went on to warn that the intention of the superpowers to demilitarise the West Bank was 'preparation for Jewish rule'.

According to Haj Amin, a Palestinian Government in the West Bank would have no *raison d'être* from either an economic or a military point of view, since it would be unable to defend either its borders or its citizens 'against the colonial covetousness of the Zionists'.[16] According to Haj Amin, Husayn, the former enemy of Palestinian independence, had now become the defender of the Palestinians, and the only safeguard against the calamity which Palestine now faced was cooperation with the Jordanian ruler.

The praise that Haj Amin lavished on Husayn, whom he had denounced for years as the enemy of Palestinian nationalism, illustrates the dramatic change that had taken place in his personal status following the establishment of the PLO, as well as his willingness to pay any price for the chance of political survival. There were other motives as well. Haj Amin's breach with Egypt had deepened since 1959, when he had been compelled to transfer the Arab Higher Institute from Cairo to Beirut. Jordan was also subject to propaganda attacks by Egypt, and Haj Amin found himself on the same side as Husayn. It should also be remembered that the majority of Palestinians were living under Jordanian rule, and they constituted the vast majority of Jordan's subjects. Many of them did not see Husayn as their legitimate ruler, and in the West Bank demonstrations were held against his regime. In addition, Husayn's position in the Arab world was shaky. Haj Amin might therefore have hoped that the *rapprochement* with Jordan would enable him to attain a more secure position in anticipation of future changes.

On 1 March 1967, Haj Amin travelled from Beirut to Jerusalem, and was received with honour at the airport on the outskirts of the city. It was widely reported in the press that among those who turned out to greet him were the Jerusalem District Governor, regional police and army commanders, and Palestinian notables. From the airport, Haj Amin made his way to *al-Haram al-Sharif*, where he visited the graves of Sharif Husayn Ibn 'Ali, Musa Kazim al-Husayni, 'Abd al-Qadir al-Husayni and Muhammad 'Ali, all in the vicinity of the al-Aqsa mosque. When he arrived at the mosque to pray, he was welcomed by the local shaikhs and cheered by the mass of worshippers. Husayn made a special gesture toward Haj Amin by putting an official state car at his disposal.[17] In the evening, Haj Amin travelled to Amman, where he was received by the king to discuss the measures that would be taken by the Jordanian Government and Arab Higher Institute in order to eliminate Shuqairy's influence among the Palestinians. Haj Amin told journalists at the end of the talks that he supported the king's Palestinian policy, while the Egyptian media reported that the two had discussed the establishment of a rival organisation to the PLO.[18] In an interview given to Zuhir al-Maradini six years later, Haj Amin recalled his impressions of this meeting with the king. He claimed that Husayn repeated the following sentence a number of times: 'This country is your country, and we need your under-standing and advice.' Haj Amin emphasised in the interview that he had felt 'the king's earnest desire to do all that he could to find a solution to the Palestinian problem'.[19]

The following day, Haj Amin visited the Muslim *waqf* building in Jerusalem, close to the place from which he had escaped thirty years previously. He had then been forty years old, and had enjoyed the status of leader and national hero. He returned an old man, with a multitude of failures behind him. A large number of Palestinians arrived to welcome him, including political activists and heads of Muslim religious institutions.[20] During his stay, the King put at Haj Amin's disposal in Jerusalem his palace at Beit Hanina (which the King rented from a local resident). On 15 March, after meetings with Palestinian figures and office-holders in the Jordanian administration, Haj Amin left Jordan for Mecca in order to fulfil the religious precept of *haj*. In mid-April, he returned to Beirut.[21]

Shortly before his death, Haj Amin recalled his visit to Jeru-salem: 'While the plane flew around Jerusalem's airport, I saw the Dome of the Rock smiling at me. I left a part of myself in every corner of the city and on every one of its hills.'[22]

The PLO's popularity among the Palestinians had grown enor-mously even before Haj Amin's visit, and it appears to have been involved in organising the demonstrations that broke out on both sides of the Jordan at the end of 1966 and the beginning of 1967, following the IDF's raid on the village of Samu'. The Hashemite regime hoped that Haj Amin's visit, together with the appoint-ment of his supporters to positions in the administration and to the parliament, would reduce the PLO's influence over the Palestinians living in Jordan.[23] In actual fact, Haj Amin's influence over the Palestinians, especially over the educated among them, was not what it had once been. One may nevertheless assume that had Haj Amin continued his activities in the Palestinian centres of population in Jordan with the backing of the Hashemite regime, he would have produced important long-term results. Shortly after his visit to Jordan, however, a number of developments took place in the region that were to alter completely the political and military reality.

LAST EFFORTS TO SURVIVE

Despite the efforts to achieve a reconciliation between the Arab rulers at the three summit conferences held in 1964 and 1965, there was no lessening in their mutual hostility. The conflict between the radical and conservative states continued, and there was also a series of bilateral rivalries: between Egypt and Saudi Arabia, against the background of Egypt's involvement in Yemen; between Syria and Egypt, as a continuation of the disintegration of the UAR, and Nasser's unwillingness to respond to the national water carrier project that was designed to transport water from northern Israel to the Negev region in the south; and in the propaganda war between Egypt and Jordan.

Nasser was accused on all sides of failing to take action, and of hiding his army behind the UN emergency force. In the second half of May, he expelled the UN emergency forces that divided Egypt and Israel, and then ordered the closing of the Straits of Tiran. The mutual mud-slinging between Egypt and Jordan stopped immediately, and Husayn arrived in Cairo for a reconciliation with Nasser.

On 30 May, the two leaders signed a mutual-defence pact. This turnabout in Egyptian-Jordanian relations brought in its wake a change in the relations between Husayn and Shuqairy. For months, the king had been vilified by Shuqairy. Now, after the signing of the agreement between Husayn and Nasser, the PLO leader spoke warmly of the Jordanian and Egyptian rulers. In response to Nasser's request, Husayn returned to Amman with Shuqairy, and the Jordanian press, which only yesterday had denounced the PLO leader, now honoured him, while Haj Amin's name disappeared from its pages.[24] Shuqairy was once again active in Jordan, and his ardent speeches about the impending war, in the course of which the Jews were to be thrown into the sea, echoed throughout the region. The feeling prevalent throughout the Arab world at this time was that the coming war would end in Israel's utter defeat. This mood was to undergo a radical change in just a few days.

The Six Day War broke out on 5 June 1967, and led to the conquest of the West Bank and Gaza Strip by the Israeli army. As a result of the war, Shuqairy's prestige declined enormously, and he became the target for severe criticism from Arab rulers. Although he was not invited to the conference of Arab Foreign Ministers held in Khartoum at the beginning of August, he nevertheless made a dramatic appearance there, accompanied by Shafiq al-Hut. After Shuqairy threatened to appeal to Arab public opinion from the great mosque in Khartoum, the Foreign Ministers withdrew their objections and agreed to his participation in the conference. He also took part in the summit conference of Arab heads of state that met in Khartoum at the end of August and the beginning of September, and influenced the decisions which were taken not to conduct negotiations with Israel, not to recognise the Jewish state, and not to make peace with it. After submitting a protest about the supposedly moderate positions of the Arab states, he left the summit conference. On 24 December 1967, Shuqairy was forced to resign from his positions as head of the PLO and representative of Palestine in the Arab League. Yahya Hamudah was appointed in his place.[25]

The agreement reached between Egypt and Jordan in May and the loss of the West Bank to Israel in June brought about changes in the relations between Jordan and the PLO. Husayn became an honoured member of the inter-Arab club, and spokesman for the Arab states in the world and at the UN. This situation, combined with his desire to frustrate any attempt on the part of Israel to perpetuate the occupation of the West Bank, led Husayn into close cooperation with the PLO, as a result of which he agreed to the establishment of operational PLO bases in Jordan. Although there was no place for Haj Amin in this new arrangement, he continued his political and religio-political involvement.

Shuqairy's declining prestige reopened the way for Haj Amin's return to political activity. In the days preceding the Six Day War, he had almost disappeared from sight; now, after Israel had conquered territories from Egypt, Jordan, and Syria, his voice was heard once again. For Haj Amin, the Israeli occupation served to prove his claim that the Jewish state intended to expand at the expense of the Arab states. He repeated his warning to leaders of the Muslim world, that if they did not rouse themselves and unite ranks, Muslims would face serious danger.[26] King Husayn acceded to Haj Amin's request and, on 16 September 1967, a World Islamic Congress was held in Amman to discuss the 'consequences of Zionist aggression'.[27]

Although Husayn gave his patronage to the Congress, he himself did not attend. He was represented by the Court Minister, Akram Zu'aytir. Other participants included the Prime Minister, Sa'ad Jum'ah, the Director of the King's Office, Sharif Husayn Ibn Nasser, the Speaker of the Jordanian Parliament, Sa'id al-Mufti, and delegations from different countries including Turkey, Uganda, Pakistan, and Somalia. Haj Amin, who headed the Congress, delivered a long speech in which he reiterated Israel's expansionist intentions, and repeated that it was not only the al-Aqsa mosque in Jerusalem that was in danger, but the Arabian peninsula and region's other countries as well.

At the end of his speech, Haj Amin stressed two points: first, opposition to Shuqairy's plans, which meant 'the establishment of a flimsy entity named Palestine which our enemies will exploit as a convenient instrument for the realisation of their aim – the severing of the ties of brotherhood between the two banks'; second, an appeal to the Palestinians living in the West Bank and Gaza Strip 'not to fall prey to the enemy's temptations and promises', and to maintain their 'firm stand' (*sumud*) against the Israeli occupation.

In an attempt to strengthen the impression made by the Islamic Congress, its organisers arranged a further conference which was held on 18 September. Attended by Muslim and Christian religious and intellectual figures from Jordan and the other Arab states, this conference emphasised Muslim–Christian solidarity in the face of 'the barbaric and inhuman acts being perpetrated by the Zionists in their desecration of the holy places'. This text was formulated by Haj Amin. Likewise, it was Haj Amin who directed the conference and who described the fraternal relations between Christians and Muslims in occupied Jerusalem. In the name of the conference, he sent telegrams to the UN Secretary General, to the Pope, and to other world figures, with a call to liberate the holy places and 'return them to Husayn'.[28]

Haj Amin's speeches at the congresses held in Amman reflected his changing fortunes. Over the previous three years he had been courted by the king then dismissed, and finally summoned to Amman once again. The possibilities open to him were already restricted; and as he could no longer choose freely, he gave his services to anyone who was still interested in them.

Husayn, traumatised by the loss of the West Bank, knew of the contacts between representatives of the residents of the occupied territories and the Israeli authorities, and he feared that if they reached a political settlement, his demand for the return of the West Bank would be undermined. Hoping that the PLO and Fatah could be used to prevent such a settlement, he allowed a massive presence of their units in his kingdom. However, it also suited Husayn's purposes to have Haj Amin operating in Jordan and speaking out, not in favour of Palestinian independence in the territories to the west of the Jordan, but rather for 'their return to Husayn'. But if Husayn believed that Haj Amin would succeed in counteracting the rise of the PLO in Jordan, the following years were to prove just how mistaken this calculation was.

Even after the conference of Arab leaders at Khartoum, hostile relations still prevailed between the radical states under the leadership of Egypt and the conservative states led by Saudi Arabia. Haj Amin, who had always called on the Arab states to adopt extreme positions, now found refuge with the moderate conservative states. In the struggle that took place in 1968 between Saudi Arabia and Egypt, Haj Amin served the interests of the Saudis, who continued to fund his various activities. In July he issued a declaration from Beirut stating that the Egyptian Government 'is harming Arab unity'.[29]

Jordan remained Haj Amin's principal area of activity, and he visited Amman on a number of occasions after Shuqairy's resignation, particularly after Yasser Arafat became head of the PLO's Institute Committee in February 1969. The PLO, within which the various Palestinian organisations were united, filled the political vacuum which the Israeli occupation had created in the West Bank, and was seen as the legitimate representative of all the Palestinians. Although Haj Amin's chances of recapturing the leadership appeared slim, he did not give up the idea of establishing an organisation that would recognise his authority, and now concentrated his activities on Muslim religious groups. At the beginning of 1969, shortly before the fifth congress of the Palestine National Council in Cairo, he held talks with Muslim groups in Jordan, during which he raised the idea of founding an organisation to be called *al-Fatah al-Islami*.[30] As usual, Haj Amin planned to place one of his relatives at the head of the new organisation – this time his son-in-law, Muhi al-Din al-Husayni.[31]

155

This initiative apparently came about as a result of Haj Amin's loss of influence over the various political groups. He now tested his strength among the religious Palestinian elements in Jordan, in particular with the Muslim Brotherhood, who disapproved of the fact that the struggle for independence was being carried out by secular organisations alone. Encouraged by the Jordanian authorities, who wished to prevent a PLO monopoly over the Palestinian cause, Haj Amin made every effort to establish a military power-base for himself. However, *Al-Fatah al-Islami* never became a factor of any consequence, and it probably never numbered more than a few hundred members. In the summer of 1969, units of Arafat's Fatah attacked the *al-Fatah al-Islami* base in the al-Wahda'at refugee camp, killing three and disarming the rest. The new organisation thus suffered a crippling defeat before ever taking part in any armed activity.[32]

During his stay in Jordan, Haj Amin met with various leaders of the Hashemite regime. On 14 April 1969 he was received by the Prime Minister, 'Abd al-Man'im al-Rifa'ai, for what was described as a 'discussion of the recent developments in the Palestinian issue'. The meeting was also attended by Haj Amin's confidant, Emil al-Ghouri who, in August 1969, was appointed Minister of Labour and Social Affairs in the Jordanian Government.[33] Haj Amin held similar meetings during his visits to Amman, which became more frequent as the tension between the Jordanian security forces and units of the PLO increased. These units did not accept the authority of the Jordanian law or police, and operated as a rival armed force to the Jordanian army, posing a threat to the regime.[34]

At the beginning of 1969, even before the relations between Husayn and Arafat reached breaking point, Haj Amin reorganised the *al-Jihad al-Muqaddas* units. Unlike the *al-Fatah al-Islami* group, this organisation had roots that stretched back to the disturbances of the 1930s and 1940s, and it was now to constitute part of the effort to form a Palestinian force under the aegis of Jordan. After a few months, however, the *al-Jihad al-Muqaddas* units ceased to operate, and their members joined Arafat's Fatah organisation. Haj Amin himself would certainly not have voluntarily relinquished the separate existence of a force loyal to him. The initiative behind the disarmament of the *al-Jihad al-Muqaddas* units apparently came from Arafat, who visited Jedda at the beginning of June and persuaded the Saudis to stop funding Haj Amin's units. After losing Saudi Arabian support, Haj Amin was forced to visit Jordan in an attempt to reach an understanding with Arafat and other Fatah commanders. An agreement was indeed reached, at least formally, by which the *al-Jihad al-Muqaddas* units would be disbanded and their members transferred to Fatah.[35]

In practice, however, units of *al-Jihad al-Muqaddas* continued to exist, despite the agreement between Haj Amin and the leaders of Fatah. In one of the clashes which occurred in Jordan during the course of 1969, a Fatah unit seized four members of the *al-Jihad al-Muqaddas* and confiscated their weapons. Fatah also fought other Palestinian terrorist groups in Jordan during this period, in an effort to unite the armed Palestinian activity under its control.[36]

Haj Amin continued to set up militant units of both a religious and a secular nature. At the beginning of 1970, he was occupied with establishing an organisation in Jordan by the name of the Jerusalem Muslim Congress, whose headquarters were situated in one of the Jabal Amman city squares. He also planned to set up another paramilitary organisation in Jordan with the support of the Muslim Brotherhood.[37]

Meanwhile, relations between Husayn and Fatah continued to deteriorate, while the prestige of Fatah and the other Palestinian organisations increased as a result of the growing number of terrorist penetrations into Israel. Husayn and Haj Amin were now both in competition with the various factions of the PLO for leadership of the Palestinian struggle. Although the threat to the Jordanian regime from the PLO factions continued to increase, Husayn strove to avoid an armed confrontation with them for as long as possible. However, incidents between these factions and the Jordanian security forces in the capital and other towns became more frequent, and by the autumn of 1970 the disturbances that were later to be known as 'Black September' had become inevitable.

The Jordanian army's attacks on the PLO began in September 1970, in the vicinity of the capital, Amman, and continued in the Ajlun region until July 1971. Thousands of PLO members were killed in these attacks, and a huge number fled to Lebanon. Some of those escaping even crossed over the border into Israel and turned themselves over to the IDF.[38]

Haj Amin was greatly shocked by the massacre of thousands of his people. Strange as it may seem, however, this did not lead him to come out in support of his slaughtered brothers. The hope he cherished, that with Husayn's support he could rebuild his position, made it difficult for him even to distinguish between killed and killers. At one of the most tragic moments in the history of the Palestinians, Haj Amin had only this to say:

> It is almost impossible to conceive of the fratricidal struggle and mutual massacre that recently took place in Jordan between residents of the same country, the same people and the same homeland. Neither the nation nor history can possibly forgive even a single one of those responsible for this act.
>
> The present phenomenon of internal fighting in Jordan, and the mutual massacres in Amman, Irbid, al-Zarka, and other towns is worse than the case of the residents of Constantinople, who argued among themselves about the question of whether the angels are male or female, while the Sultan Muhammad al-Fatih laid siege to their city ...
>
> While the residents of Constantinople argued with words, we fight each other with artillery, missiles, tanks, and guns, and massacre one another, while the enemy looks on and laughs at our expense. Moreover, he is preparing himself well for further conquests of our land and country, and for a further expulsion of our people.
>
> The fact that the number of those killed by their brothers' lead bullets is greater than the number of those killed by the lead bullets of their Israeli enemies is a cause for sorrow and tears.
>
> It is almost impossible to believe, yet true. The time has come to bring this dreadful disaster and terrible destruction to an end.[39]

The scales were weighted on the one hand with the well-being of the Palestinian people, and on the other with Haj Amin's personal interest. He preferred the latter, and continued to support the Hashemite regime that had only recently slaughtered his people. At that time, the king was the only person to extend Haj Amin assistance, and he did not have the courage to reject it, despite Husayn's responsibility for the spilling of so much Palestinian blood.

While the battles with the PLO were still in progress, Husayn proposed to Haj Amin that he settle in Jordan.[40] Palestinian figures in the West Bank who had returned from Amman later reported that the Jordanian ruler had repeated his offer to Haj Amin to move to Jordan and to serve as his personal advisor.[41]

Husayn was not content with his army's massacre of the Palestinians. He also sought to derive the maximum political benefit from the resultant situation. The PLO was now concentrated in Lebanon, and before it had the chance to recover, Husayn decided to pursue a plan aimed at establishing a new relationship between Jordan and the Palestinians living in the West Bank. According to his plan, later known as the Federation Plan, which he announced on 15 March 1972 at the Basman palace, two districts were to be created in the framework of the United Arab Kingdom: the district of Jordan and the district of Palestine. Each was to have autonomous legislative, judicial and administrative institutions, although the king was to remain sovereign and ultimate ruler.[42]

The plan caused a storm in the Arab world. It was interpreted as showing an intention on the part of Husayn to eliminate the Palestinian problem and to accept the existence of Israel. Husayn was accused of damaging the Arab front at the very moment when it needed to unite, in view of the Nixon–Brezhnev summit meeting. The reaction of the conservative countries, such as Saudi Arabia and Kuwait, was relatively moderate, while, within the PLO, the reaction was angry and threatening. The PLO saw in the plan an attempt to end the Palestinians' hope for independence, by re-establishing the kingdom of Jordan on the West Bank on the ruins of the PLO. The organisation labelled Husayn a traitor, and voices were heard calling for the destruction of the Hashemite regime. A few days after the publication of the plan, a mine exploded in Amman, killing four people. A PLO spokesman in Beirut announced that this was the beginning of the campaign to overthrow Husayn.[43]

The only voice not heard was Haj Amin's. In the past, events which posed much less of a threat to the fate of Palestine had sent him rushing to publish statements in the name of the Arab Higher Institute and to send protests and memoranda to Arab rulers. Now he fell silent; not one word was heard about this plan, which sought to put an end to the aspiration for an independent Palestine.

Perhaps Haj Amin hoped that Husayn would place him at the head of the Palestine district in the confederation framework. In actual fact, Husayn's plan disappeared from the political agenda almost as suddenly as it had arrived. Haj Amin declined Husayn's invitation and refused to settle in Amman, although he did maintain his contacts with the Hashemite regime. For a place of permanent residence, he preferred Lebanon, both because his freedom of activity was unlikely to be restricted in the Lebanese capital, and because settling permanently in Amman would clearly have made him a servant of the king, something that would have lost him the sympathy of those Palestinians who still supported him.

Even if the Arab states and the PLO had been prepared to accept the Federation Plan, its implementation would have been dependent first and foremost on the agreement of Israel, which was in control of the West Bank – the Palestinian part of the planned federation. Husayn's Federation Plan may possibly have been a sign to Israel that he was prepared to reach an agreement, and that the exclusion of the PLO from his kingdom had created an opportunity for such an arrangement. Israel, however, rejected the king's plan.

Under these circumstances, Husayn saw no reason to continue to pay the price of bad relations with the Arab world and the PLO for a plan which, in any case, had no chance of being implemented. Instead, he began to search for ways to improve his relations with the radical Arab states and with the PLO. After he had shown a willingness to 'repent', Egypt agreed to renew diplomatic relations with Jordan which had been severed following the publication of Husayn's Federation Plan. Following the summit meeting held in Cairo between 10–12 September 1973, which was attended by Sadat, Assad and Husayn, Syria also considered improving its ties with Jordan, having broken them off in response to the events of 'Black September'.[44]

In a continuation of his efforts to end his isolation within the Arab world, Husayn also made a good-will gesture to the PLO. On 19 September 1973, the Jordanian press reported that Husayn had issued a general amnesty for all political prisoners, detainees and wanted persons. Included in the amnesty were senior members of the PLO, for instance, Abu Da'ud (Muhammad Da'ud), Salih Rifa'at and Hamdi Mattar, who had been sent to Jordan to attack leaders of the regime. To give further emphasis to this gesture, Husayn personally supervised the release of the senior PLO figures, and even proposed to Abu Da'ud that he take up permanent residence in Jordan.[45]

With the beginning of this reconciliation between Husayn and the PLO, Haj Amin realised that his efforts to reassume leadership of the Palestinians by exploiting the rivalry between Jordan and the PLO had failed. He sent a message to Husayn on behalf of the Arab Higher Institute thanking him for his gesture toward the PLO. He also expressed his hope that the king's measures would help in the 'liberation of the al-Aqsa mosque and the remaining occupied Arab lands'.[46]

The Yom Kippur War (known to the Arabs as the 'October War'), although resulting in the conquest of additional Arab territory by the IDF, was seen in the Arab world as a heroic campaign and a victory for the Egyptian and Syrian armies. Husayn, who was not included in the preparations for the war, and who did not open an additional front against Israel, once again faced criticism from the radical states and from the PLO leaders. It seems that at this stage Haj Amin decided to distance himself from Husayn and to find some way of associating himself with the PLO.

At the time of the Geneva conference, which met after the war in accordance with UN resolution 338, Haj Amin arrived in Jordan as a guest of the government. In Amman, efforts were made to enlist his support for Husayn's appearance as spokesman for the Palestinians before the conference.[47] By now, however, Haj Amin was not prepared to go along with the complete appropriation of Palestinian sovereignty by Husayn. Instead, in an attempt to improve his relations with the PLO, he invited a 'high ranking delegation' of the organisation for talks. Haj Amin was apparently angling for a cooperation agreement with the PLO leaders, and although the latter accepted his invitation in principle, they postponed such a meeting 'until the ex-Mufti of Palestine demands that his ministers in the Jordanian Government resign'.[48] This decision seems to have stemmed from the PLO leaders' wish to underline their dissatisfaction with the figure who had stood alongside Husayn during the years of great tension in their own relations with the king. Furthermore, there was more than an element of pretentiousness in Haj Amin's conduct. Although lacking any real political status, he did not visit the headquarters of the PLO in Beirut, but rather summoned a 'high ranking delegation' to come to Jordan for talks with him.

Haj Amin's loss of political influence brought with it a depreciation in his standing in the Islamic arena. A summit conference of heads of Muslim states (*Mu'tamar al-Qimmah al-Islami*), was held in Rabat in September 1969, after the fire in the al-Aqsa mosque. Participants included a PLO delegation with the status of observer, under the leadership of Khalid al-Hasan, while Haj Amin was not even invited to attend.[49]

A second summit conference of Muslim countries met in February 1974 in Lahore, Pakistan. The preparatory committee invited the leader of the PLO, Yasser Arafat, to represent the

Palestinians at the conference, and as a result Husayn refused to participate. Arafat took his place among the thirty-seven heads of state and representatives of Muslim governments. Haj Amin was also invited to the conference. Although he was seated next to Arafat, he had no official status. For many years, Haj Amin had been the central personality at extra-governmental Islamic congresses, but now the Palestinians had a different leader, one who enjoyed inter-Arab and international recognition. One of the central issues at the Lahore conference was 'Jerusalem and Palestine'. Arafat delivered a long and impassioned speech on the subject, at the end of which he presented Pakistan's Prime Minister, 'Ali Zulfiqar Bhutto, with a model of the al-Aqsa mosque to the applause of those present.[50] Haj Amin, who had striven throughout his life to achieve for the Palestinians a status equal to that of other Arab and Muslim governments, was now present at an important political occasion where a Palestinian delegation was indeed accorded such status. But the figure on the platform was not he, but another man, one who represented the hope of the future.

HAJ AMIN'S DEATH

Haj Amin's participation in the summit conference in Lahore was a last sad accord. Shortly afterwards, on 4 July 1974, he died of a heart attack in al-Mansuriyyah, Beirut, at the age of 80.[51]

The PLO leaders, who only recently had avoided meetings with Haj Amin, visited his home immediately after news of his death reached them. According to newspaper reports, Arafat arrived with 'tears in his eyes', together with Abu Iyad, Abu al-Za'im, and the secretary, Muhammad al-Sha'ar. A statement issued by PLO headquarters on the day of Haj Amin's death said:

> The Palestinian Revolutionary Command and the Palestinian masses mourn the death of the great Palestinian leader, Haj Amin al-Husayni, who passed away at 03.30 p.m. this afternoon in the American University hospital in Beirut, at the age of 90 [sic]. Throughout his life he waged a constant and bitter struggle for the Palestinian people and for the Arab nation.[52]

Sala'ah, Haj Amin's only son (there were also six daughters), who was in Spain at the time of his father's death, arrived at the family home in al-Mansuriyyah the following day. There, he received the many mourners who came to express their condolences, among them Lebanese leaders such as A'adil 'Asiran and Kamil Chamoun.[53] The funeral was held on the afternoon of 7 July, and it was afforded detailed coverage by the Lebanese press. The Lebanese President, Suleman Faranjieh, was represented by Taqi al-Din al-Sulh; and King Husayn sent 'Abd al-Mun'im al-Rifa'ai, his advisor for international affairs. Other Arab heads of state also sent representatives. Also present at the funeral were Shaikh Hasan Khalid, the Mufti of Lebanon; Shaikh Muhammad Salih al-Qaziz, the secretary general of the World Muslim Society (*Rabitat al'Alam al-Islami*); ambassadors of the Arab states; and leaders of the various Lebanese communities.[54] A large crowd, estimated at hundreds or even thousands of Palestinians and Lebanese, attended the funeral.[55]

The presence of PLO members was especially conspicuous. Its leaders took their place at the head of the procession, followed by armed PLO units and a 'resistance band'. Haj Amin was buried in the cemetery of 'The Fallen of the Palestinian Revolution'. The eulogies at his graveside included one by Shafiq al-Hut, the PLO representative in Beirut, who said:

> We are gathered here today in the name of our people, those from the occupied land and those from abroad, in admiration and humility ... We are here to return to God ... the imam of those who sacrifice themselves, the shaikh of the rebels, imam of the Palestinians, the religious fighter who has returned his soul to the Creator ... The flame which he has lit will never be extinguished ... May you rest in peace, our glorious shaikh ... The thousands of Palestinian swords will remain unsheathed until the day the flag is restored to Jerusalem.[56]

A few days later, the Popular Front for the Liberation of Palestine published a eulogy in its official organ, *al-Hadaf*. The name of Haj Amin al-Husayni, it said, 'is bound up in the history of the Palestinian struggle against the Zionist invasion. He led one of the long stages of this struggle'.[57]

Notwithstanding these eulogies, it is unlikely that there was anyone in the PLO who really viewed Haj Amin's death as a loss to the Palestinian national movement. In the preceding years his activity had declined, and the stance which he had adopted toward the relations between Jordan and the PLO had made him unpopular with members of the organisation. In effect, his death marked the demise of the Arab Higher Institute, which was now seen by many, including leaders of the PLO, as little more than a nuisance. Only the Saudi King, Faisal, was apparently genuinely saddened by Haj Amin's death and the disintegration of the Arab Higher Institute. Faisal sought to ensure the continued existence of the Institute, and proposed that Haj Amin's son, Sala'ah, be appointed chairman in his place. By this time, however, such a proposal had no chance of being accepted.[58]

The occasion of Haj Amin's death was not lacking in problems caused by the Israeli–Palestinian conflict. It was reported in the Jordanian and Lebanese press that the Supreme Muslim Council in East Jerusalem had requested permission from the Israeli authorities to bury Haj Amin in Jerusalem, but the request had been turned down.[59] Israel also refused to allow the traditional mass memorial ceremony marking the fortieth day of his death to be held.[60] An Egyptian newspaper wrote that Israel refused to allow Haj Amin to be buried in Jerusalem 'as he had requested in his will', and that he was buried in Lebanon 'until the transfer of his bones to Jerusalem after the Israeli withdrawal'.[61]

Although during the many years of his political activity Haj Amin had been the subject of a great deal of media interest, there was almost no world reaction to his death. In London *The Times* dedicated a long article to Haj Amin, describing the major events of his political career in detail. The article portrayed Haj Amin as an uncompromising man, but also as a man who had succeeded in preserving a balance within the Palestinian camp, as well as cooperation between Muslims and Christians. According to *The Times*, Haj Amin had also played a role in moderating the younger militant elements, until he changed direction and fled to Lebanon, where he became something of an oracle, sought by many for his advice. There is almost no mention in the article of his involvement with the Nazis, although Churchill is quoted as having described him as the 'deadliest enemy of the British Empire'.[62]

On the fortieth day after his death, a memorial was held in Haj Amin's honour in the Islamic faculty of the Jordanian University in Amman. Husayn directed the Prime Minister, Zaid al-Rifa'ai, to represent him at the memorial, and the eulogy was delivered by his advisor, 'Abd al-Mun'im al-Rifa'ai.[63] The Jordanian authorities did their utmost to make the memorial an impressive occasion. No other major event is known to have been organised in the region to mark this day. Having made a point of publicly honouring Haj Amin's memory after his death, the PLO leaders almost never mentioned him again.

164

Haj Amin's death did not leave a vacuum in the Palestinian camp. The PLO leaders had for some time constituted the national leadership, and since the end of the 1960s they had succeeded, better than any previous leadership, in uniting the Palestinians. Their success in this endeavour was certainly greater than Haj Amin's, whose leadership had been contested throughout his political career. The change may have been the result of different objective conditions. It was certainly affected by the different personalities of those who headed the nationalist movement. Haj Amin built the Palestinian national movement, but, in contrast to Arafat, he lacked the ability to cooperate with his rivals in the Palestinian camp, and did not succeed in establishing any form of teamwork.

The memory of Haj Amin disappeared from the Palestinian public consciousness almost without trace. No days of mourning were set aside in his memory. His name was not commemorated in the refugee camps, and no streets were named after him. No memorials were built in his memory, and no books written extolling his deeds. The only evidence of his memory were a few isolated articles which appeared here and there, mainly emphasising his activities in the 1920s and 1930s.

The PLO, which succeeded in turning 'Izz al-Din al-Qassam and 'Abd al-Qadir al-Husayni into symbols of national heroism, has completely ignored the memory of Haj Amin. Not one of the tens of PLO units bearing the names of Palestinians and Arab heroes is named after him.

Haj Amin, who more than any other Palestinian had borne the burden of leadership, and who had dedicated his long life to his people, became, at the end of his life and after his death, a symbol of defeat. His achievements have been lost to oblivion; and the Palestinians have tried to repress the failures that characterised the end of his career, along with his memory.

6

Summary

From his very first appearance on the arena of political leadership, Haj Amin's personality aroused controversy. There were those who claimed that he was the greatest Muslim and Arab leader of his time, while others argued that he was no more than a mediocre politician and cunning intriguer. While some lauded him, describing him as having sacrificed his life for pure ideals, others saw in him a man who, in his lust for power, had turned national and religious ideals into means by which to further his own, and his family's, personal interests. Likewise, while some credited him with having fashioned the Palestinian national movement and with leading it through its struggles to achievements and victories, others blamed him for its failures and defeats. The conflicting feelings which he aroused, especially among his own people, accompanied Haj Amin throughout his life, and continued after his death.

Nevertheless, almost no one denies that, in comparison with the other Arab leaders of the time, he was extraordinary. First, at a very young age he rose to religious and political leadership in a society ruled by traditional, elderly, family heads. Second, by his personality and sheer force of leadership, he put an end to the status quo that had existed between the leading Jerusalem families, and brought about the ascendancy of the Husaynis, which lasted until the 1948 war. Third, he turned rejection of the British Mandate and of Zionism, and the aspiration for an independent Arab Palestine, into principles which could not be compromised. Finally, in a society in which it was common for office-holders to enrich themselves at the expense of the public, Haj Amin stood out as a leader of great integrity.

IDEALISM AND THE LUST FOR POWER

Haj Amin's efforts to attain power and authority knew no bounds. Once he had been appointed Mufti of Jerusalem, he set his sights

166

on the leadership of the Supreme Muslim Council; and having secured both of these positions, he campaigned to replace Musa Kazim as head of the Arab Institute Committee, the highest political institution at the time. This last ambition was not realised until the death of Musa Kazim and the establishment of the Arab Higher Committee in 1936. But even before assuming the leadership of this committee, Haj Amin had begun to weave a dream of Muslim unity under his leadership. The first expression of this was the Islamic Congress which was held in Jerusalem in 1931. Some suspected that he intended to exploit this congress to attain the seat of caliph that had been abolished by Mustafa Kama'al in 1924. His activities in the 1940s in Iraq, and afterwards in Europe, also indicated a pretension to hold a position of leadership in the Arab world.

It is true that Haj Amin never tired in his endeavour to achieve power and authority; but in this he was no different from any other leader who had tasted power and not yet satiated his appetite for it. He likewise did not differ from other leaders in his tendency to see his personal ambitions, and the ideals that he sought to serve, as one and the same thing.

Haj Amin's rivals repeatedly claimed that his actions were motivated solely by egotism, and that his public activity was designed solely to serve his personal ambitions. This was certainly an exaggeration. More than any other Palestinian leader, Haj Amin believed that Britain and the Jews had from the very beginning plotted to expel the Palestinians from their lands. He believed that Britain planned to hand over the Palestinians' country to the Jews and even to help them to conquer the neighbouring Arab states. Fantastic as it was, this belief was an important motive in Haj Amin's political activity and in his violent struggle against those whom he saw as the enemies of the Palestinians. During Haj Amin's career as leader, situations continually arose which proved his far-reaching devotion to the Palestinian cause; but there were other situations which exposed his inclination to seek personal advance at the expense of the community as a whole.

This was the case in 1931, when he organised the General Islamic Congress in Jerusalem. Contrary to the position of the other organisers of the Congress, Haj Amin did not involve other families such as the al-Khalidis and al-Nashashibis, thus widening the split within the Muslim camp in Palestine. This factionalism was to be the cause of a series of politically motivated killings in the

167

course of the 1930s; in particular, the number of Arabs murdered on Haj Amin's orders rose toward the end of the 1936–39 revolt. The failure of the appeal made to Haj Amin in Lebanon by a group of Arab intellectuals from Haifa to order an end to the murders has already been mentioned. There was nothing exceptional in Arab politics about the physical elimination of political rivals, but Haj Amin went further than others. He insisted determinedly on maintaining the existence of his sole authority, and exhibited a singular lack of tolerance toward anyone who disagreed with him.

Haj Amin adopted a similar approach in Baghdad in 1940, when he established a leadership comprising Palestinian figures who had been exiled from Palestine. Jamal al-Husayni refused to join the new body on the grounds that Haj Amin had assumed dictatorial powers. Later, during his stay in Europe, Haj Amin invested enormous effort in his attempts to persuade the Germans and Italians to select him as the future leader of the Arab world rather than Rashid 'Ali. In pursuit of this aim, he was not above making groundless claims or making use of rather dubious evidence.

Haj Amin's struggle with Rashid 'Ali for recognition as leader of the Arabs was primarily concerned with the future – with the expected victory of the Axis powers in the war. Of more immediate significance was his campaign against Fawzi al-Qawuqji, after the League had appointed the latter commander of the Liberation Army at the end of 1947, a few months before the withdrawal of the British army. The Palestinians were desperate for outside assistance, and the Liberation Army, which was funded by the Arab League, was to enter the country in an effort to prevent the establishment of the Jewish state. With the future of Palestine at stake, Haj Amin badgered the League's leaders for months with his demand that the command of the Liberation Army be put in his hands, or in the hands of one of his supporters. Figures such as al-Quwwatli, the President of Syria, Taha al-Hashimi, the Iraqi Prime Minister and former Chief of Staff, and a number of Palestinian leaders, did their best to persuade Haj Amin that the best interests of the cause required that the command be given to al-Qawuqji, but without success. Haj Amin remained stubborn, even when soldiers of the Liberation Army were already involved in military exercises at the Qatana camp on the outskirts of Damascus; he even encouraged the soldiers to desert to the *al-Jihad al-Muqaddas* units. Throughout this period, he conducted a campaign of hostile propaganda against al-Qawuqji, denouncing him as a traitor and enemy of the Arabs.

With the war at its height, the League decided to set up a provisional Palestinian administration (July 1948) and, later, the All-Palestine Government (September 1948). In an attempt to reduce the opposition of Iraq and Transjordan to these decisions, those behind them chose not to include Haj Amin among the members of the administration and government. Although he was involved in the preparations for the establishment of the two bodies, Haj Amin was meant to remain behind the scenes. However, despite the advice of the Arab states, Haj Amin was not prepared to concede his place at the centre of affairs. He fled from Cairo to Gaza, where he organised a meeting of the Palestine National Council, was elected its president, and ensured his complete control of the Council and of the All-Palestine Government. When the latter was forced to move to Cairo, Haj Amin would not allow it to operate as the supreme Palestinian institution. He subjugated the government to the Arab Higher Institute, which he headed and which he refused to disband, thus depriving the former of any real substance. Instead of championing the government and demanding that the Arab states recognise its authority as the legal government of the Palestinians, Haj Amin appeared before Arab rulers and at various functions with a delegation of the Arab Higher Institute, as if the All-Palestine Government had never been constituted. The government was never held in very high esteem by the Arab states, and throughout its existence it remained in the shadows; and it was the shadow of Haj Amin, among others, which hung over it.

After the 1948 defeat, Haj Amin was more dependent than ever on the good will of the Arab rulers. The fact that the Palestinians were dispersed throughout the Arab states, and that those who remained on their land were under the rule of Jordan (in the West Bank) or Egypt (in the Gaza Strip), left him little room for manoeuvre. He nevertheless made no real effort to establish a basis for independent activity, in Lebanon for example, from which to conduct a struggle against the Arab states' appropriation of what remained of Palestine. Instead, he chose to court Arab rulers, who exploited the Palestinian issue for their own needs. The efforts which Haj Amin made to please the Egyptians up to 1957, and, later, Qassem's Iraq, were designed to preserve his personal status, and did not benefit the national cause. And when there was no further gain to be had from 'Abd al-Nasser and Qassem, Haj Amin began to seek a *rapprochement* with Husayn's Jordan.

Haj Amin's egocentricity made itself very strongly felt in January 1964, when the summit conference of Arab states decided to impose on Shuqairy the task of establishing the PLO. Although the motivation of the League's members in making this decision was not entirely unselfish, it still represented a historic turning point. Objectively, it strengthened the commitment of the Arab states to assist the Palestinians in their struggle for independence; and, subjectively, it allowed those Palestinians living in these Arab states to 'walk tall', and improved their self-image. Haj Amin, after working for years to achieve this very aim, now declared war on the summit decision to establish the PLO.

In the speeches that he delivered, and in the memoranda and statements which were published in the name of the Arab Higher Institute, Haj Amin stressed that the PLO did not represent the Palestinian people, and that the decision to establish the organisation served no purpose other than to rid the Arab states of the Palestinian problem. Here, as on previous occasions, Haj Amin's personal motives took precedence over every other consideration.

Now, however, Haj Amin resolved to take his personal struggle further than he had done before. Not content with conducting a propaganda campaign that portrayed the establishment of the PLO as an imperialistic plot to enable Israel to take over 'what remained of Palestine', he went further and joined forces with Husayn, who was the real enemy of Palestinian independence. There was, indeed, some truth in Haj Amin's claim that the Arab states were trying to prevent Palestinian independence; but instead of fighting for this independence, he chose to place himself at the disposal of a regime which had erased the name of Palestine from the map, and which, at that very moment, was busy effacing the Palestinian identity and replacing it with a Jordanian one. By dispatching his colleagues to coordinate the struggle to wipe out the PLO with the Jordanian regime, and by going to Amman himself in March 1967 to express his support for the 'unity of the two banks of the Jordan', Haj Amin acted as someone who had sold his soul to the devil.

Although no one fought more vigorously for the cause of Palestinian independence, Haj Amin's personal ambition was stronger still. In the ten years which remained of his life after the establishment of the PLO, Haj Amin never came to terms with the fact that he had not been placed at the head of the organisation. In the course of these ten years he continued his contacts with the Jordanian regime, and when that regime struck at the PLO in 1970 and thousands of Palestinians were killed by Husayn's soldiers, he did not even speak out in defence of his people.

Throughout this period Haj Amin was supported by Saudi Arabia, but he was very careful not to take any steps that might have disrupted his relations with Husayn. By this time, it was primarily his contacts with the Hashemite leader which lent his existence any political significance, and it would seem that for Haj Amin this significance took precedence over every other consideration, even the destruction of his image in the eyes of the Palestinian masses.

Of his later years, it can only be said that his old age shamed his youth. Nevertheless, he was a new type of leader, different from the conservative leaders of his time. He presaged the appearance of a new generation of leadership that was to break into the political arena from the beginning of the 1950s. Marlowe thus wrote that: 'He was the spearhead of the xenophobic, uncompromising Arab nationalism which succeeded the conservative, cynical easy-going Arab nationalism of Faisal and Abdullah, Nuri and Nahas, Riad Solh and Mardam.'[1]

ACHIEVEMENTS AND DEFEATS

As the dominating figure in the Palestinian leadership, Haj Amin left his mark on the 30 year period which stretched from the beginning of the 1920s until the end of the 1940s. Even when he held positions of a purely religious character, prior to his assumption of political leadership in 1936, Haj Amin had a great deal of influence on the political decisions of Musa Kazim and the Arab Institute Committee.

His years of leadership were characterised both by impressive achievements for the Palestinian national movement, and by enormous failures. Even before his appearance on the political scene, the important Palestinian families had united around the idea of rejecting Zionism, but mutual rivalry had nevertheless remained the dominant characteristic of their relationship. This rivalry continued, and even deepened, after Haj Amin's ascendancy, but the emphasis passed to political activity and the struggle against the Zionist enterprise. Like other Arab leaders, Haj Amin placed his family interests above those of his people. In contrast to them, however, he also succeeded in putting forward joint national objectives, which he made into focal points with which all could identify. Perhaps this is one of the explanations for the fact that the

171

Palestinian masses followed him from the very beginning of his political career. His first achievement was thus to pass the test of leadership.

A further achievement was his success in dispelling the Palestinians' sense of helplessness at their disorganisation and lack of equipment in the face of the power of the British regime and the Zionist movement. This sense of helplessness and frustration grew as the neighbouring Arab states achieved independence (even if only partial), while the Palestinians were forced to accept a regime that had undertaken to alter the national character of their country. More than any other Palestinian leader, Haj Amin recognised the Palestinians' weaknesses, and he knew that in order to meet the challenge posed by the Zionist enterprise, which had the support of the international community and world Jewry, he had to enlist the help of the Muslim world and of the Arabs of the neighbouring states in the Palestinian cause. This he did with great energy, exploiting the prevailing situation and chance opportunities.

The political aspect of the Palestinian problem was not enough to capture the hearts of Muslims throughout the world, and so Haj Amin turned to the issue of the *al-Haram al-Sharif* mosques in Jerusalem. Through long neglect, the mosques had been in a state of disrepair and certainly needed restoration, but Haj Amin placed particular emphasis on the dangers that they supposedly faced from the Jews. The restoration work continued until the end of the 1920s, accompanied by an intensive propaganda campaign in the Arab and Islamic states. This was followed by the bloody disturbances surrounding the conflict over the Western Wall, and the subsequent General Islamic Congress in Jerusalem. Haj Amin can thus be credited with having brought Jerusalem, and through it the problem of Palestine, to the attention of millions of Muslims throughout the world.

By directing his appeal to the Arab masses in the region over the heads of their rulers, Haj Amin succeeded in fashioning a public opinion that the governments could not ignore. Politicians in the Arab world began to compete among themselves in issuing declarations of support for the Palestinian cause. Commitment to this cause gained strength, and when the moment of truth arrived, the governments were forced to take into consideration the attitude of the masses to both the Palestinian issue and to Haj Amin.

This was exemplified at the end of 1939, when the pro-British regime in Iraq found itself obliged to give Haj Amin, the anti-

British exile who had fled to Baghdad from Beirut, a royal welcome. Such constraints probably also explain the decision of the Arab League states in June 1946 to leave the position of president of the Arab Higher Institute vacant for Haj Amin. Britain demanded that the Arab states prevent Haj Amin from reassuming political leadership, but his popularity eliminated any possibility of acceding to this demand.

There were more important tests in the period before and after the British left Palestine: those Arab governments which were undecided about whether or not to invade the country were obliged to take into account public opinion that overwhelmingly supported extending military aid to the Palestinians. The same atmosphere prevailed in other Arab states, and the primary 'copyright' for this belonged to Haj Amin.

In actual fact, Haj Amin's leadership of the Palestinians came to an end with the establishment of the State of Israel and the defeat of the Arabs in the 1948 war. The defeat occurred *despite* the deep involvement of the Arab states in the Palestinian issue, and not *because* of it (as Haj Amin repeatedly claimed afterwards). In any case, Haj Amin, more than any other person, was responsible for making the Palestinian issue a central topic on the agenda of the neighbouring countries, and for turning the conflict into a regional struggle. Just as there is no truth in Haj Amin's claim that the Palestinians would have defeated the Jews in the 1948 war but for the involvement of the Arab armies, so is there none in the argument that Haj Amin was responsible for this defeat. The failure of the Arab effort during this period resulted from other factors, as, for instance, the competition between Arab rulers, political differences between countries, the weakness of the Arab armies, and, above all else, the weakness of Arab society. All of these factors doomed to failure from the very beginning Haj Amin's efforts to overcome the Jews, by enlisting the might of the Arab and Muslim world.

Haj Amin attempted, unsuccessfully, to create a real sense of Arab solidarity over the Palestinian issue. If any solidarity was created, it was purely declaratory, and when this had to be translated into action, rivalry overcame solidarity. Without extensive aid, Haj Amin had no chance of meeting the challenge posed by the institutions that had been established by the Zionist movement (the Jewish National Fund, Jewish Foundation Fund, Settlement Training, and other voluntary bodies). The Arab attempts to establish similar bodies (for instance, the Arab National Fund, and the Arab Treasury) were unsuccessful.[2] The same happened to the Muslim Congresses. Although when founded they were intended to be permanent institutions, they disappeared shortly after being constituted. The reasons for this almost certainly lie in the individual nature of Arab society, and in the absence of any real identification on the part of the individual with the extended society. This also explains the indifference shown by the Palestinian public to the mutual aid institutions that Haj Amin sought to set up, as well as the trifling amount of aid that the Arab world extended to the Palestinians.

Despite these difficulties, Haj Amin managed to unite the majority of Palestinians around the nationalist aims, and to make the Palestinian issue the concern of millions of Arabs and Muslims. These achievements were undoubtedly an expression of his charismatic leadership and of his skills of organisation and rhetoric.

For a period of thirty years, Haj Amin was active in trying to involve the Arab states in the Palestinian cause, and was responsible, more than any other figure, for turning a local conflict – between the Jews and the Arabs in Palestine – into a regional one. His influence on the course of events until 1948 was decisive, and it continued to be felt during the years that followed.

Haj Amin succeeded in creating beliefs and myths which are still held today. From the beginning of the 1920s, he formulated and circulated the idea of a Zionist plan to expand at the expense of the Arab states, an idea that he himself probably did not initially believe. It is probable that he simply wished to persuade those Arab states which were indifferent to the Palestinian cause that the Zionist threat was also directed against them, and that their fate was thus bound up with that of Palestine. Nevertheless, what apparently began as nothing more than a stratagem became, over the years, a belief rooted deep in the consciousness of millions of people in the Arab and Muslim world. This belief was reinforced when Israel occupied territories following the wars with the Arab states. Although Israel has repeatedly insisted that it is not interested in territorial expansion but in establishing peaceful relations with its neighbours, the suspicions that Haj Amin aroused have remained. Even the current PLO leaders, who have disassociated themselves from their predecessors' thinking and methods of propaganda, are convinced of the truth of various myths, as, for example, that the two blue stripes on the Israeli flag symbolise the Nile and the Euphrates rivers.[3]

Another subject that is still influenced by Haj Amin's doctrine is the problem of moving the refugees out of their camps and resettling them in the Arab countries. Plans along these lines, put forward immediately after the 1948 war, were strongly opposed by Haj Amin and the Arab Higher Institute which he headed. Whenever the subject was discussed by the UN Conciliatory Committee (composed of representatives from the US, France and Turkey), or by any other body or forum, Haj Amin objected violently and demanded that it be removed from the agenda. He defined the plan to resettle the refugees as 'a plot to eliminate the problem of Palestine'. Haj Amin influenced the evolution of an all-Arab consensus regarding the 'right of return' (*Haq al-'Aawadah*), which has become almost sacred, so much so that no one in the Arab world now dares to question it. Even the moderates among the Arab states and within the PLO are not prepared to abandon this principle.

Until Arafat's appearance, no Palestinian so influenced the course of his people's history as did Haj Amin. As we have said, this influence continued to be felt after his loss of political prominence, and even after his death. One cannot overstate Haj Amin's achievements from the point of view of the national interests of the Palestinians. However, there was another side to Haj Amin, one that prevented the exploitation of these achievements.

This other side was his determined obstinacy, his insistence on measuring things in terms of all or nothing. This was the case both in 1922–23, when the British, in an effort to placate the Arabs, proposed elections to a legislative council and advisory council; and in 1922, when Churchill's White Paper was issued, limiting the significance of the Balfour Declaration. Haj Amin fought anyone who was inclined to accept the British proposals, and worked determinedly and consistently to prevent the constitution of the Council. Had it in fact been established, it is possible that the Palestinians, at that early stage, would have already taken their first step toward independence.

It was also Haj Amin's maximalist approach that led to his failure in the revolt of 1936–39. By leading a propaganda campaign during the first half of the 1930s against the moderate line adopted by the traditional political leadership under Musa Kazim, he contributed to the appearance of a young and militant opposition. Although Haj Amin's aim was to undermine the status of Musa Kazim, the elderly chairman of the Arab Institute Committee, the force of opposition which he created was unwilling to restrict itself to a struggle against the traditional leadership, and steered toward a confrontation with the British. Haj Amin joined the wave of radicalism, and in 1937 began to fight on two fronts, against both the Jews and the British. Had he used the strength of his authority to prevent the outbreak of an armed struggle against the British, he would probably have made political gains, and have widened the circle of support for the Palestinian cause in London. As it was, he brought about even closer cooperation between the British and Jews in Palestine, with all the repercussions that this was to have for future developments.

The British Government's publication of the White Paper on 17 May 1939 presented another opportunity to alter the course of history. This document would probably have stifled the Zionist enterprise, leading to the establishment, in a further ten years, of state institutions with an Arab majority. Once again, it was Haj Amin who opposed the anti-Zionist proposal, contrary to the opinion of many within the Palestinian camp and the Arab world. Although at the time he was virtually alone in his utter rejection of the White Paper, Haj Amin still succeeded in forcing his opinion on some of the members of the Arab Higher Committee who met in Beirut to sign a decision rejecting the British document.

He adopted a similar position toward the attempts by US representatives at the UN to remove their support for the partition plan. As a result of the efforts of Arab heads of state at the UN, these representatives proposed, in March 1948, that the partition plan be suspended, and that an international trusteeship be imposed in Palestine. Haj Amin attacked the American initiative, and hindered Arab efforts at the UN. By doing this, he paradoxically aided the continued execution of the partition plan.

Although Haj Amin's position on the discussions at the UN carried little weight, the accusations levelled at him by members of his own camp that his involvement weakened the Palestinian cause were not ungrounded. On the other hand, it is doubtful that there is any basis to the arguments prevalent in the Arab world that the Palestinians' behaviour in the 1948 war contributed to the defeat, and that the cooperation between Haj Amin and the Axis powers caused the Allied countries to support the establishment of the State of Israel.

In the collection of articles that he published in 1954, and in his memoirs, written during the last years of his life in Beirut, Haj Amin repeatedly praised the consistent struggle waged by the Palestinians against the British and Jews over the years, and the heroism that, in his eyes, they displayed in the 1948 war. He claimed that the Arab failure in the war derived from two factors. The first was the plan contrived by Britain and the Jews at the end of the First World War to build Jewish strength in Palestine and, at the right moment, to expel the Arabs from it. According to Haj Amin, this plan was carried out systematically over the years; the British excluded the Palestinians from the battlefield, helped in their expulsion, and determined the outcome of the war in favour of the Jews. The second cause was the disunity that Britain sowed in the Arab world, which prevented the Arab states from uniting in order to win the war. Haj Amin claimed that Arab rulers did as the British wanted, and that the decisions that were taken by the Arab League between the years 1946–48, decisions that were designed to enable the Jews to achieve victory and establish a state of their own, were dictated by British agents. He even went as far as to hint that the whole invasion was aimed at securing this purpose.

The truth is that at various times, especially after 1939, Britain did its utmost to prevent Jews from immigrating to Palestine, and to halt the Zionist enterprise. The years of the Second World War, and those immediately following it, were characterised by a struggle against British rule waged by the Jewish Yishuv in Palestine and the Jewish underground organisations, a struggle that contributed to Britain's decision to end the Mandate and remove its forces from the country.

Haj Amin's description of the division within the Arab world accurately portrays the reality of the time, but there is no truth in his claim that there was a connection between this division and a British policy to assist the Jews to establish their state. At the time, Britain's attitude to Zionism was hostile. While continuing shipments of arms to the Arab countries, it prevented arms from reaching the Jewish Yishuv; and, after the establishment of the State of Israel in 1948, it introduced an embargo on arms shipments to the new state. As regards the Arab states, even those subject to British influence were united by the decision to prevent the establishment of the State of Israel. The Zionist enterprise and the establishment of the state were the challenges faced by the Arab states, and the bond which held the rival Arab rulers together.

Haj Amin chose to disregard all this, just as, in his collection of articles, he chose to disregard the decisive role played by Abdullah in preventing the Palestinians from gaining independence. For his own personal convenience, with an eye to preserving his political options for the future, he avoided levelling any accusations against

177

the Arab countries. The picture painted by Haj Amin showed only the 'British devil' which seduced Arab politicians into working against the interests of the Arab world.

IN THE SERVICE OF THE AXIS POWERS

Haj Amin's treatment of the chapter of his political career in which he aided the Nazis is also lacking in sincerity. From time to time he explains that he had no choice but to go to Germany, although at the same time making it clear that he believed that the Axis powers would assist the Palestinians to realise their national goals. Similarly, despite the fact that he repeatedly denies having had any part in the Final Solution, he does not conceal his efforts to prevent Jews escaping from the Nazi inferno. His memoirs, which appeared in the quarterly *Filastin*, even include a detailed description of these efforts, in which he notes with pride that by preventing Jews from leaving Europe he had kept the Jewish Yishuv in Palestine from increasing its strength.

Three months before his death, Haj Amin met with Sala'ah Khalaf (Abu-Iyad), one of the heads of the PLO and *Fatah*. Abu-Iyad described the meeting as follows: 'When I rebuked him for involving himself with Germany, he explained his motives to me. Embittered by the actions of the English in Palestine, and hunted by the Mandatory authorities, it seemed natural to him to join the opposing camp.'[4]

In response to Haj Amin's comments, Abu Iyad noted that:

> Like many other Arab nationalists, particularly in Egypt and Iraq, Haj Amin believed that the Axis powers would win the war and would then grant independence to Palestine as a mark of thanks to those who had assisted them in the struggle. I pointed out to him that such illusions were based on a rather naïve calculation, since Hitler had graded the Arabs fourteenth after the Jews, in his hierarchy of 'races'. Had Germany won, the regime which it would have imposed on the Palestinian Arabs would have been far more cruel than that which they had known during the time of British rule.[5]

'Naïvety' was not one of Haj Amin's characteristics. Moreover, for the purposes of the current discussion it is irrelevant whether or not Hitler and Mussolini would have honoured their commitments to grant independence to the Arabs. Haj Amin certainly believed that he would benefit from an Axis victory, and he did not launch his propaganda campaign on Berlin radio until this benefit had been promised to him, in writing, by Berlin and Rome. He had no doubt that if Germany were to win the war, it would settle accounts with its enemies – Britain and the Jews. In any case, Haj Amin's hatred of the Jews provided a sufficient motive for his association with their greatest oppressors. His speeches on Berlin radio were congruous with the Nazi murderers: 'Kill the Jews wherever you find them – this pleases God, history and religion.'[6]

His hatred of Jews – and not just of Zionism – was fathomless, and he gave full vent to it during his period of activity alongside the Nazis (October 1941 – May 1945). His claim that his cooperation with the Nazis was prompted only by the struggle against the British is groundless. For Haj Amin, Germany was first and foremost the embodiment of anti-Jewish sentiment. Germany's defeat caused him great sadness, and for years after the war he continued to express his desire for cooperation between the Arabs and Germany – as he wished to see it. In an interview in December 1951, with the German quarterly, *Zeitschrift für Geopolitik*, he said: 'The Arab people are bound by ties of friendship to Germany, a country they admire ... Both peoples have always worked together amicably, in a cooperation which has never ceased ... Above all, my wish is that Germany should attain the political prominence it deserves.'[7]

There was surely no more committed devotee of Nazi Germany among the Arab leaders than Haj Amin, who openly yearned for a renewal of Germany's greatness of the war years.

It should be stressed, however, that large parts of the Arab world shared this sympathy with Nazi Germany during the Second World War. As the number of German victories increased, so too did the attempts of Arab politicians to make secret contacts with it. One of the ways in which this sympathy was expressed at the time was by naming Arab children after Nazis such as Hitler and Rommel.

By his actions, Haj Amin expressed the longing of many leaders within the Arab world for a German victory. While these leaders generally preferred to wait for this victory to be won, Haj Amin, whose relations with Britain were in ruins, did what others only dared to think.

Although after the war Haj Amin's critics argued that his activity among the Nazis helped the Jews to enlist sympathy in the West, the claim lacked any real substance. World sympathy for the

Jews after the war derived from what the Germans had done to them, and not from Haj Amin's pro-Nazi propaganda.

Haj Amin's popularity among the Palestinian Arabs and within the Arab states actually increased more than ever during his period with the Nazis. When he returned to the Middle East from Europe, Arab leaders hurried to greet him, and the masses welcomed him enthusiastically. It was only after the defeat of 1948 that the need arose for someone to blame. To a certain extent, Haj Amin was chosen as the scapegoat.

A MISERABLE ENDING

Until the age of sixty, Haj Amin was too involved in his political activities to find the time to write down in an orderly fashion the ideas that he had sought to promulgate. In contrast, during the last twenty years of his life, he wrote a great many articles and memoirs about past events. The style of writing was generally apologetic, and was often intended as a response to the attacks of his many critics, who claimed that he was the major cause of the calamities that had plagued the Palestinian Arabs.

Marlowe claims that Haj Amin was one of the most able politicians in the Middle East.[8] This holds true if one distinguishes between the gifted politician and the statesman able to foresee future events. Haj Amin was certainly not much of a great statesman. If he had been, he would have acted with greater prudence, avoiding the gambles and ventures that brought him, from time to time, to the brink of disaster. He would also have been more likely to give an honest picture in his memoirs of the negative role that the Arab rulers played in the history of the Palestinian Arabs. But as a politician, trapped by the compulsive need to pursue power and office, even the writing of his memoirs was subject to immediate political manipulation. The desire to avoid angering Arab regimes and the effort he made to make himself agreeable to rulers, whether conservative or radical, turned him, at the end of his life, into a pathetic figure. From the heights, where he stood as the first real leader of the Palestinian Arabs, as president of World Islamic Congresses, and on platforms on which he played the role of future leader of the Middle East, Haj Amin deteriorated to a position of complete degradation. In his last years, he often appeared at the courts of the Saudi Arabian and Jordanian kings, where he laboured to hinder the progress of the Palestinian national movement which, in the 1960s, set out on its way once again. This time, the long journey began without him. He could not come to terms with this, and was thus fated to end his life denigrated and completely forgotten.

Nonetheless, it was Haj Amin who laid the foundations for that very national movement which has since gone on with generations of new leaders at its head. There is almost nothing in the PLO doctrine, or in the national charters of the Palestine National Council, which had not already been conceived and given expression by Haj Amin, but the PLO does not even take the trouble to pay lip service to Haj Amin for this. This is a sad fate for a man who, during his lifetime, embodied more than any other, the appearance of the Palestinian national movement and its decades of struggle.

Notes

FOREWORD

1. Zeine n. Zeine, *The Emergence of Arab Nationalism* (Beirut, 1966), pp. 60-1; George Antonius, *The Arab Awakening* (London, 1938), p. 79.
2. For Arab political organisations, see ibid., pp. 108-12.
3. Yossef Gurni, *Ha-She'elah Ha-Aravit Ve-Ha-Ba'ayah Ha-Yehudit* [The Arab Question and the Jewish Problem] (Tel Aviv, 1985), pp. 30-1.
4. For the support of members of the British administration for Arab activity against Zionism, see R. Meinertzhagen, *Yoman Mizrah Ha-Tikhon 1917–1956* [Middle East Diary, 1917–1956], translated into Hebrew by Aharon Amir (Haifa, 1973), pp. 55-6, 71-5.

CHAPTER 1

1. Shlomo Ben-Elkanah, 'Mimtsa'im Hadashim Le-Motsa'ah Shel Mishpahat al-Husayni Ha-Yerushalmit' [New Findings Concerning the Origin of the Jerusalem al-Husayni Family], *Keshet*, 61, 1973–74, pp. 121–35; Eliyahu Eilat, *Haj Muhammad Amin al-Husayni: Mufti Yerushalayim Li-She'avar* [Haj Amin al-Husayni: Ex-Mufti of Jerusalem] (Tel Aviv, 1968), p. 18; see also, Biyan Nuwayhid al-Hut, *al-Qiyyadat Wa al-Mu'assat al-Siyassiyyah Fi Filastin: 1917–1948* [Political Leadership and Institutions in Palestine 1917–1948] (Second Edition: Acre, 1984), p. 201. The author interviewed Haj Amin at his home in Beirut shortly before his death. Haj Amin told her that he was born in 1897. This later date does not appear in any earlier source.
2. Ben-Elkanah, ibid.; Joseph B. Schechtman, *The Mufti and the Fuehrer: The Rise and Fall of Haj Amin el-Husseini* (New York, 1965), pp. 15–16.
3. Ibid. According to Jbara, 'Abd al-Latif was born in 1703/4. See Tyasir Jbara, *Palestinian Leader Hajj Amin al-Husayni: Mufti of Jerusalem* (Princeton, NJ, 1985), pp. 6–14.
4. Ibid.
5. Al-Hut, ibid.
6. For this period in Haj Amin's life, see Eilat, pp. 18–21; M. Asaf, *Toledot Hit'orerut Ha-Aravim Be-Eretz Yisrael U'Verihatam* [History of the Awakening of the Arabs in Palestine and Their Flight] (Tel Aviv, 1967), p. 252, note 1176, and pp. 264–5, note 1359 (below, Asaf, *Toledot*); Ya'acov Shim'oni, *Aravi'ey Eretz Yisrael* [The Arabs of Palestine] (Tel Aviv, 1947), p. 215; Gad Frumkin, *Derekh Shofet Bi-Yerushalayim* [The Path of a Judge in Jerusalem] (Tel Aviv, 1954), p. 206; M. P. Waters, *Mufti over Middle East* (New York, 1942), p. 7; Yehuda Taggar, *The Mufti of Jerusalem and Palestine Arab Politics: 1930–1937*, unpublished Ph.D. Thesis (University of London, 1973), pp. 12–13.
7. Al-Hut, p. 202; Jbara, p. 16.
8. Jabara, pp. 16–17.
9. Frumkin, ibid.; Taggar, p. 14; Eilat, p. 20. According to Sir Alec Kirkbride, Haj Amin was working at the time as a British informer. See Yuval Arnon-Ohanah, *Harav Mi-Bayit: Ha-Ma'avak Ha-Penimi Ba-Tenuah Ha-Palestinayyit, 1929–1939* [Destruction from Within: The Internal Struggle Within the Palestinian Movement, 1929–1939] (Tel Aviv, 1981), p. 37.

10. For the meeting of the Congress and its decisions, see Muhammad 'Izzat Darwaza, *al-Qadiyyah al-Filastiniyyah Fi Mukhtalif Marahalihah* [The Palestinian Issue in its Various Periods] I (Beirut, 1959), pp. 35–6; Yehoshua Porat, *Tsemihat Ha-Tenuah Ha-Leumit Ha-Aravit-Palistinayyit, 1918–1929* [The Emergence of the Palestinian Arab National Movement, 1918–1929] (Jerusalem, 1971), pp. 71–3 (below, Porat, *Tsemihat*); Antonius, pp. 440–2).

11. The slogans of the two clubs appeared on their stationery. See Porat, *Tsemihat*, pp. 60–1; and al-Hut, pp. 86–7.

12. See al-Hut, pp. 86–9; for the clubs, see Porat, *Tsemihat*, pp. 59–63.

13. Al-Hut, p. 211.

14. Eilat, pp. 24–5; Porat, *Tsemihat*, pp. 71, 80–1; Muhammad 'Izzat Darwaza, *Hawla al-Harakah al-'Arabiyyah al-Hadithah* [About the Modern Arab Movement] III (Sidon, 1959), p. 37 (below, Darwaza, *Hawlah al-Harakah*). In his memoirs, published in 1967, Darwaza claims that during the 1920 revolt Haj Amin headed a group of youngsters who instigated the disturbances. See Muhammad Amin al-Husayni, *Zikhronot, Filastin* [Memoirs, Palestine] (Beirut), 73, April 1967, p. 10 (below, al-Husayni, *Zikhronot*).

15. Al-Hut, p. 118.

16. Norman Bentwich, *England in Palestine* (London, 1932), p. 49; Maurice Perlman, *Mufti of Jerusalem: The Story of Haj Amin El-Husseini* (London, 1947), p. 12; see also, Eilat, p. 26; Schechtman, pp. 20–1.

17. Taggar, pp. 18–19; Eilat, p. 26; al-Hut, pp. 203–4.

18. Ibid.; Porat, *Tsemihat*, p. 155; Taggar, p. 21.

19. Darwaza, p. 51; Taggar, p. 23.

20. Al-Hut, p. 204; Porat, *Tsemihat*, p. 156; Eilat, p. 29; Elie Kedourie, *The Chatham House Version and Other Middle-Eastern Studies* (London, 1984), p. 66.

21. *Ginzat Ha-Medinah* [Israel State Archives], below ISA (Jerusalem), F/649, Herbert Samuel Papers, the High Commissioner to the First Secretary, 11 April 1921; Taggar, p. 24.

22. Porat, *Tsemihat*, pp. 157–8.

23. Al-Hut, p. 205.

24. *A Survey of Palestine*, prepared in December 1945 and January 1946 for the Information of the Anglo-American Committee of Inquiry, II (Government Printer, Palestine, Jerusalem, 1946) pp. 900–1; Al-Hut, p. 206.

25. Porat, *Tsemihat*, pp. 159–65.

26. Ibid., p. 112; Asaf, *Toledot*, pp. 86, 89, 94, 100, 104; Eilat, p. 33.

27. Porat, *Tsemihat*, pp. 167, 210–15; see also, Muhammad Amin al-Husayni, *Haqa'iq 'An Qadiyyat Filastin* [Truths about the Palestinian Issue] (Third Edition: Cairo, 1957), pp. 115–19, (below, al-Husayni, *Haqa'iq*).

28. See quotes from the opposition press, Eilat, pp. 50–3. See also the way in which the Supreme Muslim Council rejected the criticism levelled against it: *al-Jami'ah al-'Arabiyyah*, 29 Dec. 1930.

29. Al-Hut, p. 299.

30. Al-Hut, pp. 218–21; Porat, *Tsemihat*, p. 210; Philip Mattar, 'The Role of the Mufti of Jerusalem in the Political Struggle over the Western Wall, 1928–1929', in *Middle Eastern Studies (MES)*, XIX, No. 1, Jan. 1983, pp. 104–18.

31. Porat, *Tsemihat*, pp. 213–14; Christopher Sykes, *From Balfour to Bevin*, translated by S. Goren (Tel Aviv, 1966), pp. 101–3. On this subject see also al-Hut, ibid. See also note 27.

32. Sykes, ibid.; John Marlowe, *The Seat of Pilate* (London, 1959), pp. 113–15.

33. Mattar, ibid.; al-Hut; al-Husayni, *Zikhronot*, 102, September, 1969, p. 42.

34. Darwaza, *Hawla al-Harakah* II, pp. 61–2. This is also the version adopted by *al-Jami'ah al-'Arabiyyah*, 10 Nov. 1928. The treatment of the incident was limited to a report of what had occurred; see *al-Jami'ah al-'Arabiyyah*, 27 Sept. 1928; *Filastin* (Jaffa), 28 Sept. 1928; see also Mattar, ibid.

35. Al-Hut, ibid., and also list 24, p. 867. (It is worthwhile noting the fact that although

Haj Amin was the dominant figure at the Congress, Musa Kazim headed the list of representatives.)

36. *Al-Jami'ah al-'Arabiyyah*, 5 Nov. 1928.
37. Sykes, ibid.; Porat, *Tsemihat*, pp. 217–18.
38. Sykes, pp. 108–11; Yehoshua Porat, *Mi-Mehumot Li-Meridah: Ha-Tenuah Ha-Leumit Ha-Aravit Palestinayyit 1929–1939* [The Palestinian Arab National Movement: From Riots to Rebellion, Volume II, 1929–1939] (Tel Aviv, 1978) (below, Porat, *Mehumot*).
39. Great Britain, *Report of Commission on the Palestine Disturbances of August 1929* (London, 1930), pp. 71–8.
40. *Al-Jami'ah al-'Arabiyyah*, 6–28 Feb. 1930; for a different description, the source of which is apparently Haj Amin, see al-Hut, p. 234. See also, Porat, *Tsemihat*, pp. 220–1.
41. See the coversation between David Ben-Gurion and Musa al-'Alami: David Ben Gurion, *Pegishot Im Manhigim Araviyyim* [Meetings With Arab Leaders] (Tel Aviv, 1967), p. 34.
42. The Mufti's journal, quoted by Taggar, p. 74.
43. *Al-Jami'ah al-'Arabiyyah*, 9 Feb. 1930.
44. Porat, *Mehumot*, p. 40; Porat, *Tsemihat*, pp. 220–1. Many years after the event, Haj Amin emphasised that the office had been given to Musa Kazim because of his age. See al-Hut, ibid.
45. Porat, *Mehumot*, pp. 42–5; al-Hut, pp. 238–9; *al-Jami'ah al-'Arabiyyah*, 10 and 14 May 1930; Taggar, pp. 95–8.
46. *Al-Jami'ah al-'Arabiyyah*, 22 Feb. 1931; al-Hut, pp. 240–2.
47. Ibid., p. 243; Porat, *Mehumot*, pp. 25–6.
48. Martim Kramer, *Islam Assembled: The Advent of the Muslim Congresses* (New York, 1986), p. 126.
49. For criticism of Haj Amin shortly before the Congress, see *Mir'at al-Sharq*, 6 Dec. 1931. See also the journal of Akram Zu'aytir, quoted by al-Hut, pp. 244–5; *al-Jami'ah al-'Arabiyyah*, 16 Dec. 1931; Kramer, p. 127.
50. Ibid.
51. Ibid., p. 128.
52. For the discussions of the Congress, see *al-Jami'ah al-'Arabiyyah*, 18–25 Dec. 1931; Kramer, pp. 132–40; Al-Hut, pp. 245–6.
53. Ibid., p. 247; Porat, *Mehumot*, pp. 27–8; Kramer, pp. 192–3.
54. *Al-Jami'ah al-'Arabiyyah*, 13 May 1932.
55. Ibid., 12 Aug. 1932.
56. Ibid., 2 Aug. 1931, 2 Sept. 1931.
57. Government of Palestine, *Reports on Agricultural Development and Land Settlement in Palestine by Lewis French* (April 1932), p. 20, quoted by Porat, *Mehumot*, p. 56.
58. *Al-Jami'ah al-'Arabiyyah*, 25 Aug. 1931.
59. *Mir'at al-Sharq*, 29 March 1933. See also the report of the British Investigator, 1 April 1933 – quoted by Porat, *Mehumot*, p. 61.
60. Quoted by al-Hut, p. 288; for the differences of opinion at the conference in Jaffa, and Haj Amin's position, see ibid., pp. 284–90; and Porat, *Mehumot*, pp. 59–61, 82–3.
61. For the controversy over the election of a chairman for the Executive Committee, and the rivalry surrounding the municipal elections, see Emil al-Ghouri, *Filastin 'Ibra Sittin 'Aman* [Palestine Through 60 Years] Part I (Beirut, 1972), pp. 188–90, 199–204; Porat, *Mehumot*, pp. 67, 84–6.
62. For the founding of the parties and their manifestos, see al-Hut, pp. 301–14; Porat, *Mehumot*, pp. 84–104, 150–5.
63. See Y. Vashitz, *Ha-Aravim Be-Eretz Yisrael* [The Arabs of Palestine] (Merhavia, 1947), p. 383; Asaf, *Toledot*, p. 123; Sykes, p. 132.
64. Zvi Elpeleg, *Meor'aot 1936–1939: Peraot o Mered* [The Disturbances of 1936–1939: Riots or Rebellion] *Sekirot* (Shiloah Institute, Tel Aviv University), Jan. 1977, pp. 5–6 (below, Elpeleg, *Meor'aot*).

65. Ibid.; *Arkhiyyon Toledot Ha-Haganah* [Haganah Archives] (Tel Aviv), File 103; *al-Jami'ah al-'Arabiyyah*, 10 July 1935.
66. See Vashitz, pp. 175–6; *al-Liwa*, 10 March 1935; *al-Jami'ah al-Islamiyyah*, 15 March 1935; *al-Difa* (Jaffa), 17 and 20 March 1936; *al-Jami'ah al-'Arabiyyah*, 20 June 1934, 16 Sept. 1934.
67. Elpeleg, *Meor'aot*, p. 6; *al-Jami'ah al-'Arabiyyah*, 16 and 19 Aug. 1934.
68. Taggar, pp. 325–8; concerning 'Izz al-Din al-Qassam and his activities, see al-Hut, pp. 317–28; Elie Kedourie and Sylvia G. Haim (eds.), *Zionism and Arabism in Palestine and Israel* (London, 1982), pp. 52–88.
69. Al-Hut, ibid.; Asaf, *Toledot*, p. 280 (note 1490); Porat, *Mehumot*, pp. 164–7.
70. Subhi Yasin, *al-Thawrah al-'Arabiyyah al-Kubra: 1936–1939* [The Great Arab Revolt 1936–1939] (Cairo, 1959), pp. 14–22; al-Hut, pp. 326–7.
71. Al-Hut, pp. 319–20; *Davar*, 21 Nov. 1935; *Ha-Aretz*, 22 Nov. 1935; Porat, *Mehumot*, p. 107.
72. See, for example, *al-Jami'ah al-Islamiyyah*, *Filastin* (Jaffa), 23 Nov. 1935.
73. Conversations with Faisal al-Husayni, the son of 'Abd al-Qadir, in Jerusalem, Nov.–Dec. 1984; Porat, *Mehumot*, pp. 161–2.
74. Porat, *Mehumot*, pp. 173–5; *al-Jami'ah al-'Arabiyyah*, 22 Oct. 1935; al-Hut, p. 314; Robert John and Sami Hadawi, *The Palestine Diary*, I (Beirut, 1970), p. 250 (below, John-Hadawi).
75. On the subject of the Legislative Council, see Porat, *Mehumot*, pp. 175–93; Moshe Sharett (Shertok) *Yoman Medini* I [Political Diary] (Tel Aviv, 1968), pp. 73–5.
76. Taggar, p. 372; Porat, ibid, p. 191.; al-Hut, p. 333.
77. Quotation from Akram Zu'aytir's memoirs – al-Hut, pp. 333–4.
78. For the beginning of the 1936 disturbances, see Beracha Habas (ed.), *Sefer Meor'aot 1936* [Book of 1936 Disturbances] (Tel Aviv, 1937), pp. 3–13, 419–21; *Filastin* (Jaffa), *al-Liwa*, 19 April 1936; *Davar*, *Ha-Aretz*, 20 April 1936.
79. Message from the High Commissioner, Wauchope, to the Colonial Office, Taggar, p. 370.
80. *Arkhiyyon Toledot Ha-Haganah* [Haganah Archives] (Tel Aviv), Arab Office Files – Taggar, ibid.
81. *Filastin* (Jaffa), 26 April 1936; al-Hut, pp. 335–6.
82. Memoirs of Husayn Fakhri al-Khalidi – al-Hut, pp. 336–7.
83. *Al-Liwa*, 8 May 1936; *Filastin* (Jaffa), 9 May 1936; al-Hut, pp. 337–9.
84. *Al-Liwa*, 15 May 1936; Porat, *Mehumot*, pp. 203–4; Asaf, *Toledot*, pp. 135–6.
85. Yuval Arnon-Ohanah, *Falahim Ba-Mered Ha-Aravi Be-Eretz Yisrael: 1936–1939* [Felahin in the Arab Revolt in Palestine: 1936–1939] (Tel Aviv, 1978), p. 34; Shim'oni, pp. 296–7; Asaf, *Toledot*, p. 41; Porat, ibid., pp. 205–6, 231–4; al-Hut, p. 353.
86. *Al-Liwa*, 22 June 1936; Porat, ibid.
87. Ben Gurion, p. 99.
88. Moshe Sharett, *Yoman Medini* [Political Diary] II (Tel Aviv, 1971), pp. 126–7.
89. Al-Hut, p. 362.
90. Palestine Royal Commission Report – presented by the Secretary of State for the Colonies to Parliament by command of His Majesty, July 1937, Cmd. 5479 (Jerusalem, 1937), p. 100; Akram Zu'aytir, *Yawmiyyat al-Harakah al-Wataniyyah al-Filastiniyyah 1935–1939* [Diary of the Palestinian National Movement, 1935–1939] (Beirut, 1980), pp. 257–62; Yehuda Slutsky and others, *Sefer Toledot Ha-Haganah* [History of the Haganah] II, Vol. II (Tel Aviv, 1963), p. 714.
91. *Filastin* (Jaffa), 27 July 1936.
92. *Al-Liwa*, 13 and 14 Oct. 1936; *Filastin* (Jaffa), 14 and 16 Oct. 1936.
93. *Al-Liwa*, 20 Aug. 1937; *Filastin* (Jaffa), 1 Sept. 1937.
94. Yuval Arnon-Ohanah, pp. 279–88; Ezrah Danin (ed.), *Te'udot U-Demuyot: Mi-Ginzey Ha-Kenufiyyot Ha-Araviyyot Bi-Meor'aot 1936–1939* [Documents and Portraits: Archives of the Arab Bands from the 1936–1939 Disturbances] (Tel Aviv, 1944).
95. Al-Hut, pp. 366–7; for a list of the Palestinian participants see ibid., pp. 894–6.

96. Al-Hut, pp. 376–7; John-Hadawi, I, p. 278. According to Porat (*Mehumot*, pp. 276–8) the murder was carried out by members of the 'Ikhawan al-Qassam' under the command of Muhammad al-Salih.
97. Al-Hut, p. 373. According to Porat (*Mehumot*, pp. 278–9), Jamal al-Husayni escaped to Syria.
98. In his memoirs, Haj Amin claims that he attempted to reach Syria, but that he was forced by the French security forces to enter Lebanon. See al-Husayni, ibid., 74, May 1967, pp. 9–11; see also, al-Hut, pp. 373–4; Porat, *Mehumot*, p. 280.
99. See previous note.
100. For a detailed analysis of the revolt, see Ezra Danin.
101. Ibid., pp. 135–6, 144–7; Yuval Arnon-Ohanah, pp. 127–40; *Ha-Aretz*, 9–13 March 1939, 4–12 June 1939.
102. According to Hanna Asfur, who attended the Haifa conference. See al-Hut, p. 403.
103. Ibid., pp. 383–5. For a discussion of the influence of the revolt see Uriel Dann, 'Emirat Ever Ha-Yarden 1921–1946', *Sekirot*, Feb. 1982, pp. 11–12.
104. Issah al-Safri, *Filastin al-'Arabiyyah Bayn al-Inti'dab Wal-Sahayuniyyah* [Arab Palestine: Between the Mandate and Zionism] II (Jaffa, 1937), pp. 140–1, 170; Porat, *Mehumot*, pp. 245–6; al-Hut, p. 357. For the failure of the 'Round Table' talks in the eyes of the Arabs, see *Filastin* (Jaffa), 19–24 March 1939.
105. Regarding his non-inclusion in the delegation, Haj Amin wrote that he did not want his 'personal problem to stand in the way of the delegations, on which some of them placed great hope'. Al-Husayni, ibid., 76, July 1967, p. 38.
106. Porat, *Mehumot*, pp. 340–1; Yehoshua Porat, *Be-Mivhan Ha-Ma'ase Ha-Politi: Eretz Yisrael, Ahdut Aravit U-Mediniyyut Britaniyyah 1930–1945* [The Test of Political Action: Palestine, Arab Unity and British Policy, 1930–1945] (Jerusalem, 1985), p. 190. Haj Amin blamed the British and the US Governments for the failure of the conference. See al-Husayni, ibid., p. 39.
107. *Akhir Sa'a*, 25 April 1973; for the complete text of the committee's decision, see al-Hut, pp. 766–74; Porat, *Mehumot*, p. 346.
108. Dr 'Izzat Tannus' diary – al-Hut, p. 397.
109. Al-Husayni, *Haqa'iq*, p. 46.
110. Al-Husayni, ibid.
111. Al-Husayni, ibid., 127, Oct. 1971, p. 8; *Akhir Sa'a*, ibid.; Porat, *Mehumot*, ibid.

CHAPTER 2

1. Lucas Hirshowitz, *Ha-Reich Ha-Shlishi Ve-Ha-Mizrah Ha-Aravi* [The Third Reich and the Arab East] translated into Hebrew from the Polish by A. Cana'ani (Tel Aviv, 1965), pp. 35–6, 42–4, 90–3. For Haj Amin's connections with Mussolini during the 1930s and his attempts to gain the Italian leader's assistance in order to poison Tel Aviv's water sources, see *Yediot Ahronot*, 21 Dec. 1986.
2. John-Hadawi, I, p. 330; al-Hut, p. 431; Philip Mattar, 'Amin al-Husayni and Iraq's Quest for Independence, 1939–1941', *Arab Studies Quarterly*, VI, No. 4, Fall 1984, pp. 267–81 (below, Mattar, *Iraq*).
3. Majid Khadduri, *Independent Iraq 1932–1958: A Study in Iraqi Politics* (2nd edn.; London, 1960), p. 163 (below, Khadduri, *Iraq*).
4. His mental condition was reported by the French High Commissioner in Lebanon, Gabriel Puaux. See Mattar, *Iraq*, pp. 269–70; Majid Khadduri, *Arab Contemporaries* (Baltimore, 1973), p. 76.
5. Khadduri, *Iraq*, ibid.; 'Uthman Kama'al Hada'ad, *Harakat Rashid 'Ali al-Qailani* [The Movement of Rashid 'Ali al-Qailani] (Sidon, 1941), p. 6; Mattar, *Iraq*, pp. 267–81.
6. Ibid., p. 275. See also Eleazar Bari, *Ha-Ketsunah Ve-Ha-Shilton Ba-Olam Ha-Aravi* [Officers and the Regime in the Arab World] (Tel Aviv, 1966), p. 32.
7. Al-Hut, pp. 448–51; Mattar, *Iraq*, pp. 275–6; Shim'oni, p. 315; Schechtman, pp. 96–8.

8. Mattar, ibid.; Khadduri, *Iraq*, pp. 164–5; al-Hut, ibid.; Hirshowitz, p. 143.
9. Ibid., pp. 77, 89–90; Mattar, ibid., p. 275; Khadduri, ibid., pp. 171–2; al-Husayni, *Zikhronot*, 77, August 1967, p. 24; Musa Alami, *Palestine is My Country* (London, 1969), pp. 127–8.
10. Al-Husayni, ibid., 79, Oct. 1967, p. 52; Mattar, ibid., p. 278; Hirshowitz, pp. 87–95. On other occasions, Haj Amin's emissary to Germany was a secretary by the name of Dr Mustafa al-Wakil. See al-Hut, pp. 452–3; Khadduri, ibid., pp. 179–80.
11. Hada'ad, pp. 25–33; Mattar, ibid.
12. Hirshowitz, pp. 118, 333–5; Khadduri, ibid., pp. 378–80.
13. Hirshowitz, pp. 106–8; Mattar, *Iraq*, p. 279.
14. Ibid., pp. 279–81; al-Husayni, ibid., 76, July 1967, p. 44; David Niv, *Ma'arakhot Ha-Irgun Ha-Zva'i Ha-Leumi* [The Campaigns of the Irgun Zva'i Leumi Group] III (Tel Aviv, 1967), pp. 73–4.
15. Hirshowitz, pp. 115–16, 142–50.
16. Ibid. Haj Amin claims in his memoirs that his involvement was at the initiative of Nuri al-Sa'id who, on 19 February 1941, rebuked him for not bringing about a reconciliation between the politicians and the hawkish generals. See al-Husayni, ibid., 77, Aug. 1967, pp. 20–4.
17. Hirshowitz, pp. 150, 165.
18. Al-Husayni, ibid., 79, Oct. 1967, p. 52; Khadduri, *Iraq*, p. 224.
19. Al-Husayni, ibid., p. 50.
20. Nissim Kazzaz, 'Du'ah Va'adat He-Hakirah Mi-Ta'am Memshelet Iraq Al Meor'aot 1–2 Yuni 1941' [Report of the Iraqi Government's Commission of Inquiry into the Events of 1–2 July, 1941] *Pa'amim*, 8, 1981, pp. 46–59.
21. Al-Hut, p. 454.
22. Ibid.; al-Husayni, ibid., 80, Nov. 1967, pp. 15–16.
23. Hirshowitz, p. 217.
24. Al-Husayni, ibid., 82, Jan. 1968, p. 14; Hada'ad, pp. 138–41, 172–5; Khadduri, *Iraq*, pp. 235–6; al-Hut, p. 455; Hirshowitz, pp. 218–20.
25. Al-Husayni, ibid., 80, Nov. 1967, pp. 16–17; Ibid., 81, Dec. 1967, pp. 14, 17–19.
26. Ibid.
27. Ibid., 104, Nov. 1969, pp. 13–15; see also the interview given by Haj Amin to Zuhir al-Maradini, *al-Dustur* (London), 29 Nov. 1982.
28. *Ha-Aretz*, 28 Oct.1941; Daniel Carpi, 'The Mufti of Jerusalem, Amin el-Husseini, and His Diplomatic Activity during World War II', *Studies in Zionism*, VII, Spring 1983, pp. 104–5.
29. Al-Husayni, ibid., 82, Jan. 1968, p. 15; Carpi, pp. 105–7.
30. Al-Husayni, ibid., 85, April 1968, pp. 14–17; Hirshowitz, pp. 223–9; Carpi, pp. 108–10; al-Hut, pp. 457–9; Interview given by Haj Amin to Zuhir Maradini, *al-Dustur* (London), 29 Nov. and 6 Dec. 1982.
31. Al-Hut, pp. 451–2; see also the exchange of letters between Haj Amin and Shawkat and the evidence of al-Sabbagh – ibid., pp. 777–8; see also, Hirshowitz, pp. 236, 268–76; Mattar, *Iraq*, p. 276.
32. Interview with Habib Cana'an, *Ha-Aretz*, 1 March 1970; Hirshowitz, ibid. See also, Fritz Grobba, *Männer und Mächte im Orient* (Göttingen, 1967), p. 299.
33. For Haj Amin's plans concerning North Africa and his activity in the Balkans, see Carpi, pp. 118–31; *Sefer Toledot Ha-Haganah* [History of the Haganah] C, Part 1, pp. 109–14.
34. Ibid.; al-Husayni, ibid., 93, Dec. 1968, pp. 5–6; ibid., 142, Jan. 1973, p. 4; ibid., 163, Oct. 1974, p. 4.
35. Carpi, pp. 130–1; Hirshowitz, pp. 322–3; *Sefer Toledot Ha-Haganah* [History of the Haganah] III, Part 1, p. 111; *New York Times (NYT)*, 31 Jan. 1946.
36. Al-Hut, pp. 460–1.
37. Al-Husayni, *Haqa'iq*, p. 121.
38. Al-Husayni, *Zikhronot*, 103, Oct. 1969, p. 19; ibid., 105, Dec., 1969, p. 4.
39. Ibid., 89, Aug. 1968, p. 16; ibid., 105, Dec. 1969, pp. 4–5.

40. Ibid., 112, July 1970, pp. 5–7.
41. Ibid., pp. 6–8; Ibid., 143, Feb. 1973, pp. 4–7; See also, *Ha-Aretz*, 4 June 1961, 27 April 1961.
42. Al-Husayni, ibid., p. 6.
43. Al-Husayni, ibid., 118, Jan. 1971, p. 12; see also, Hirshowitz, p. 323.
44. For Haj Amin's efforts to flee Germany, see al-Husayni, ibid., pp. 13–14; ibid., 119, Feb. 1971, pp. 4–5.
45. Ibid.; *Ha-Aretz*, 4 April 1946, 29 Nov. 1945 and 25 Oct. 1945.
46. Al-Husayni, ibid. See also, ibid., 149, Aug. 1973, p. 4.
47. Ibid., 120, March 1971, p. 7; ibid., 151, Oct. 1973, pp. 4–5; For his escape from France, see al-Hut, p. 460; Schechtman, pp. 167–90; Jbara, p. 186; Khadduri, *Iraq*, p. 242.
48. *Ha-Aretz*, 12, 13, 16, 18, 21 June 1946; al-Husayni, ibid., 121, April 1971, p. 5.
49. For the French Foreign Ministry's statement, see al-Husayni, ibid., 150, Sept. 1973, p. 6.
50. *Ha-Aretz*, 21 June 1946; see also, al-Husayni, ibid., 151, Oct. 1973, pp. 4–9.
51. Ibid., pp. 5–6; ibid., 121, April 1971, p. 5; Schechtman, p. 178.
52. Al-Husayni, ibid., 119, Feb. 1971, p. 6.
53. For his escape, see ibid., 122, May 1971, pp. 6–8; ibid., 123, June 1971, pp. 4–5; Ibid., 151, Oct. 1973, p. 4.
54. Ibid., 124, July 1974, pp. 4–5.
55. Al-Hut, pp. 469, 477; Yossef Nevo, *Abdullah Ve-Aravi'ey Eretz Yisrael* [Abdullah and the Arabs of Palestine] (Tel Aviv, 1975), p. 33.
56. Al-Hut, pp. 469–71; Assaf, *Toledot*, p. 166.
57. Ahmad al-Shuqairy, *Hiwa Wa-Asrar Ma'a al-Muluq al-Ru'assah* [Dialogue and Secrets with Monarchs and Presidents] (Beirut), pp. 81–96; al-Hut, ibid.; al-Husayni, ibid., 128, Nov. 1971, p. 6.
58. Nevo, p. 28; Asaf, ibid., pp. 166–7. For the text of the League's charter, see Ahmed M. Gomaa, *The Foundation of the League of Arab States* (London, 1977), pp. 274, 295–301.
59. Emil al-Ghouri, who was the secretary of the Husayni party, and other figures, justified their opposition to the establishment of a new committee by pointing to the absence of Haj Amin from the country. See al-Hut, pp. 470–2.
60. *Filastin* (Jaffa), 8 Feb. 1946; al-Hut, pp. 477–8.
61. For the activity surrounding the establishment of a Palestinian representation to the League, see al-Hut, pp. 536–43. See also, Nevo, p. 28; Asher Goren, *Ha-Leegah Ha-Aravit* [The Arab League] (Tel Aviv, 1954), p. 382.
62. Al-Hut, p. 555. See *Me-Ahorey Ha-Pargod, Va'ada Parlamentarit Iraqit Al Ha-Milhamah Be-Yisrael* [Behind the Curtain: The Iraqi Parliamentary Commission on the War Against Israel] translated into Hebrew by S. Segev (Tel Aviv, 1954), pp. 38–42; al-Husayni, ibid., 123, June 1971, p. 6; ibid., 127, Oct. 1971, p. 7.
63. Al-Hut, p. 544.
64. Ibid., pp. 474, 543–5.
65. Al-Husayni, ibid., 155, Feb. 1974, pp. 11–15; al-Hut, pp. 559–65; Nevo, pp. 32–3.

CHAPTER 3

1. See Nevo, pp. 12, 20.
2. Robert W. Macdonald, *The League of Arab States* (Princeton University, 1965), pp. 350–1; see Sykes, pp. 300–2; Yossef Amitai, 'Medinot Arav U-Milhemet Eretz Yisrael: 1945–1948, Mi-Me'oravut Medinit Le-Hit'arvut Zvai't' [The Arab States and the War over Palestine: 1945–1948, From Political to Military Involvement'], *Iyunim Be-Heker Ha-Mizrah Ha-Tikhon* (Haifa University), April 1976, pp. 21, 40; al-Hut, pp. 571–3; Nevo, p. 44.
3. Jbara, p. 187; al-Hut, p. 580; 'Arif al-'Arif, *al-Nakba: Nakbat Bayt al-Muqaddas Wa al-Fardus al-Mafqud 1947–1952*, I [The Calamity: The Calamity of Jerusalem and the

Lost Paradise, 1947–1952, Volume I] (Beirut, 1956), pp. 14–16; *Ha-Aretz*, 20 Dec. 1947.

4. Jbara, ibid., Nevo, p. 45; al-Hut, pp. 535, 580.
5. Segev, pp. 38, 54; al-Husayni, ibid., 152, Oct. 1973, p. 7.
6. Al-Hut, p. 580; Nevo, ibid.
7. Haj Amin claimed that the Arab Higher Institute sent 1,000 Palestinian youngsters to Qatana for training. See al-Husayni, ibid., 135, June 1972, pp. 4–6; Jbara, ibid. For the conflict between al-Qawuqji and Haj Amin, see Muhammad Nimr al-Hawari, *Sir al-Nakba* [The Underlying Reasons for the Calamity] (1955), p. 103; Fawzi Qawuqji, *Manazamat al-Tahrir al-Filastiniyyah – Markaz al-Abhath, Filastin Fi Muzakarat al-Qawuqji* [Palestine in the Memoirs of al-Qawuqji], II (1975), pp. 130–1; Khaldun Sati' al-Husri (ed.), *Muzakarat Taha al-Hashimi 1942–1955* [The Memoirs of Tala al-Hashimi, 1942–1955], II (Beirut, 1978), pp. 158–78; al-Hut, pp. 614–15.
8. Al-Husayni, ibid. Two British soldiers cooperated with the Arabs in the explosion in Ben Yehuda Street. See *Davar*, 16 Sept. 1948.
9. Al-Hut, pp. 580–3; al-'Arif, A, pp. 33–6; Segev, pp. 18–22.
10. In their books, mentioned above, Taha al-Hashimi and Muhammad Nimr al-Hawari describe Haj Amin's stubbornness and the negative feelings that he evoked among members of the League and within the Palestinian camp.
11. Al-Hussayni, *Haqa'iq*, p. 21.
12. Segev, pp. 17–18, 54.
13. For the understanding reached between Britain and Transjordan regarding the conquest of Palestine, see Glubb, pp. 62–6. For the split between representatives of the Jewish Yishuv and King Abdullah, see Ze'ev Sherf, *Sheloshah Yamim* [Three Days] (Tel Aviv, 1959), pp. 62–4. See also, al-Husayni, ibid., pp. 21, 29, 36.
14. Al-Husayni, *Zikhronot*, 159, June 1974, pp. 4–6; ibid., 134, May 1972, p. 5.
15. Amitai, pp. 44–7. For Abdullah's contacts with Palestinian opponents of Haj Amin, see Nevo, pp. 46–52.
16. Segev, pp. 22–4, 57–9; Amitai, pp. 44–6.
17. Muhammad Khalil, *The Arab States and the Arab League*, II (Beirut, 1962), pp. 553–4 (below, Khalil); al-Hut, p. 588; al-Husayni, ibid., 99, June 1969, pp. 5–7; al-Husayni, *Haqa'iq*, pp. 69–72.
18. Al-Husayni, *Zikhronot*, 167, Feb. 1975, pp. 6–10.
19. Al-Husayni, ibid., 162, Sept. 1974, p. 6; *Haqa'iq*, pp. 21–2.
20. Sherf, p. 63; Nevo, pp. 79–80.
21. Segev, pp. 18–21.
22. Al-Husayni, *Zikhronot*, 165, Dec. 1974, pp. 6–7. The Soviet Union reacted with displeasure to the declaration of the US representative, and demanded the continued execution of the partition plan. See *Al Ha-Mishmar*, 11 and 12 March 1948; *al-Tali'a*, March, 1975, pp. 134–5; al-Hut, p. 621.
23. Al-Husayni, ibid., 166, Jan. 1975, pp. 5–7; Thomas Mayer, 'Egypt's Invasion of Palestine', *MES*, XXII, No. 1, Jan. 1986, p. 23.
24. *Al-Tali'a*, ibid. According to a different source, it was King Farouk who insisted on carrying out the invasion 'with or without al-Nuqrashi's agreement'. See al-Hashimi, II, pp. 216–7.
25. Jon and David Kimche, *Both Sides of the Hill: Britain and the Palestine War* (London, 1960), p. 107. See also, Nevo, p. 68.
26. Al-Hashimi, II, pp. 217–21; Kimche, Jon and David, p. 108; Nevo, p. 69.
27. *Sefer Toledot Ha-Haganah* [History of the Haganah] III, Part 2, pp. 1359, 1364–70. The commander of the Egyptian invading force was ordered to take over large areas in order to prevent them being seized by the Legion. See Kimche, Jon and David, p. 164.
28. Ibid., p. 109. For the meetings and discussions see Segev, pp. 26–7; al-Hashimi, ibid.; Amitai, p. 49; Nevo, pp. 69–70.
29. Al-Hut, p. 641.
30. Nevo, pp. 87–8; Abdullah al-Tal, *Zikhronot Abdullah al-Tal* [The Memoirs of Abdullah al-Tal], translated into Hebrew from the Arabic by Yehoshua Halamish (Tel Aviv, 1964), pp. 167–8 .

31. *Ha-Aretz*, 23 May 1948; Nevo, ibid.
32. 'Aziz Shihada, 'Megamot Ha-Hakikah Ha-Yardenit Ba-Gada Ha-Ma'aravit' [Trends in Jordanian Legislation in the West Bank], *Ha-Mizrah Ha-Hadash*, III, 1970, p. 166.
33. General Glubb relates that he was present when an emissary of 'Abd al-Qadir al-Husayni arrived in Ramallah and purchased ammunition for the fighters at the Kastel from the local residents. Glubb, p. 80. Al-Hawari claims that Arab families were forced to set up militias in order to protect themselves against members of the *al-Jihad al-Muqqadas*. See al-Hawari, p. 106.
34. After he failed in the assault on Mishmar Ha-Emeq, al-Qawuqji announced to Arab journalists that he had conquered it. In reply to a question regarding how long it would take before he would overcome the whole Jewish section of Palestine, al-Qawuqji replied that the conquest of Mishmar Ha-Emeq had lasted 90 minutes and that all that was required was to multiply that period of time by the number of Jewish settlements. See Kirkbride, p. 157.
35. In his memoirs, Haj Amin relates that because of an argument between al-Qawuqji and the commander of the Liberation Army in Jaffa, 'Adil Nijim al-Din, the latter gathered his men and robbed shops, confiscated cars and guns, and left the town. See al-Husayni, ibid., 169, April 1975, pp. 10–12. See also, al-Hut, pp. 630–3; al-Hawari, pp. 185–7; Glubb, ibid. For the end of the role of the Liberation Army on 22 November 1948, see al-Husayni, ibid., 174, May 1975, p. 8.
36. Sala'ah al-'Aqa'ad, *Qadiyyat Filastin: al-Marhala al-Harija, 1945–1956* [The Palestinian Issue – The Critical Stage, 1945–1946] (Cairo, 1968), pp. 72–4; Hani al-Hindi, *Jaysh al-Inqaz* [The Liberation Army] (Beirut, 1974), p. 85; al-Hawari, p. 165.
37. At the end of May he also visited the al-Aqsa mosque, where the masses received him with cries of 'King of Transjordan and Palestine'; when someone in the crowd shouted 'Long live Haj Amin', he was removed by soldiers of the Legion and arrested. See *Ha-Aretz*, 1 June 1948; see also, Nevo, p. 89.
38. Al-Husayni, *Haqa'iq*, pp. 80–4. (For more detail, see the following chapter.)
39. Radio Damascus, 16 May 1948 – *Ha-Aretz*, 17 May 1948. It was reported that Abdullah proposed that Haj Amin come to Amman and put himself at the disposal of the king. See *Ha-Aretz*, 24 May 1948. Al-Husayni, ibid., pp. 82–3.
40. After the Baludan conference, five members were appointed to the Institute. However, a few months after Haj Amin returned from Europe and assumed the leadership, he announced the addition of a further five members. See al-Hut, pp. 586–94, 905.
41. Ibid., pp. 589–90. See also the report of the Egyptian consul in Jerusalem to the Foreign Ministry in Cairo concerning the predicament of the Palestinians in the absence of the Institute from the country – Ahmad Farraj Tai'a, *Safahat Matu'ah 'An Filastin* [Forgotten Papers Concerning Palestine], pp. 96–7 (below, Ahmad Farraj); also al-Hut, pp. 592–3.
42. It should be remembered that during the disturbances of 1936–39 as well, most of the Palestinian activists left for the neighbouring countries (apart from those who were arrested or who fled from warrants for their arrest).
43. *Ha-Aretz, Davar*, 18 May 1948.
44. Nevo, p. 87.
45. *Davar*, 21–24 Dec. 1948, 13 Jan. 1949; Schechtman, pp. 236–7; Nevo, p. 116; *Middle East Journal (MEJ)*, III, 1949, p. 195.
46. Al-Tal, pp. 268, 288–9; Glubb, pp. 133, 192; Jbara, pp. 188–9; Nevo, p. 88.
47. Folke Bernadotte, *To Jerusalem* (London, 1951), pp. 129–31; Nevo, pp. 96–8.
48. Nevo, pp. 97–8; Khalil, II, pp. 566–8.
49. According to R. Musairi, the *Ha-Aretz* correspondent for Arab affairs, the administration did not begin to operate because of the strident objections from Amman. See *Ha-Aretz*, 19 Sept. 1948. A different researcher, relying on documents of the Arab Higher Institute in the PLO's research centre in Beirut, argues that the Institute also had its reservations about the civil administration – first, because of the dependence of this body on the Arab League; and second, because it constituted an infringement of the authority of the Arab Higher Institute. See Samih Shabib, 'Muqaddamat al-

Mussadarah al-Rasmiyyah Lil-Shakhsiyyah al-Wataniyyah al-Filastiniyyah 1948–1950' [Background to the Formal Denial of the Palestinian National Identity, 1948–1950] *Shuun Filastiniyyah*, 129–31, Aug.–Oct. 1982, pp. 73–4.

50. National Archives (Washington), Department of State, Secret File, 890 i.00/9–348. 3 Sept. 1948 (below, NA).

51. *Ha-Aretz*, 3 Aug. 1948.

52. According to al-Hawari, Ahmad Hilmi was invited to Cairo under the pretext of dealing with the issue of the Arab National Bank, and that while there he was persuaded to accept the position of Prime Minister. See al-Hawari, p. 271; Nevo, p. 99.

53. *NYT*, 25–29 Sept. 1948. Al-Hawari claims that members of the League convinced Abdullah's representatives that by establishing the All-Palestine Government they would be able to rid themselves of Haj Amin. See al-Hawari, pp. 271–2; see also Ahmad Farraj, pp. 150–1; Nevo, ibid.; *Ha-Aretz*, 26 Sept. 1948; *Davar*, 24 Sept. 1948.

54. See the previous note. For a list of members of the government, see Nevo, Appendix 5, p. 126.

55. NA Department of State, 890 i.01/9–2048. 22 Sept. 1948. See also, UP News Agency report from Cairo – *Davar*, 27 Sept. 1948.

56. Ibid.; Nevo, p. 100; *Ha-Aretz*, 27 Sept. 1948.

57. *Al-Ahram*, 23–26 Sept. 1948; Goren, p. 201; Nevo, p. 99; *Davar*, 26 Sept. 1948.

58. *Ha-Aretz*, *Davar*, 26 Sept. 1948; *al-Ahram*, 26 Sept. 1948; Nevo, ibid.

59. Al-Hawari, p. 273; *Davar*, 26 Sept. 1948; *NYT*, 24–25 Sept. 1948.

60. *Ha-Aretz*, 27 Sept. 1948; Ahmad Farraj, pp. 150–1.

61. Al-Hawari, pp. 277–8; Ahmad Farraj, pp. 100–1.

62. *Ha-Aretz*, 29 Sept. 1948; Radio Ramallah, 29 Sept. 1948 – *Davar*, 29–30 Sept. 1948.

63. Al-Hawari, p. 275.

64. See al-Husayni, ibid., pp. 83–4; al-Hawari claims that Haj Amin arrived in Gaza disguised as a woman. See al-Hawari, p. 282; *NYT*, 29 Sept. 1948.

65. Interview with Musa al-Surani in Gaza, in November 1967. See also, Zvi Elpeleg, 'Palestin Atsma'it Bi-Svak Ha-Yerivut Ha-Bayn-Aravit: 1946-1948' [An Independent Palestine in the Web of Inter-Arab Rivalry: 1946–1948] *Sekirot*, Feb. 1982, p. 32.

66. Interview with Kama'al Hasaniyyah in his hotel in 'Umar al-Muhktar Street, Gaza, in December 1980.

67. Al-Husayni, ibid., pp. 83–6; al-Hashimi, II, pp. 241–2; see also, Husayn Abu al-Namil, *Qita'a Raza 1948–1967: Tatawurat Iqtisadiyyah Wa-Siyassiyya Wa-Ijtimaiyyah Wa-'Asqariyyah* [The Gaza Strip 1948–1967: Economic, Political, Social and Military Developments] (Beirut, 1979), pp. 22–5. According to a different version, he returned to Egypt only after the middle of October. See Shabib, p. 79.

68. Al-Hawari, pp. 275–83; Radio Near East termed the conference as the 'Parliament', and announced in its broadcasts that Haj Amin had arrived in Gaza in order to participate in the Palestinian 'Parliament' – *Davar*, 30 Sept. 1948; for a description of the welcome that Haj Amin received from the local residents in Gaza, see Shabib, p. 75; Abu al-Namil, ibid. Interview with Hamdi al-Husayni (one of the representatives at the conference) in Gaza, in December 1980. See also *Ha-Aretz*, 3 Sept. 1948.

69. Issam al-Shawa, who was serving as a district officer in Jenin at the time, describes how representatives who were to participate in the conference in Gaza were prevented from attending. Together with other regional officers, he was summoned to the commander of the Iraqi force in the region, Brigadier Tahir al-Zubaydir, who told them to inform those present not to 'go to [Ahmad Hilmi] in Gaza, and if they do then they will have to stay there'. Interview with Issam al-Shawa in Gaza, Dec. 1980.

70. *Al-Ahram*, 1 Oct. 1948; see also, Abu al-Namil, pp. 21–2, who emphasises that in light of Abdullah's claim that the All-Palestine Government was not a representative body, Haj Amin was careful to invite to the conference heads of representative institutions of the Palestinian Arabs; for the participants in the Palestine National Council, see also, Shabib, pp. 75–7.

71. Ibid.; al-Hawari, ibid.; *al-Ahram*, ibid.; Nevo, p. 101.

72. *Al-Ahram*, 4 Oct. 1948. As President of the Palestine National Council, Haj Amin

secured for himself a right of veto over all important matters. See *Davar*, 6 Oct. 1948. The conference also elected Hasan Abu al-Sa'ud and Michael 'A'aza as deputy presidents. See Abu al-Namil, p. 23; Shabib, ibid.; Nevo, ibid.; Issam Sakhnini, *Filastin al-Dawlah* [Palestine: The State] (2nd edn., Acre, 1986); pp. 220–3.

73. According to Khalil, II, p. 579; the committee that worked on the formulation of the declaration was comprised of Munif al-Husayni, Akram Zu'aytir, Anwar Nusseibeh and Issah Nahlah. See *al-Ahram*, 3 Oct. 1948; see also, *Herald Tribune (HT)*, 3 Oct. 1948.

74. Nevo, pp. 108–9; Shabib, pp. 77–9.

75. Nevo, pp. 112–13.

76. *NYT*, 3 Oct. 1948; according to a different source, he was even compelled to participate in a conference organised by the Hashemite regime in Amman. See Shabib, pp. 77–8; *Davar*, 3 Oct. 1948.

77. He was replaced by Akram Zu'aytir. See *Davar*, 24 Sept. 1948; Nevo, p. 126.

78. *Davar*, 29 Sept. 1948; Nevo, ibid.

79. *Ha-Aretz*, *Davar*, 29 Sept. 1948.

80. Ahmad Farraj, p. 154. Al-Khalidi later changed his mind and was appointed Minister of Health.

81. See note 45, above.

82. *Ha-Aretz*, 26 Sept. 1948.

83. Radio Cairo, 2–3 Oct. 1948 – Summary of Arabic broadcasts, No. 55; *al-Ahram*, 3 Oct. 1948.

84. Telegram from the US Embassy in Egypt to the State Department in Washington – NA Department of State, Division of Communications and Records, 1433, 4 Oct. 1948.

85. NA Department of State, 867N. 01710 – 243, 2 Oct. 1948.

86. Radio Damascus, 4–5 Oct. 1948 – Summary of Arabic broadcasts, No. 56; see also the telegram from the US Embassy in Cairo to the State Department – NA Department of State, Division of Communications and Records, 1439, 3 Oct. 1948. The Secretary of State's response was that the US would not recognise the All-Palestine Government, 'that was not established in accordance with the rules, elections were not held and it does not control the territory which it claims'; see also, *al-Ahram*, 6 Oct. 1948.

87. *Davar*, 6 Oct. 1948.

88. Radio Monte Carlo, 11–12 Oct. 1948 – Summary of Arabic broadcasts, No. 62.

89. See note 84; see also, Abu al-Namil, p. 24.

90. The Egyptian Gazette, 5 Oct. 1948. The Palestine National Council conference in Gaza elected a Supreme Council composed of Haj Amin (president) and two other members – the Prime Minister and the President of the Palestine Supreme Court. For the Supreme Council's authority, see Appendix F.

91. Shabib, p. 77; *al-Ahram*, 9 Oct. 1948.

92. Ibid., 20 and 25 Oct. 1948.

93. Ahmad Mu'awad, *Sarakha Illah al-Sama* [Cry to Heaven] (Jerusalem), p. 35. Among the tens of passports that I checked, I found many with entrance permits to Egypt, and a few with Saudi Arabian permits. In an interview that I held with him in Gaza in November 1967, Bashir al-Rais (who held the position of Minister of Education in the Legislative Council in Gaza) claimed that other countries did not recognise the passports.

94. *Al-Ahram*, 28 Sept. 1949.

95. For the publication of regulations and appointments to offices by the Egyptian President, the Minister of War and the various governors, see *Ida'arat al-Haqim al-Ida'ari al-A'am – Qita'a Raza, al-Waqa'ah al-Filastiniyyah – al-Jeridah al-Rasmiyyah Li-Qita'a Raza* [The Administration of the General Administrative Governor – Gaza Strip. The Palestinian Official Gazette for the Gaza Strip. Collections of Orders, Rules and Statements], Majmu'at al-Awarma Wal-Anzima Wal-I'ala'anat, I (Dir al-Nil, 1957), II (Dir al-Nil, 1961), III (Dir Shushah, 1966). See also, Abu al-Namil, p. 13; al-Husayni, ibid., p. 87.

96. *Davar*, 6 and 8 Oct. 1948.
97. Al-Hashimi, B, p. 242. According to the source, the Iraqi Prime Minister arranged for the decision to be published in the press, and presented the Regent with an established fact.
98. *NYT*, 13 Oct. 1948; *al-Ahram*, 16 Oct. 1948.
99. Ibid.; *Davar*, 14 Oct. 1948; Goren, pp. 201–2.
100. Zrubavel Gilad (ed.), *Sefer Ha-Palmah*, II [Book of the Palmah, Vol. II] (Tel Aviv, 1955), pp. 625–46, 871–5; see also, *Davar*, *Al Ha-Mishmar*, 19–22 Oct. 1948.
101. *Davar*, 12 Oct. 1948.
102. The UN Press Officer who reported this added that the majority of the UN observers were removed from the town. *Davar*, 19 Oct. 1948.
103. Interview with Kama'al Muhammad Hasaniyyah in Gaza, December 1980.
104. *HT*, 22 Oct. 1948.
105. *Davar*, 24 Oct. 1948. There is no confirmation of this statement from other sources, and if the General Secretary indeed made such a declaration, then he did so of his own accord. In any case, decisions along this line were not taken by the government, nor by the Arab Higher Institute.
106. *Davar*, 2 Nov. 1948.
107. *HT*, 2 Nov. 1948; *Davar*, ibid.
108. According to a different version, it was attended by 200 people – see Shabib, p. 79; according to another version, 1000 people – see al-'Arif, IV, p. 877; and according to a different version, 2000 people – see Radio Ramallah, 1 Dec. 1948 – summary of Arabic broadcasts, No. 107. See also the telegram from Welles Stabler to the acting Secretary of State: Department of State, *Foreign Relations of the United States: 1948*, V (Washington, 1976), pp. 1645–6 (below, FRUS).
109. After the establishment of the All-Palestine Government, Muhammad al-Ja'abri was, according to him, included in a delegation that went to thank King Farouk for the establishment of the government. See the interview given to *Al Ha-Mishmar*, 19 Dec. 1971.
110. Radio Ramallah, 1 Dec. 1948 – Summary of Arabic broadcasts, No. 107; *Al Ha-Mishmar*, 3 Dec. 1948.
111. Shabib, pp. 79–80; Nevo, pp. 112–15; Radio Ramallah, 2 Dec. 1948 – Summary of Arabic broadcasts, No. 108.
112. Nevo, ibid.; Shihadah, p. 166.
113. Radio Ramallah, 7 Dec. 1948 – Summary of Arabic broadcasts, No. 113; 23 Dec. 1948 – Summary of Arabic broadcasts, No. 127; Nevo, ibid.; Shabib, pp. 80–1.
114. Ibid., p. 80. See also the telegram from Amman to the State Department in Washington: FRUS V (1948), pp. 1642–3.
115. Ibid., p. 1667.
116. *Davar*, 8, 12, 22 Dec. 1948; *Ma'ariv*, 23 Dec. 1948.
117. *MEJ*, III, 1949, p. 196.
118. Ibid., p. 197.
119. Goren, p. 142.
120. Shabib, p. 80.
121. Nevo, p. 116.
122. Shabib, p. 81; Sakhnini, pp. 231–2.
123. The cease-fire agreement between Israel and Egypt was signed on 24 February 1949. It was the first of four agreements with Arab states. For the cease-fire agreements see Shabtai Rosen, *Sefer Ha-Hozim La-Mizrah Ha-Tikhon: Osef Heskemim, Amanot, U-Veritot-Zva'iot* [Collection of Agreements, Charters, and Military Alliances of the Middle East] (Tel Aviv: Ma'arakhot Publishing House, 1956), pp. 11–68. See also, Khalil, II, pp. 585–614.
124. Abu al-Namil, p. 26.
125. Ibid., pp. 26–7.
126. Ibid.
127. p. J. Vatikiotis, *The Modern History of Egypt* (London, 1969), pp. 366–7.

THE GRAND MUFTI

128. Against the background of the breakup of the Muslim Brotherhood organisation and the establishment of the new government in Cairo, it was made clear to the All-Palestine Government that it was not wanted in Egypt. Ahmad al-Shuqairy was sent to Beirut in order to look into the possibility of transferring the government to the Lebanese capital. See *Davar*, 13 Jan. 1949.
129. Shabib, p. 82.
130. Ibid., pp. 82–3; Public Record Office (London). Foreign Office, 371/75076–7194, E13646, 7 Nov. 1949 (below, PRO FO). See also, ibid. E14057, from 14 Nov. 1949.
131. See previous note.
132. *Al-Ahram*, 27 Oct. 1948. For Tawfiq Abu al-Huda's comments at the press conference in Beirut on 21 April 1950, see Sakhnini, p. 230.
133. *Al-Misri*, 27 Oct. 1948.
134. NA Department of State, Foreign Service of the US, Cairo 515, 786.00/3 – 2250, 22 March 1950.
135. Telegram from the US Embassy in Cairo to the State Department in Washington. Cairo Embassy to Sec. State Washington, telegram no. 294, 27 March 1950.
136. *Al-Ahram*, 28 March 1950; Cairo Embassy to Sec. State Washington, telegram no. 301, 28 March 1950.
137. Decision No. 473, see Khalil, II, p. 171.
138. *Al-Joumhouriah* (Egypt), 16 July 1958.
139. Ibid., 22 July 1958.
140. Yehoshua Harkabi (ed.), *Arav Ve-Yisrael*, collection of translations from Arabic, No. 3–4 (Tel Aviv, 1975), p. 12 (below, Harkabi, *Kovetz*).
141. *Al-Ahram*, 1 July 1963.
142. *Al-Joumhouriah* (Egypt), 11 July 1963.
143. Al-Husayni, ibid., pp. 84–7.

CHAPTER 4

1. PRO FO 371/75363–7085, E 2676, 22 Feb. 1949.
2. Ibid.
3. PRO FO 371/75048–7085, E 10532, 27 Aug. 1949.
4. Message to the Foreign Office signed by J.W. Hall, PRO FO 371/75363–7085, 8 March 1949.
5. Since the expulsion of Abdullah's father, Husayn Ibn 'Ali, from his homeland in Hejaz, there were continual mutual territorial demands between the kingdoms of Saudi Arabia and of Transjordan. See Goren pp. 110–11.
6. PRO FO 371/75048–7085, E 8989, 19 July 1949.
7. *Ha-Aretz;* 23 Sept. 1949; *al-Ahram*, 21–29 Sept. 1949; PRO FO 371/75333–7085, E 12237. 3 Oct. 1949; PRO FO 371/75333–7085, E 11948, 26 Sept. 1949.
8. PRO, ibid.; *al-Misri*, 26 Sept. 1949.
9. PRO FO 371/75333–7085, E 12022, 4 Oct. 1949.
10. Ibid., E 12022/1015/31, from 8 Oct. 1949.
11. Ibid., E 12352, from 12 Oct. 1949.
12. Ruhi 'Abd al-Hadi was appointed Foreign Minister; Musa Nasser, transport; Khalusi al-Khayari, agriculture and trade. Raghib al-Nashashibi was later appointed Minister for Refugees. See Shabib, p. 83.
13. Radio Ramallah, 16 Aug. 1949 – Summary of Arabic broadcasts, No. 80. For a different version, see *Ha-Aretz*, 19 Aug. 1949. In April 1950, Raghib al-Nashashibi was appointed Minister of Agriculture in Sa'id al-Mufti's Government. See Shabib, ibid.; *MEJ*, IV, 1950, pp. 339–40.
14. Anne Sinai and Allen Pollack (eds.), *The Hashemite Kingdom of Jordan and the West Bank* (New York, 1977), pp. 27–8; there were approximately 100,000 Palestinian refugees in East Transjordan at the time. See ibid.
15. *Ha-Aretz*, 16 Dec. 1949.

194

16. Ibid., 7–12 and 20 March 1950.
17. *Al-Ahram*, 10 March 1950.
18. During my conversations with Palestinians who had moved from Jordan to Israel within the framework of family unification – in my capacity as Military Governor of the 'triangle' area of Northern Israel at the beginning of the 1950s – some related that on a number of occasions Jordanian officers had tied villagers with ropes and led them forcibly to the polls.
19. Shabib, pp. 83–4; *MEJ*, IV, 1950, p. 339.
20. Ibid., p. 340.
21. Ibid.; Shabib, p. 84.
22. Shabib, p. 85; Radio Beirut, 16 May 1950 – Summary of Arabic broadcasts, No. 250; *Ha-Aretz*, 12 and 15 May 1950; *MEJ*, IV, 1950, p. 334.
23. *Ha-Aretz*, 15 May 1950.
24. See the article in *al-Akhbar* (Egypt), 17 May 1950; see also the statement by the Egyptian Prime Minister during the conference of the Arab League, according to which, in accordance with the League's charter, the Arab states viewed Palestine as an independent state – *al-Ahram*, 28 March 1950.
25. Macdonald, pp. 353–4; Shabib, p. 85; Sakhnini, p. 225.
26. *Jerusalem Post (JP)*, *al-Ahram*, 21 Dec. 1950.
27. *Ha-Aretz*, 3–8 Jan. 1951; Richard P. Mitchell, *The Society of the Muslim Brothers* (London, 1969), pp. 72–9.
28. *Ha-Aretz*, 11 Feb. 1951; see also Jbara, p. 190; Schechtman, pp. 251–61; *al-Ahram*, 13 Feb. 1951.
29. Radio Monte Carlo, 29 April 1951 – Summary of Arabic broadcasts, No. 457; Schechtman, ibid.
30. According to certain sources, Ahmad Hilmi did not attend the Political Committee's session in Damascus in May 1951 due to illness, or because he feared creditors of the Arab National Bank, which had gone into liquidation. See Radio Monte Carlo, 15 May 1951 – Summary of Arabic broadcasts, No. 465; *Ha-Aretz, al-Ahram*, 17 May 1951.
31. Ibid.; *Ha-Aretz*, 17 and 21 May 1951.
32. Radio Monte Carlo, 22 May 1951 – Summary of Arabic broadcasts, No. 470.
33. For a description of the murder, see Schechtman, pp. 243–4; Glubb, pp. 277–81.
34. Ibid.
35. *Ha-Aretz, Al Ha-Mishmar*, 26 July 1951.
36. *Ha-Aretz*, 6 and 16 Aug. 1951; Radio Beirut, 15 Aug. 1951 – Summary of Arabic broadcasts, No. 528.
37. Abdullah al-Tal escaped from Jordan and found political asylum in Cairo. See Glubb, ibid.; *Ha-Aretz*, 6 Sept. 1951.
38. Ibid.; Schechtman, pp. 243–4; Kirkbride, pp. 164–8; *Middle East Record (MER)*, III, 1967, p. 395.
39. *Ha-Aretz*, 31 Aug. 1951.
40. Ibid., 25 Feb. 1952.
41. Radio Monte Carlo, 6 March 1952 – Summary of Arabic broadcasts, No. 697.
42. Radio London (Arabic), 1 Aug. 1952 – Summary of Arabic broadcasts, No. 817.
43. Schechtman, pp. 256–61; *NYT*, 1 and 19 March 1952.
44. Al-Husayni, *Haqa'iq*, pp. 89–90.
45. Jbara, p. 190; *MEJ*, IX, 1955, p. 58.
46. In the Autumn of 1952, the League's Political Committee discussed the issue of the All-Palestine Government and decided 'to retain the Government since it serves as a moral symbol of Palestine'. Radio Beirut, 15 Sept. 1952 – Summary of Arabic broadcasts, No. 856.
47. Radio Damascus, 26 Aug. 1952 – Summary of Arabic broadcasts, No. 838.
48. Radio Cairo, 24 Nov. 1953 – Summary of Arabic broadcasts, No. 1213.
49. Radio Cairo (Hebrew), 22 Nov. 1953 – Summary of Arabic broadcasts, No. 1211.
50. Ibid.; Radio Cairo (Hebrew), 17 Dec. 1953 – Summary of Arabic broadcasts, No.

1233; Radio Cairo (Hebrew), 11 Dec. 1953 – Summary of Arab broadcasts, No. 1228; Radio Damascus (Hebrew), 7 Dec. 1953 – Summary of Arabic broadcasts, No. 1224.

51. Radio Cairo, 25 Nov. 1953 – Summary of Arabic broadcasts, No. 1214; *MEJ*, VIII, 1954, pp. 84, 186.
52. *Al-Mawsu'ah al-Filastiniyyah* [The Palestinian Encyclopedia], IV (Damascus, 1984), p. 142; *Hotem*, 12 June 1986.
53. Ehud Ya'ari, *Mitsrayim Ve-Ha-Fedayeen: 1953–1956* [Egypt and the Fedayeen: 1953–1956] (Giva'at Havivah, 1975), pp. 10–11 (below, Ya'ari, *Mitsrayim*).
54. *Al-Waqa'ah al-Filastiniyyah*, I, pp. 140–1. For the curfew orders, see ibid., pp. 72, 82, 92, 96, 105, 370, 1147–9, 1160–1.
55. Ya'ari, *Mitsrayim*, pp. 12–16.
56. An additional factor behind the raid was the internal situation within Israel and the need to revive confidence in the strength of the IDF. See *MEJ*, IX, 1955, p. 166.
57. Ya'ari, ibid., p. 18.
58. Ibid., pp. 12–19; Moshe Dayan, *Yoman Ma'arekhet Sinai* [Diary of the Sinai Campaign] (Tel Aviv, 1967), p. 11.
59. For the Bandung conference, see Vatikiotis, pp. 390–1. For photographs and text concerning Haj Amin's presence at the conference see al-Husayni, ibid., pp. 185–7. According to Haj Amin, the head of the Syrian delegation, Khalid al-'Azam, also proposed that he join their delegation. See al-Husayni, *Zikhronot*, 108, March 1970, pp. 8–9; *Al-Mawsu'ah al-Filastiniyyah*, IV, p. 142.
60. Al-Husayni, ibid., and 143, Feb. 1973, pp. 9–10; Vatikiotis, ibid.; *Davar*, 20 April 1955.
61. Ibid., 22–25 April 1955; Vatikiotis, ibid.; Schechtman, p. 263.
62. *Davar*, 24 April 1955.
63. On his way from Bandung to Cairo, Haj Amin stayed with the Palestinian delegation in Pakistan and delivered speeches about the Palestinian question to groups of Muslims. See al-Husayni, *Haqa'iq*, p. 187.
64. *Al-Ahram, Davar*, 18 Oct. 1955.
65. For 'Abd al-Nasser's speeches and the part played by the Palestinians in the campaign, see al-Husayni, ibid., pp. 23–6, 150; *Zikhronot*, 97, April 1969, p. 17.
66. Uriel Dann, *Iraq under Qassem: A Political History, 1958–1963* (Jerusalem, 1969), pp. 69–76, 156–63.
67. For the Arab Higher Institute's memorandum to the Arab Governments and for Qassem's declaration, see *Jewish Observer and Middle East Review (JO)*, 15 and 1 Jan. 1960 and 2 Sept. 1960.
68. *Ruz al-Youssef*, 17 Aug. 1959; *Davar*, 18 Aug. 1959.
69. Abdullah al-Tal, the Chief-of-Staff of the Jordanian army, and 'Ali Abu Nuwar, a senior officer, were involved in subversive activities against the regime in Amman and received political asylum in Egypt. See *Davar*, 20 Aug. 1959; *al-Ahram*, 5 April 1960; Ehud Ya'ari, *Fatah* (Tel Aviv, 1970), p. 24 (below, Ya'ari, *Fatah*).
70. Jbara, p. 191; *al-Hayat*, 12 and 13 Aug. 1959; *Davar*, 1 Sept. 1959; *JP*, 16 March 1960.
71. *Davar*, 23 Dec. 1959.
72. Ibid., 28 Jan. and 16 March 1960; *JP*, 27 Jan. 1960. At an earlier stage, Haj Amin tried to seek assistance from the Syrian regime in achieving the same objective. See the message sent from the British embassy in Damascus to London: PRO FO 371/121483, 20 Feb. 1956, and *Akhbar al-Usbu'ah* (Syria), quoted in PRO FO 371/121505, 30 Jan. 1956.
73. *Davar, JP*, 16 March 1960.
74. *Davar*, 4 July 1961; Schechtman, p. 271; *al-Zaman*, 5 July 1961.
75. John Marlowe, *Arab Nationalism and British Imperialism* (London, 1961), pp. 192–3; *Davar*, 1 Sept. 1959.
76. Ibid., 20 Oct. 1961, 27 Oct. 1961.
77. Ibid., 24 April 1962.
78. Al-Husayni, *Zikhronot*, 73, April 1967, p. 15; Schechtman, pp. 272–4; *JP*, 4 May 1962; *Davar*, 7 May 1962.

79. *Sawt al-Ahrar, al-Thawra* (Iraq), 9 May 1962; *Davar*, 10 May 1962.
80. Al-Husayni, ibid.; Schechtman, pp. 274–6; *JP*, 30 May 1962.
81. Schechtman, pp. 278–81; al-Husayni, ibid.; Radio Damascus, 15 April 1963 – Summary of Arabic broadcasts, No. 5078.
82. For the Palestinian organisations established during this period see Ya'ari, ibid., pp. 26–7.
83. *Ma'ariv*, 15 Sept. 1963; Harkabi, *Kovetz*, No. 3–4, p. 21. The background to this summit conference was the Israeli project to transport water from the sources of the Jordan southwards, and the mutual accusations between Syria and Egypt concerning this project. The establishment of the PLO was intended as a substitute for the lack of any response to the Israeli project. For the conference, see Avraham Sela, *Ahdut Mi-Tokh Pirud Ba-Ma'arekhet Ha-Bayn-Aravit* [Unity Amongst Division in the Inter-Arab Arena] (Jerusalem, 1983), pp. 26–36.
84. Ya'ari, ibid., pp. 34–5. For the reasons behind *Fatah*'s fears concerning the establishment of the PLO, see Abu Iyad, *Le-Lo Moledet* [Without a Homeland], translated into Hebrew from the Arabic by Norit Peled (Jerusalem, 1979), p. 75.
85. Radio Amman, 28 March 1960 – Summary of Arabic broadcasts, No. 3333; See *Filastin* (Jordan), 17–30 March 1960.
86. The Institute's delegation which arrived in Amman included Emil al-Ghouri, Munif al-Husayni, Issah Nahlah and Shaikh Tawfiq Tibi. *Davar, al-Manar, Filastin* (Jordan), 31 March 1961; *al-Jihad*, 2 April 1961; see also, *al-Thawra* (Iraq), 4 May 1962.
87. Radio Beirut and Radio Amman, 25 April 1962 – Summary of Arabic broadcasts, No. 3973; *al-Jihad, Filastin* (Jordan), 14–29 April 1962.
88. Ibid.; Radio Beirut, 26 April 1962 – Summary of Arabic broadcasts, No. 3974; *Filastin* (Jordan), 4 May 1962.
89. *Davar*, 30 Aug.–2 Sept. 1960; Sinai–Pollack, p. 355; Ze'ev Bar-Lavi, 'Ha-Mishtar Ha-Hahashami 1949–1967 U-Ma'amado Ba-Gada Ha-Ma'aravit' [The Hashemite Regime 1947–1967 and Its Status in the West Bank] *Sekirot*, September 1981, p. 34.
90. Al-Husayni, ibid., 73, April 1967, p. 15.
91. *Al-Difa* (Jordan), 6 Feb. 1964.
92. Ibid., 30 March 1964; Schechtman, pp. 281–2; *JO*, 24 April 1964.
93. *Akhbar al-Usbu'ah* (Jordan), 3 April 1964; *al-Difa* (Jordan), 26 March and 31 March 1964.
94. *Amman al-Masa*, 6 April 1964.
95. Radio London, 11 April 1964 – Summary of Arabic broadcasts, No. 87; *al-Jihad*, 14 April 1964.
96. Ibid.; *al-Manar*, 1 May 1964; *al-Difa* (Jordan), 1 March 1964; Ibid., 28 April 1964 – Daily Newspaper Collection, No. 100; *al-Hayat*, 19 May 1964 – Daily Newspaper Collection, No. 118. See *Akhbar al-Usbu'ah* (Jordan), 3 April 1964.
97. *Al-Jihad*, 14 April 1964; *al-Manar*, 20 April, 1 and 26 May 1964; *Filastin* (Jordan), 22 May 1964 – Daily Newspaper Collection, No. 120; *Filastin* (Jordan), 28 May 1964 – Daily Newspaper Collection, No. 125; *Akhbar al-Usbu'ah* (Jordan), 8 May 1964 – Daily Newspaper Collection, No. 110.
98. *Al-Musawwar*, 24 April 1964 – Daily Newspaper Collection, No. 108.
99. *Al-Hayat*, 19 May 1964 – Daily Newspaper Collection, No. 118; *al-Hayat*, 14 May 1964 – Daily Newspaper Collection, No. 116.
100. *Ruz al-Yussef*, 13 April 1964 – Daily Newspaper Collection, No. 104; *al-Joumhouriah* (Egypt), 15 April 1964 – Daily Newspaper Collection, No. 108.
101. Harkabi, *Kovetz*, No. 3–4, pp. 23–45; Ya'ari, ibid., pp. 34–5; *al-Jihad*, 14 April and 26 May 1964–3 June 1964.
102. Ibid.
103. Harkabi, *Kovetz*, No. 3–4, pp. 84–117; Sela, p. 40.

CHAPTER 5

1. Saudi Arabia, which supported the existence of the Arab Higher Institute, sought to retain this body even after Haj Amin's death. See *al-Hawadith*, 12 July 1974.
2. His memoirs were published in this monthly magazine under the title, *Safahat Min Muzakarat al-Sayid Muhammad Amin al-Husayni*.
3. It appears that it was Haj Amin's personal status that prevented the break up of the Institute, even after the establishment of the All-Palestine Government and the founding of the PLO.
4. *Al-Hayat*, 19 June 1965.
5. *Ruz al-Youssef*, 21 Sept. 1964 – Appendix to the Daily Newspaper Collection No.228 (from 2 Oct. 1964). On the discussions of the second summit conference and Haj Amin's declaration concerning these discussions, see *al-Kifa'ah*, 11–30 Sept. 1964; *al-Akhbar* (Egypt), 26 Jan. 1965; Sela, p.46.
6. Interview with Haj Amin, see *al-Hayat*, 19 June 1965; *Akhbar al-Usbu'ah* (Jordan), 5 Nov. 1965, Daily Newspaper Collection No. 358.
7. *Akhbar al-Usbu'ah* (Jordan), 28 Jan. 1966 – Daily Press Collection No.46.
8. *Al-Akhbar* (Egypt), 21 June 1966.
9. *Al-Joumhouriah* (Egypt), 11 Oct. 1966.
10. Ya'ari, *Fatah*, pp.118–19; *Los Angeles Times*, 3 June 1965; *Ma'ariv*, 30 Sept. 1965; *Davar*, 6 Feb. 1967.
11. Ya'ari, ibid., pp.12–13.
12. *Al-Manar*, 15 June 1966. The speech can also be found in a Jordanian Government publication under the title, *al-Husayn Yursim Ma'alim al-Tariq, Nas al-Khitab al-Sa'ami Alazi Alqa'ah Jala'lat al-Maliq al-Husayn al-Mu'azim Fi Hariji Ma'ahad al-Mu'alimin Wa al-Mu'alimat Fi Ajlun* ['Al-Husayn Outlines the Way'. The complete version of the royal presentation delivered by His Majesty, King Husayn, at the graduation ceremony of the Ajlun Teachers' College (Tuesday, 14 June 1966)], pp.8–11; see also, Sela, p.65; *MEJ*, XX, 1966, p.506.
13. On measures for a joint struggle between the Jordanian Government and Haj Amin against the PLO and Shuqairy, see *Filastin* (Lebanon), 9 March 1967 – Daily Newspaper Collection No. 1065; *Filastin* (Lebanon), 23 March 1967 – Daily Newspaper Collection No. 1079. See also, *MER III*, 1967, p.395; *al-Manar*, 3 Feb. 1967; Radio Amman, 23 Feb. 1967 – Summary of Arabic broadcasts, No. 88; Radio PLO, 25 Feb. 1967 – Summary of Arabic broadcasts, No. 89.
14. *Al-Manar*, *Filastin* (Jordan), 5 Feb. 1967; *Davar*, 6 Feb. 1967; *Akhbar al-Usbu'ah* (Jordan), 10 Feb. 1967.
15. Ibid. For the *rapprochement* between Haj Amin and Husayn, see Bar-Lavi, p.44.
16. *Akhbar al-Usbu'ah* (Jordan), 24 Feb. 1967.
17. Radio Amman, 1 March 1967 – Summary of Arabic Broadcasts, No.97; *al-Manar*, *Filastin*, *al-Difa* (Jordan), 2–6 March 1967; *Ha-Aretz*, 2–12 March 1967.
18. Ibid.; *Davar*, 2–3 March 1967; *JP*, 2 March 1967.
19. *Al-Dustur* (London), 6 Dec. 1982; Zuhir al-Maradini interviewed Haj Amin in February 1973 in al-Mansuriyyah, a suburb of Beirut, and claims that the interview was published as a result of the meeting between Husayn and Arafat, following the latter's expulsion from Beirut in the Summer of 1982.
20. *Al-Manar*, *al-Difa*, *Filastin* (Jordan), ibid.
21. *Al-Hayat*, 18 April 1967; *Filastin* (Jordan), 17 March 1967; *al-Manar*, 6 March 1967.
22. *Al-Dustur* (London), 6 Dec. 1982.
23. *MER*, 3, 1967, p.394; *Ha-Aretz*, 6 Feb. and 6 March 1967.
24. *Al-Quds*, 31 May 1967; *al-Akhbar* (Iraq), 31 May 1967.
25. Ahmad al-Shuqairy, 'Ziqriyyat 'An Mu'tamar al-Qimma Fi al-Khartum' [Memoirs from the Khartoum Summit Conference], *Shuun Filastiniyyah*, 4, Sept. 1971, pp.90–9; *al-Watha'iq al-Filastiniyyah al-'Arabiyyah*, C, 1967, pp.668–9; *MER*, III, 1967, p.262–4.

26. *Al-Alam* (Rabat), 8 July 1967; *al-Watha'iq al-Filastiniyyah al-'Arabiyyah*, III, 1967, pp. 474–5.
27. *Ha-Aretz*, 17–18 Sept. 1967; *al-Dustur* (Jordan), 16–21 Sept. 1967.
28. Ibid.; *al-Difa* (Jordan), 19 Sept. 1967; *al-Watha'iq al-Filastiniyyah al-'Arabiyyah*, III, 1967, pp. 712–16; Radio Amman, 17 Sept. 1967 – Appendix to Summary (B) of Arabic Broadcasts, No. 475 (from 17 Sept. 1967); *MER*, III, 1967, p. 296.
29. *Yediot Ahronot*, 8 July 1968; *Ma'ariv*, 29 June 1969.
30. *Ma'ariv, Ibid.*, 27 Feb. 1970; *al-Hayat*, 15 April 1969.
31. *Ma'ariv*, 29 June 1969. In May 1973, Muhi al-Din al-Husayni was appointed Minister of Transport in the Government of Zaid al-Rifa'ai. See *al-Ray*, 27 May 1973.
32. *Ma'ariv*, 27 Feb. 1970; *MER*, V, 1969–1970, p. 294.
33. *Al-Hayat*, 15 April 1969; *Ha-Aretz*, 1 March 1970; *MER*, V, 1969–1970, p. 819.
34. For the PLO's violent activities in Jordan, see *MEJ*, XXIV, 1970, p. 505–6; XXV, 1971, pp. 68–72, 236–7, 511–12; *NYT*, 20 Nov. 1969.
35. *MER*, V, 1969–1970, p. 245; *al-Hayat*, 13 June 1969.
36. *Ma'ariv*, 2 July 1969.
37. Ibid., 27 Feb. 1970; *Ha-Aretz*, 1 March 1970.
38. *MER*, V, 1969–1970, pp. 833–70.
39. Al-Husayni, *Zikhronot*, 115, October 1970, p. 9.
40. *Ma'ariv*, 27 Feb. 1970.
41. Ibid.; *Ha-Aretz*, 20 April 1971.
42. Zvi Elpeleg, 'Tokhnit Ha-Federatsiyyah Shel Husayn: Gormim U-Teguvot' [Husayn's Federation Plan: Factors and Responses] *Sekirot*, December 1977, pp. 1–19.
43. Ibid.; *MEJ*, XXVI, 1972, p. 298; *Ha-Aretz, Davar, Ma'ariv, Yediot Ahronot*, 16–21 March 1972.
44. *Al-Sayad*, 20 Sept. 1973; *al-Ray*, 11–13 Sept. 1973; Sela, p. 105.
45. *Al-Ray*, 19–28 Sept. 1973; *al-Sayad*, 27 Sept. 1973.
46. *Al-Ray*, 25 Sept. 1973.
47. *Ha-Aretz*, 3–5 Dec. 1973. For the conference, see United States Department of State, *The Quest for Peace: Principal United States Public Statements and Related Documents on the Arab–Israeli Peace Process 1967–1983* (Washington, 1984), pp. 44–9.
48. *Al-Sayad*, 27 Dec. 1973.
49. *Al-Nahar, al-Anwar*, 23–25 Sept. 1969.
50. *Al-Nahar, al-Anwar*, 22 –25 Feb. 1974; *Yediot Ahronot*, 1 March 1974; *JP*, 20 Feb. 1974; Nehemia Levtzion, 'International Islamic Solidarity and its Limitations', *Jerusalem Papers on Peace Problems*, No. 29, 1979; Afak Haydar, 'The Islamic Summit Conference of 1974; An Assessment', *Asian Profile* (Hong Kong), III, No. 4, August 1975, pp. 391–404; Reyazul Hasa, 'The Islamic Summit Conference', *Iqbal Review* (Iqbal Academy, Pakistan), XV, No. 1, April 1974, pp. 43–4.
51 *Davar, Ha-Aretz, Ma'ariv, Yediot Ahronot, JP*, 5 July 1974; *NYT*, 6 July 1974.
52. *Al-Hayat*, 5 July 1974.
53. Ibid., 6–7 July 1974.
54. *Al-Nahar, al-Sharq, al-Hayat, al-Ray, Davar, Ha-Aretz*, 8 July 1974.
55. *JP*, 8 July 1974; for an anomalous and exaggerated version, according to which tens of thousands attended the funeral, see Jbara, p. 192.
56. *Al-Hayat*, 8 July 1974.
57. *al-Hadaf*, 13 July 1974.
58. *Al-Hawadith*, 12 July 1974.
59. *Al-Dustur* (Jordan), *al-Sharq, Ha-Aretz, Davar*, 8 July 1974.
60. *Ha-Aretz*, 1 Sept. 1974.
61. *Akhir Sa'a*, 17 July 1974.
62. *The Times*, 6 July 1974.
63. *Al-Ray*, 27 Aug. 1974. For the comments of 'Aja'aj Nuwyhed and Akram Zu'aytir, see *Shuun Filastiniyyah*, 36, Aug. 1974; *al-Hawadith*, 16 Aug. 1974.

SUMMARY

1. Marlowe, *Pilate*, p. 5.
2. Joseph Nevo, 'The Arabs of Palestine 1947–1948: Military and Political Activity', *MES, XXIII*, No.1, Jan. 1987, p. 4; Nevo, pp. 33–6.
3. See, for example, Arafat in an interview with *Playboy*, see ibid., p. 64.
4. Abu Iyad, p. 63.
5. Ibid., pp. 64–6.
6. Schechtman, p. 296.
7. Ibid., pp. 294–5.
8. John Marlowe, *Rebellion in Palestine* (London, 1946), p. 73.

APPENDICES

Appendix A

THE ARAB HIGHER COMMITTEE'S DECISION REJECTING
THE 1939 WHITE PAPER*

The Higher Committee convened to discuss the wording of the White Paper published by the British Government, and the new declaration of policy towards Palestine which it contains. The Committee is aware that this declaration is based on proposals previously put forward by the British Government at the London conference, which were unanimously rejected by the Arab–Palestinian delegation and by representatives of the Arab states as failing to meet Arab demands. Moreover, the Committee is aware that in this declaration the British Government has reconsidered a number of important points that it previously proposed and which were rejected [by the Arabs].

Accordingly, the Committee has hastened to announce that in regard to this political plan it shares the [negative] position adopted by the Arab representatives at the London conference. A declaration detailing the Committee's comments and the reason for this rejection will be published shortly.

Date: 18.5.39.

Signed (from left to right): Muhammad Amin [al-Husayni], Fu'ad Saba, Jamal al-Husayni, Dr Husayn al-Khalidi, Muhammad 'Izzat [Darwaza] and Alfred Rok.

* *Source*: al-Husayni, *Zikhronot*, 127, Oct. 1971, p. 8. Translated from the Hebrew.

Appendix B

LETTER FROM THE MUFTI OF JERUSALEM TO HITLER, DATED 20 JANUARY 1941*

Your Excellence,

England, that bitter and cunning enemy to the true freedom of the Arab nation, has never ceased to forge fetters in which to enslave and subjugate the Arab people, either in the name of a deceitful League of Nations or by the expression of perfidious and hypocritical humanitarian feelings, but with the actual aim of effecting her imperialist machinations, which are camouflaged by principles of democracy and of deceitful internationalism.

By geographical coincidence, the Arab people find themselves at the centre of a land and sea crossroads which, according to the English, is the major intersection of the English Empire's 'transport lines'. As a result, England has spared no effort in piling obstacle upon obstacle on the path of the Arab nations towards liberation and advancement. It can even be said that the relative peace which has existed between France and England over the last 100 years is largely founded on the pact of silence between the two powers to continue to enslave the Arab populations in accordance with a heinous partition agreement which created a kind of equilibrium between their respective aspirations, without damage to the sensitive artery of the 'holy' British transport lines! This division of influence between France and England was created in order to break the rebelliousness and response of the Arabs in the face of various strong powers. However, English policy could not for long ignore the resurrection of Arab nationalism, and hence their relentless efforts to place new obstacles in the way of the Arabs towards the achievement of their independence and freedom. This is the picture of the terrifying history of the last decades, years that have presented to the eyes of the world the spectacle of a bitter and prolonged struggle.

In the spirit of the motto 'divide and rule', the English resolved to bring millions of Indians from British India to Iraq and to settle them among the local Arab population. This plan failed after a bloody revolt, and England was compelled to yield. Since then, she has been obliged to concern herself primarily with exploiting the Iraqi oil. King Faisal the First agreed to a *modus vivendi*, and

---

* *Source*: Translated from the Hebrew edition of Hirshowitz, *The Third Reich and the Arab East*.

signed a treaty with England, and, despite the opposition of the majority of the Iraqi people, sold the relative independence of Iraq in return for oil concessions. It was Turkey's ambition to annex Musul to its territory which compelled the late king to adopt this policy.

As regards Syria, she was liberated by France so that the latter could destroy her national unity and weaken her economically, the object being to suppress with greater ease the national spirit which stirs her. After eighteen years of struggle, Syria succeeded in winning from France the lame treaty of 1936 which gave recognition to her independence in return for unilateral concessions. Simultaneously, England barred Syria's path to freedom by signing a treaty with Turkey which neutralised the influence of the Franco-Syrian treaty. This was done with the agreement of the Jews, who feared the presence of an independent Syria as neighbour to a Palestine in revolt. At the same time, the Anglo-French-Turkish agreement against the Axis was born. The early 1936 campaign regarding Alexandria and Antioch should have led to the departure of France from the above-mentioned region, which was to be transferred to Turkey, and also the nullification of the 1936 treaty between France and Syria. England once again played a 'very democratic' role at the expense of Syria, acting contrary to the recommendations of the committees of inquiry appointed by the League of Nations, which supported the Syrians.

And now for Egypt: the English have been in Egypt 'temporarily' since 1882, as the result of a revolt by the people who demanded that the *Khedive* create a national constitution to halt the prodigality of the prince and determine a budget to meet the country's interests and needs. Notwithstanding this, the supposedly democratic England occupied Egypt in order to save the *Khedive's* throne, on the pretext of imposing order in Alexandria. In actual fact, however, perfidious Albion was at that very time devising plots, arousing intrigue, and using its agents and provocateurs to stir up disturbances and disorder. The truth is that the English were primarily interested in the Suez Canal ... and the transport routes of the empire. Egypt was compelled to wait until 1936 to gain a lame treaty, in return for certain concessions. However, it was not England's generosity which was responsible for this, but the undermining of the balance of forces in the Mediterranean region – Italy had become stronger and too dangerous to British 'interests'.

And after the other Arab states – Palestine. His Excellence is well aware of the problem faced by this country, which has also suffered from the deceitful actions of the English. They attempted to place an additional obstacle before the unity and independence of the Arab states by abandoning it to world Jewry, this dangerous enemy whose secret weapons – finance, corruption and intrigue – were aligned with British daggers. For twenty years we have confronted these various forces face to face. Full of unvanquished faith, the Arabs of Palestine fought with the most elementary means. The Palestinian problem united all of the Arab states in a mutual hatred of the English and Jews. If mutual hatred is a prerequisite for national unity, it can be said that the problem of Palestine hastened this unity. From an international point of view, the Jews owe allegiance to England in the hope that, after her victory, she will be able to realise their dreams in Palestine and in the neighbouring Arab countries. The aid to be extended to the Arabs in their war against the Zionist aspirations will, therefore, cause the Jews to lose heart. The Jews of America especially, seeing their dream shattered to pieces, will be so discouraged that they will cease to support Britain with such enthusiasm and will reconsider their position before the catastrophe.

Your Excellence, please do not be angered by my brief presentation here of the history of the conflicts between the Arabs and England. It seemed to me necessary to make manifest the cardinal causes which arouse the Arab world against the English. In particular, I felt it imperative to assert that these causes have deep roots in primordial interests and vital problems, and not in futile questions with superficial and transitory effects. The warm sympathy felt by the Arab peoples towards Germany and the Axis is an established fact. No propaganda can refute this truth. Freed from certain material impediments, the Arab peoples will be ready to serve the common enemy his just deserts, and to take their place enthusiastically alongside the Axis in order to fulfil their part in bringing about the well-deserved defeat of the Anglo-Jewish coalition.

Your Excellence! Arab nationalism is greatly indebted to you for raising the Palestinian question in your impressive speeches on a number of occasions. I wish to reiterate my gratefulness to His Excellence and to assure him that the Arab people feel friendship, sympathy and a great admiration for His Excellence, the great Fuehrer, and the courageous German people.

I am thus taking the opportunity to dispatch my private secretary to the German Government in order to establish relations in the name of the strongest and largest organisation in the Arab world, such as are necessary for sincere and faithful cooperation in all areas.

Allow me to add that the Arabs are willing to put all their weight behind the campaign, and to shed their blood in the holy war for their national rights and aspirations, on condition that certain interests of a moral and material order are assured. The cunning and power of the enemy require that certain essential cautionary measures be taken, and the war measures must be well considered in order to achieve a victory. This is a necessary caution, especially since England is compelled to struggle with all her might, because of the strategic strength of the Arab states, which is likely to endanger the transport lines of the empire and sever the contact between India and the Mediterranean region and Turkey through the Persian Gulf, and thus end the exploitation of the flow of oil for the benefit of England.

I close with wishes for long life and happiness for His Excellence, and for a shining victory and prosperity for the great German people and for the Axis in the near future.

Your Excellence, please accept these expressions of great friendship, recognition and esteem.

Appendix C

THE GARRISON COMMANDER DID NOT CONTROL HIS
SOLDIERS (THE CONQUEST OF JAFFA IN 1948)*

The soldiers refused to obey orders given by their commanders regarding posting to the fighting fronts. In addition, a force of twenty-seven volunteers from the town of Hamat [Syria] refused orders from their headquarters, and insisted on operating in the town [Jaffa] on only one front, although the fighters needed to be divided between a number of fronts. The force operated for two days, but, having been provided with clothing, machine-guns, ammunition, transport and food by the National Committee, left the town with all this equipment. The force now refuses to follow the orders of the Garrison Force.

(In the second part of his book, *The Destruction of Palestine* [p.

* *Source:* al-Husayni, *Zikhronot*, 169, April 1975, p.13. Translated from the Hebrew.

116], Brigadier Muhammad Fa'iz al-Qasri, an officer of the Liberation Army, recalled that Mulazim Awal [Lieutenant] 'Abd al-Jaba'ar al-Qaysi incited Mulazim [Second-Lieutenant] Hamud al-Khatib's soldiers against their commander in Jaffa, calling on them to revolt and abandon their positions.)

In conclusion, the force which went to defend Jaffa not only did not help to achieve the objective for which it came, but indeed constituted an instrument for the destruction of the previous defence system [*al-Jihad al-Muqaddas* under the authority of the Arab Higher Institute] *and caused many of the residents to flee the town*. This was because they did not trust [the Liberation Army] to defend Jaffa and prevent its fall into enemy hands.

Appendix D

STATEMENT BY THE SECRETARY GENERAL OF THE ARAB LEAGUE, CONCERNING THE SETTING UP OF THE ALL-PALESTINE GOVERNMENT, 10 JULY 1948*

The Political Committee of the League of Arab States has discussed the project of setting up a provisional civil administration in Palestine. Following consultations with the Palestinian organisations concerned, and having reached agreement therewith, it has approved the following:

First: A provisional civil administration shall be set up in Palestine, [whose functions shall be] to manage the public civil affairs and [to provide] the necessary services, on condition that it shall not have competence at present over the higher political affairs.

Second: The administrative machinery shall be entrusted to a Council composed of a president and nine members, each of whom shall supervise and run one of the following civil departments:

1. The Presidency of the Council and the General Administrative Affairs. This Department shall perform the duties previously performed by the Secretary-General of the Palestine Government, and supervise the officers of areas, towns and districts.

*Source: Muhammad Khalil, *The Arab States and the Arab League: A Documentary Record. Vol. II International Affairs*, pp. 566–8. See Zvi Elpeleg, 'Palestin Atsmayit Bi-Svakh Ha-Yerivut Ha-Bayn-Aravit: 1946–1948' [An Indpendent Palestine in the Web of Inter-Arab Rivalry: 1946–1948], *Sekirot*, Feb. 1982, pp. 48–51.

2. The Judiciary. This Department shall supervise the office of the Attorney-General, and the civil courts in towns and districts.
3. Health Services [Department]. This shall supervise hospitals, first-aid [centres], public health services, quarantines, etc.
4. Social Affairs [Department]. This shall supervise the affairs for the refugees, distressed persons, workers, education, etc.
5. Communications [Department]. This shall comprise public roads, communications, and the Telegraph, Post and Telephone Offices.
6. The Treasury. This [Department] shall comprise everything related to financial affairs, and the offices of income tax, municipal and rural taxes, customs, and the Public Audit Office.
7. National Economy [Department]. This shall comprise everything related to matters of supply, import and export, and the two offices of trade and industry.
8. Agricultural Affairs [Department]. This shall comprise everything related to agricultural affairs, and the offices of forestry, veterinary (services), and fishing, etc.
9. Internal Public Security [Department]. This Department shall supervise everything related to the regular police, the maintenance of security, municipal and auxiliary police, prisons and the national militia.
10. Publicity Affairs [Department]. This Department shall supervise the general [questions of] propaganda, publication, national guidance, newspapers, printed matter, and wireless broadcasting.

Third: The jurisdiction of the Civil Administration Council shall extend to all the areas at present occupied by the Arab armies or which may be occupied, until the whole of Arab Palestine is included.

Fourth: The 'Council of Directors' shall appoint all the officials it needs from among the Arab officials whose services have expired upon the termination of the British mandate over Palestine.

Fifth: All the above departments, together with social and other services, shall be conducted in accordance with the rules and laws in force at the time of the termination of the British mandate, with the exception of those in conflict with Arab public interest.

Sixth: The [said] Council shall, after the nomination and appointment of its members, meet on the summons of its President; during its meetings it shall determine the seat of the Civil Administration, the internal regulations of the Council and the procedure [to be followed] in conducting its affairs.

Seventh: All the services of the above civil departments shall be conducted in the interest of the whole population and in that of the occupying Arab armies.

Eighth: The Council of the [Arab] League and the Governments of the Arab countries concerned shall define the competence of the Council [of Directors] and its members, together with the competence of the military governors, who may be appointed by the occupying Arab armies in the various areas.

Ninth: The Civil Administration Council shall be guided by the decisions or directions that may be issued by the Council of the Arab League or by the Political Committee.

Tenth: Should a member of this Council resign, die or discontinue [his] work for any reason, the above Council shall nominate another member to fill the vacancy, with the approval of the Council of the [Arab] League or its Political Committee.

Eleventh: The Council of the [Arab] League shall issue a resolution [providing for] the setting up of this administrative machinery and the appointment of its members, and shall request all the inhabitants of Palestine to support it and facilitate its task.

Twelfth: This Council shall, at the first meeting held by it in Palestine, prepare its general budget, and [in doing this] shall aim at strict economy, as well as at the running of the necessary services with the least possible number of officials. The activities of [this Council] and its various departments shall be expanded following the development of its financial resources.

Thirteenth: As this administrative machinery cannot function unless assured of the necessary funds, particularly [those needed] for running the social, health and other services, and until such time as the finance departments have been firmly established and have begun to collect the various taxes, the Council of the [Arab] League or its Political Committee shall decide to grant this administrative machinery a loan, an advance or a gift, on condition that the amount [needed] shall be fixed when the Council begins its work and when the budget estimates for the first half of its financial year are submitted.

The Administration Council shall be composed as follows:

1. Presidency of the Council and of the General Administrative Affairs: Ahmad Hilmi Pasha.
2. Internal Public Security: Jamal al-Husayni.
3. Social Affairs: 'Awni 'Abd al-Hadi.
4. Health Services: Dr Husayn Fakhri al-Khalidi.
5. Communications: Sulayman Tuqan.
6. The Judiciary: 'Ali Hasna.
7. National Economy: Raja'i al-Husayni.
8. Publicity Affairs: Yusuf Sahyun.
9. Agricultural Affairs: Amin 'Aql.

In announcing this decision, the Political Committee hopes that it will herald the beginning of an era during which Palestinians will be able to conduct their own affairs, as well as lead to their exercising the attributes of their independence.

Appendix E

PROCLAMATION OF THE INDEPENDENCE OF PALESTINE BY THE ARAB HIGHER COMMITTEE AND THE REPRESENTATIVES OF PALESTINE MEETING IN CONGRESS, 1 OCTOBER 1948*

Acting on the basis of the natural and historic right of the Arab people of Palestine to freedom and independence – a right for which they have shed the noblest blood and for which they have fought against the imperialistic forces, which, together with Zionism, have combined to meet [these people] and prevent them from enjoying that [right],

We, members of the Palestine National Council, meeting in the city of Gaza, proclaim on this day, the 28th of Dhi al-Qi'da, 1367 (A.H.), corresponding to October 1st, 1948, the full independence of the whole of Palestine as bounded by Syria and Lebanon from the north, by Syria and Transjordan from the east, by the Mediterranean from the west, and by Egypt from the south, as well as the establishment of a free and democratic sovereign State. In this [State], citizens will enjoy their liberties and their rights, and [this State] will march forward, in a fraternal spirit, side by side with its

*Source: Muhammad Khalil, *The Arab States*, II, pp. 579. See Zvi Elpeleg, ibid., p. 52.

sister Arab States, in order to build up Arab glory and to serve human civilization. [In doing this, they] will be inspired by the spirit of the nation and its glorious history, and will resolve to maintain and defend its independence. May God bear witness to what we say.

Appendix F

THE PROVISIONAL BASIC LAW OF THE ALL-PALESTINE GOVERNMENT

(Approved by the National Council during its third and fourth sessions in Gaza, 2–3 October 1948)*

Section 1 This Law shall be entitled: The Provisional Basic Law of the All-Palestine Government.

Section 2 In accordance with this Law, the All-Palestine Government shall consist of:

1. A National Council
2. A Council of Ministers
3. A Supreme Council.

Section 3 (a) This Law shall remain in force until the establishment of a Founding Assembly, which shall establish the constitution and the nature of the regime.

(b) The National Council shall set a date for the holding of elections to the Founding Assembly.

Section 4 (a) The National Council shall consist of representatives from those representative institutions in Palestine invited to attend the first conference.

(b) In the event of the death of a member, or his resignation, or the disqualification of his membership by a decision of the Council, the Council Secretariat shall be authorised to propose the candidacy of a different member, whose election shall be ratified by the Council.

(c) The presence of fifty Council members shall be required to constitute a quorum.

Section 5 The Supreme Council shall consist of:

*Free translation from the Hebrew.

1. The President of the National Council – President.
2. The Head of the Council of Ministers – Member.
3. The President of the Supreme Court – Member.

Section 6 The National Council shall be convened every six months by order of its President; the President of the Council shall be authorised to order ordinary and extraordinary meetings of the Council at his discretion; nevertheless, if a written request to summon an extraordinary meeting be referred to him by fifty members of the Council, the President shall order a meeting of the Council at a place determined by him, within 7 days of the submission of the request.

Section 7 The Council Secretariat shall consist of The President, his two deputies, and two secretaries, elected by the [National] Council; the Secretariat shall be active for the duration of the existence of the Council.

Section 8 In accordance with this Basic Law, the All-Palestine Government shall be considered the legal body authorised to operate the branches – the legislature, the judiciary, and the executive – within the boundaries of the whole territory of Palestine [as they existed] before the termination of the British Mandate on 15 May 1948;

The judiciary shall be completely autonomous and shall be independent of the legislature and of the executive; its independence shall be guaranteed by a special law to be passed at a later time.

Section 9 The Council of Ministers, the executive branch of the Government, shall draw its authority from the National Council, in accordance with this Basic Law; the Council of Ministers shall be responsible to [the National Council], and shall operate for as long as it enjoys the confidence [of the National Council].

Section 10 The resignation of the Council of Ministers shall be submitted to the President of the Supreme Council; after the Supreme Council has accepted the resignation, its President shall impose the task of forming a new Council of Ministers on a suitable candidate.

Section 11 All international agreements, political treaties, financial loans and economic licences decided upon by the Council of Ministers shall be valid upon ratification by the National Council; notwithstanding this, the National Council shall have the authority to take an extraordinary decision granting a power of attorney to the Council of Ministers to undertake a loan without the need for a [subsequent] discussion in the [National] Council.

Section 12 (a) The Council of Ministers shall prepare and submit the Government's budget proposal for the current year for ratification by the National Council.

(b) The Council of Ministers shall not be authorised to allocate any monies without the approval of the National Council, [and shall be authorised to do so only] in accordance with the budget framework decided upon.

(c) The National Council shall be entitled to take decisions on extraordinary issues, in regard to which it shall grant power of attorney to the Council of Ministers to allocate monies necessary for the continued execution of the Government's activities, within the framework of an extraordinary budget for a period of not more than six months; the budget shall be presented to the next meeting of the National Council for ratification.

(d) In the event that the budget is approved after the new fiscal year, the Council of Ministers shall be authorised to continue the allocation of monies on the basis of the previous fiscal year.

Section 13 The National Council shall possess sole legislative authority, and shall have the authority to ratify or reject legislative proposals submitted to it by the Council of Ministers; notwithstanding this, the Council of Ministers shall be entitled to issue all orders, laws, regulations and directives connected with the war effort by means of emergency legislation without waiting for a meeting of the [National] Council, provided that such a meeting is not scheduled for that time; the Council shall discuss these matters at its earliest subsequent meeting.

Section 14 The Council of Ministers shall submit those laws and regulations prepared by it for discussion and ratification by the National Council; notwithstanding this, every member of the National Council shall be entitled to submit to the Council of Ministers, by means of the Council Secretariat (in which he is a member), any legislative proposal or regulation which he requests to be ratified; if the Council of Ministers shall refuse to submit the [member's] proposal to the National Council, and if thirty members of the National Council demand to review the proposal, then [the proposal] shall be submitted through its President.

Section 15 Jerusalem is the capital of the [All-Palestine] government; [however] Under the force of prevailing circumstances, and with the agreement of the President of the National Council, the

Council of Ministers shall be authorised to choose a temporary alternative seat for the government.

Section 16 A National Defence Council shall be established, and shall consist of the President of the National Council, the head of the Council of Ministers, and the Minister of Defence; [this] Council shall be entirely free to adopt any measures necessary to defend the borders of Palestine and to secure its unity, and to impose peace and security within it.

Section 17 The Supreme Council shall be authorised to do the following:

(a) Accept the resignation of the Council of Ministers.

(b) Grant pardons and approve or commute death penalties; however, during a hearing regarding a death penalty imposed by the President of the Supreme Court (who is a member of the Supreme Council), his place (on the Council) shall be taken by the Minister of Justice.

(c) Supervision of the implementation of laws ratified by the National Council and on behalf of the Council of Ministers, in accordance with section 14 of [this] Basic Law.

(d) Acceptance of [diplomatic] credentials and state representatives.

Section 18 The Basic Law shall be valid upon its ratification by the National Council; which shall have the authority to amend the Basic Law or replace it as the general national interest requires, by a majority of two thirds of those present at a legal meeting.

Appendix G

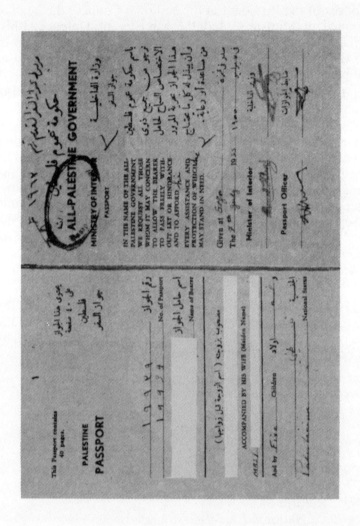

Photograph of 'All-Palestine Government' Passport Issued in Gaza in 1955.

Chronology

1895–97: Haj Amin's birth.

1918: Two Palestinian clubs established – *al-Nadi al-'Arabi* and *al-Muntada al-Adabi*.

4–5 April 1920: Disturbances during the Nabi Musa procession.

31 May 1920: Palestine Arab Society established in Damascus.

13 December 1920: Arab-Palestine Executive Committee established.

21 March 1921: Death of the Mufti Kamil al-Husayni in Jerusalem.

8 May 1921: High Commissioner's announcement to Haj Amin regarding his appointment as Mufti.

9 January 1922: Haj Amin elected President of Supreme Muslim Council.

24 September 1928: Western Wall incident.

November 1928: Muslim Conference in Jerusalem; the Society for the Protection of al-Aqsa and the Islamic Holy Places established.

19 November 1928: Publication of White Paper concerning the status of the communities at the Western Wall.

August 1929: Riots in Jerusalem, Hebron and Safed.

October 1930: Passfield's White Paper.

7–17 December 1931: General Islamic Congress held in Jerusalem.

January 1932: Youth Congress founded.

4 August 1932: *Al-Istiqlal* party founded.

March 1933: Non-Cooperation Congress held in Jaffa.

March 1934: Death of Musa Kazim al-Husayni.

December 1934: National Defence Party founded.

March 1935: Palestine Arab Party founded.

June 1935: Reform Party founded.

October 1935: National Bloc Party founded.

20 November 1935: 'Izz al-Din al-Qassam killed.

25 November 1935: Political parties in Palestine send memorandum containing an ultimatum to High Commissioner.

19 April 1936: National conference in Nablus; beginning of strike and revolt; Arab Higher Committee established under leadership of Haj Amin al-Husayni.

215

10 October 1936: General strike ends after intervention by Arab heads of state.

July 1937: Peel Commission report published.

August 1937: Renewal of revolt.

13 October 1937: Haj Amin escapes from Jerusalem.

17 May 1939: MacDonald's White Paper published.

13 October 1939: Haj Amin escapes from Lebanon to Iraq.

28 February 1941: 'Secret Committee' established by Haj Amin in Baghdad.

29 May 1941: Rashid 'Ali's revolt in Iraq crushed; Haj Amin escapes to Iran.

11 October 1941: Haj Amin escapes to Rome via Turkey.

6 November 1941: Haj Amin arrives in Germany.

28 November 1941: Hitler–Haj Amin meeting.

22 March 1945: Arab League established.

19 May 1945: Haj Amin escapes from Germany to France, via Switzerland.

April 1946: Anglo-American Commission's report published.

28–29 May 1946: Haj Amin escapes from France to Cairo.

End of May 1946: Conference of Arab heads of state at Inshas, following report of the Anglo-American Commission.

8–12 June 1946: Arab League Council session in Baludan (Syria).

September 1946: London conference; rejection of Morrison–Grady plan.

September 1947: UNSCOP report; Arab League's Political Committee meets in Sofar (Lebanon).

7–15 October 1947: Arab League Council meets in 'Aley (Lebanon).

29 November 1947: UN General Assembly's partition resolution.

7–16 February 1948: Palestinian demands put forward to Arab League Council meeting in Cairo.

26 April 1948: Transjordanian Parliament's decision to invade Palestine.

30 April 1948: Arab League decides on invasion of Palestine by Arab armies after British evacuation.

4 July 1948: Bernadotte report published.

10 July 1948: Arab League announces establishment of provisional Palestinian administration.

20 September 1948: Arab League decides to establish Palestine Government.

22 September 1948: Arab Higher Committee announces establishment of the All-Palestine Government.

27–28 September 1948: Haj Amin leaves in secret for Gaza from Cairo.

30 September 1948: Palestine National Council conference in Gaza.

1 October 1948: First Palestine Congress in Amman.

Mid-October 1948: Palestine Government recognised by Arab states; escape of ministers to Egypt.

1 December 1948: Jericho Congress.

11 April 1950: Elections on both banks of the Jordan to the Jordanian Parliament.

24 April 1950: Jordanian Parliament decides to annex West Bank to the Kingdom of Jordan.

10 February 1951: Haj Amin heads the World Islamic Congress in Karachi.

20 July 1951: Abdullah assassinated in Jerusalem.

April 1955: Bandung conference, with the participation of Haj Amin.

August 1959: Haj Amin leaves Cairo for Beirut.

29 June 1963: Death of Ahmad Hilmi 'Abd al-Baqi.

September 1963: The Arab League appoints Ahmad Shuqairy to represent the Palestinian cause.

January 1964: Arab states summit decides to establish the PLO.

28 May 1964: Palestine National Council conference held in Jerusalem.

September 1964: Second Arab summit decides to establish the Palestine Liberation Army.

1 March 1967: Haj Amin arrives from Beirut to Jerusalem and Amman as Husayn's guest.

5–10 June 1967: Six Day War.

16 September 1967: World Islamic Conference in Amman, headed by Haj Amin.

24 December 1967: Shuqairy resigns as head of the PLO.

15 March 1972: Husayn's 'Federation Plan' – Haj Amin does not respond.

December 1973: Following Yom Kippur War, Haj Amin attempts a reconciliation with the PLO.

4 July 1974: Haj Amin's death.

7 July 1974: Haj Amin's funeral.

Bibliography

ARCHIVES

Department of State, Washington
Foreign Office (FO), London
Hagana Archives, Tel Aviv
Israel State Archives, Jerusalem: Herbert Samuel Papers, Mufti
   Archives
National Archives (NA), Washington
Public Record Office (PRO), London

NEWS AGENCIES AND RADIO STATIONS

Radio Amman, Radio Beirut, Radio Cairo, Radio Cairo (Hebrew),
Radio Damascus, Radio Damascus (Hebrew), Radio London, Radio
London (Arabic), Radio Monte Carlo, Radio PLO, Radio Ramallah,
UP.

INTERVIEWS

Bashir al-Rais, Gaza, November 1976.
Faisal al-Husayni, the son of 'Abd al-Qadir, East Jerusalem, Novem-
   ber–December 1984.
Hamdi al-Husayni (one of the representatives at the Palestine National
   Conference in October 1946), Gaza, December 1980.
Issam al-Shawa, Gaza, December 1980.
Kama'al Mahmud Hasaniyyah, at his hotel, 'Umar al-Muhktar Street,
   Gaza, December 1980.
Musa al-Surani, Gaza, November 1967.

NEWSPAPERS

DAILIES

Arabic

Al-Ahram (Egypt)

218

Al-Akhbar (Egypt)
Al-Akhbar (Iraq)
Al-Alam (Rabat)
Al-Difa (Jaffa), continued as a Jordanian daily published in Jerusalem, between 1948–67
Al-Dustur (Jordan)
Al-Hayat (Lebanon)
Al-Jami'ah al-'Arabiyyah (Jerusalem – twice weekly)
Al-Jami'ah al-Islamiyyah (Jaffa)
Al-Jihad (Jordan)
Al-Joumhouriah (Egypt)
Al-Kifa'ah (Jordan)
Al-Liwa (Jerusalem)
Al-Manar (Jordan)
Al-Misri (Egypt)
Al-Nahar (Lebanon)
Al-Quds (Jordan)
Al-Ray (Jordan)
Al-Sharq (Lebanon)
Al-Thawra (Iraq)
Al-Zaman (Iraq)
Filastin (Jaffa), continued as Jordanian daily published in Jerusalem, between 1948–67
Mir'at al-Sharq (Jerusalem – twice weekly)
Sawt al-Ahrar (Iraq)

English

Egyptian Gazette (Egypt)
Herald Tribune (US)
Jerusalem Post (Jerusalem)
Los Angeles Times (Los Angeles)
New York Times (New York)
The Times (London)

Hebrew

Al Ha-Mishmar
Davar
Ha-Aretz
Ma'ariv
Yediot Ahronot

WEEKLIES

Akhbar al-Usbu'ah (Jordan)
Akhbar al-Usbu'ah (Syria)
Akhir Sa'a (Egypt). An important series of articles concerning Haj Amin
  were published from 26 July 1972 by Kama'al Jala'al al-Din
Al-Dustur (London)
Al-Hadaf (Lebanon, Syria)
Al-Hawadith (London)
Al-Musawwar (Egypt)
Amman al-Masa (Jordan)
Hotem (weekend Supplement to the daily *Al Ha-Mishmar*)
Jewish Observer and Middle East Review (London)
Ruz al-Youssef (Egypt)

PERIODICALS

Arabic

Al-Tali'a (Egypt)
Al-Watha'iq al-Filastiniyyah al-'Arabiyyah (Lebanon)
Filastin (Lebanon – bi-weekly)
Shuun Filastiniyyah (Lebanon–Cyprus)

English

Arab Studies Quarterly (US)
Asian Profile (Hong Kong)
Iqbal Review (Pakistan)
Jerusalem Papers on Peace Problems (Jerusalem)
Middle East Journal (Washington)
Middle East Record (Shiloah Institute, Tel Aviv University)
Middle Eastern Studies (London)
Studies in Zionism (Tel Aviv University)

Hebrew

Ha-Mizrah Ha-Hadash
Iyunim Be-Heker Ha-Mizrah Ha-Tikhon
Keshet
Pa'amim
Sefer Ha-Shanah (Bar Ilan University)
Sekirot

BOOKS, DOCUMENTS, AND ARTICLES

Arabic

'Abd al-Hadi, Mahadi. *Al-Masalah al-Filastiniyyah Wa Masariyyah al-Hulul al-Siyassiyyah, 1934–1974* [The Palestinian Question and Plans for a Political Solution 1934–1974] (Beirut, 1975).

Abu al-Namil, Husayn. *Qita'a Raza 1948–1967: Tatawurat Iqtisadiyyah Wa Siyasiyyah Wa Ijtimaiyyah Wa 'Asqariyyah* [The Gaza Strip 1948–1967: Economic, Political, Social and Military Developments] (Beirut, 1979).

'Alubah, Muhammad 'Ali. *Filastin Wa al-Damir al-Insani* [Palestine and the Human Conscience] (Egypt, 1964).

'Amar, Shakar. *Al-'Arab Wa Isra'il* [The Arabs and Israel] (Beirut, 1954).

'Aqa'ad, Sala'ah. *Qadiyyat Filastin: al-Marhala al-Harija, 1945–1946* [The Palestinian Issue – The Critical Stage, 1945–1946] (Cairo, 1968).

'Arif, 'Arif. *Al-Mafsal Fi Tariah al-Quds* [A Detailed History of Zionism] (Jerusalem, 1961).

—. *Al-Nakba: Nakbat Bayt al-Muqaddas Wa al-Fardus al-Mafqud 1947–1952* [The Calamity: The Calamity of Jerusalem and the Lost Paradise, 1947–1952, Volume I] I (Beirut, 1956).

'Azzam, 'Abd al-Rahman. *Al-Jami'ah al-'Arabiyyah Wal Wahdah al-A'alamiyyah* [The Arab League and Arab Unity] (Cairo, 1946).

Badawi, R. 'Sala'ah al-Naft al-'Arabi Wa Silahtuhu Bal-Qadiyyah al-Filastiniyyah' [The Arab Oil Weapon and its Relation to the Palestinian Issue], *Shuun Filastiniyyah*, 47, July 1975, pp. 102–14.

Daba'agh, Mustafa Murad. *Baladinah Filastin* [Palestine is Our Land] (Beirut, 1965).

Darwaza, Muhammad 'Izzat. *Hawla al-Harakah al-'Arabiyyah al-Hadithah* [About the Modern Arab Movement] II, III (Sidon, 1959).

—. *Al-Qadiyyah al-Filastiniyyah Fi Mukhtalif Marahalihah* [The Palestinian Issue in its Various Periods] I (Beirut, 1959).

Ghouri, Emil. *Filastin 'Ibra Sittin 'Aman* [Palestine Through 60 Years], Part I (Beirut, 1972).

Hada'ad, 'Uthman Kama'al. *Harakat Rashid 'Ali al-Qailani* [The Movement of Rashid 'Ali al-Qailani] (Sidon, 1941).

Haikal, Youssef. *Filastin Kabl Wa Ba'ad* [Palestine Before and After] (Beirut, 1971).

—. *Al-Qadiyyah al-Filastiniyyah Tahlil Wa Naqt* [The Palestinian Issue – Analysis and Critique] (Jaffa).

Hawari, Muhammad Nimr. *Sir al-Nakbah* [The Underlying Reasons for the Calamity] (1955).

221

Hindi, Hani. *Jaysh al-Inqaz* [The Liberation Army] (Beirut, 1974).

Husayni, Muhammad Amin. *Haqa'iq 'An Qadiyyat Filastin* [Truths about the Palestinian Issue] (3rd edn., Cairo, 1957).

—. *Fatwa Samahat al-Mufti al-Akhbar Bi-Sha'n Bi'ah al-Ara'adi Bi-Filastin Lil-Sahayunin* [Formal Legal Opinion (Islamic Law) of the Grand Mufti Regarding Land Sales to Zionists in Palestine] (Jerusalem, 1935).

—. 'Safahat Min Muzakarat al-Sayid Muhammad Amin al-Husayni', the memoirs of Haj Amin published in the Beirut journal *Filastin,* which expressed the opinions of Haj Amin and of the Arab Higher Institute.

Husri, Khaldun Sat'i (ed.). *Muzakarat Taha al-Hashimi 1942–1955* [The Memoirs of Tala al-Hashimi, 1942–1955] II (Beirut, 1978).

Hut, Biyan Nuwayhid. *Al-Qiyyadat Wa al-Mu'assat al-Siyassiyyah Fi Filastin: 1917–1948* [Political Leadership and Institutions in Palestine 1917–1948] (2nd edn., Acre, 1984).

Ida'arat al-Haqim al-Ida'ari al-A'am- Qita'a Raza, al-Waqa'ah al-Filastiniyyah- al-Jeridah al-Rasmiyyah Li-Qita'a Raza. Majmu'at al-Awarma Wal-Anzima Wal-I'ala'anat [The Administration of the General Administrative Governor – Gaza Strip. The Palestinian Official Gazette for Gaza Strip. Collections of Orders, Rules and Statements] I (Dar al-Nil, 1957), II (Dar al-Nil, 1961), III (Dar Shushah, 1966).

Khayriyyah Qasamiyyah (ed.), *'Awni 'Abd al-Hadi: Awraq Khasah* [The Private Papers of 'Awni 'Abd al-Hadi] (Beirut, 1974).

Khilah, Kamil Mahmud. *Filastin Wa al-Inti'dab al-Britanni, 1922–1939* [Palestine and the British Mandate 1922–1939] (Beirut, 1974).

Kiyyali, 'Abd al-Wahab (ed.). *Watha'iq al-Muqawamah al-Filastiniyyah al-'Arabiyyah Did al-Ihtilal al-Britani Wa al-Sahayuniyyah, 1918–1939* [Documents Concerning Palestinian Arab Resistance to British Occupation and Zionism 1918–1939] (Beirut, 1968).

—. *Ta'arikh Filastin al-Hadith* [The Modern History of Palestine] (Beirut, 1973).

Mahmud, Mu'in Ahmad. *Al-Amal al-Fida'i Wa Marahel Harb al-Tahrir al-Sha'abiyyah* [Activities of the Fedayeen] (Beirut, 1969).

Mawsu'ah al-Filastiniyyah [The Palestinian Encyclopedia] IV (Damascus, 1984).

Mu'awad, Ahmad. *Sarakha Illah al-Sama* [Cry to Heaven] (Jerusalem).

Muhafazah, 'Ali. *Al-'Alaqa'at al-Maniyyah al-Filastiniyyah: 1842–1945* [German–Palestinian Relations: 1842–1945] (Beirut, 1981).

Na'um al-Hasin Ibn Talal. [Husayn Ibn Talal's speech] published on behalf of the Jordanian Government under the title *al-Husayn Yursim Ma'alim al-Tariq, Nas al-Khitab al-Sa'ami Alazi Alqa'ah Jala'lat al-Malik al-Husayn al-Mu'azim Fi Hariji Ma'ahad al-Mu'alimin Wa al-Mu'alimat Fi Ajlun* [Al-Husayn Outlines the Way. The complete version of the royal presentation delivered by His Majesty, King Husayn, at the graduation ceremony of the Ajlun Teachers' College (Tuesday, 14 June 1966)].

Qailani, Musa Za'id. *Sanawat al-Ightisa'ab, Isr'ail 1948–1965* [The Stolen Years: Israel 1948–1965] (Amman, 1965).

Qawuqji, Fawzi. *Manazamat al-Tahrir al-Filastiniyyah – Markaz al-Abhath, Filastin Fi Muzakarat al-Qawuqji* [Palestine in the Memoirs of al-Qawuqji] II (1975).

Sadkah, Najib. *Qadiyyat Filastin* [The Palestinian Issue] (Beirut, 1946).

Safri, Issah. *Filastin al-'Arabiyyah Bayn al-Inti'dab Wal-Sahayuniyyah* [Arab Palestine: Between the Mandate and Zionism] II (Jaffa, 1937).

Sakhnini, Issam. *Filastin al-Dawlah* [Palestine: The State] (2nd edn., Acre, 1986).

Shabib, Samih. 'Muqaddamat al-Mussadarah al-Rasmiyyah Lil-Shakhsiyyah al-Wataniyyah al-Filastiniyyah 1948–1950' [Background to the Formal Denial of the Palestinian National Identity, 1948–1950], *Shuun Filastiniyyah*, 129–131, August–October 1982, pp. 72–87.

Shuqairy, Ahmad. *Arba'aun 'Amman Fi al-Hyat al-'Arabiyyah Wa al-Dawliyyah* [Forty Years in National and International Life] (Beirut, 1969).

—. 'Ziqriyyat 'An Mu'tamar al-Qimma Fi al-Khartum' [Memoirs from the Khartoum Summit Conference], *Shuun Filastiniyyah*, 4, September 1971, pp. 90–99.

—. *Al-Hazimah al-Kubra Ma'a al-Muluq Wal-Ru'assah: Min Bayit 'Abd al-Nasser Illah Ghourfat al-'Amaliyyat* [The Great Defeat in the Company of Monarchs and Presidents: From Al-Nasser's Home to the Operations Room] (Beirut, 1973).

—. *Hiwar Wa Asrar Ma'a al-Muluq Wa al-Ru'assah* [Dialogue and Secrets with Monarchs and Presidents] (Beirut).

—. *Min al-Qimma Illah al-Hazimah Ma'a al-Muluq Wal-Ru'assah* [From Summit to Defeat with Monarchs and Presidents] (Beirut, 1971).

—. *'Allah Tariq al-Hazimah Ma'a al-Muluq Wal-Ru'assah* [The Path to Defeat with Monarchs and Presidents] (Beirut, 1972).

Skaik, Khalil Ibrahim. *Tariah Filastin al-Hadith Munzu al-Fatrah al-'Uthamaniyyah* (Cairo, 1964).

Tai'a, Ahmad Farraj. *Safahat Matu'ah 'An Filastin* [Forgotten Papers Concerning Palestine].

Tariqi, Husayn. *Hathah Filastin* [That is Palestine] (Tunis, 1971).

'Watha'iq – al-Jalsah al-Siriyyah Li-Majlis al-Shaykh al-Ma'aqudah Fi 11 Mayu 1948 'An Masa'alat Filastin' [Documents from the Senate's

Secret Session which met to discuss the question of Palestine on 11 May 1948], *al-Tali'a*, March 1975, pp. 134–45.

Wuzarat al-Difa al-Watani – al-Jaysh al-Libnani al-Arqan al-A'amma al-Sha'aba al-Khamisah. *Al-Qadiyyah al-Filastiniyyah Wa al-Khatar al-Sahayyuni* [The National Defence Ministry – The General Head-quarters of the Lebanese Army, Fifth Department. The Palestinian Issue and the Zionist Danger] (Beirut, 1973).

Yasin, Subhi. *Al-Thawrah al-'Arabiyyah al-Kubra: 1936–1939* [The Great Arab Revolt: 1936–1939] (Cairo, 1959).

Zu'abi, Muhammad 'Ali. *Isra'il Bint Britaniyyah al-Biqr* [Israel – Britain's Firstborn] (Cairo).

Zu'aytir, Akram. *al-Qadiyyah al-Filastiniyyah* [The Palestinian Issue] (Cairo, 1955).

—. *Yawmiyyat al-Harakah al-Wataniyyah al-Filastiniyyah 1935–1939* [Diary of the Palestinian National Movement, 1935–1939] (Beirut, 1980).

Zurayq, Custantine. *Ma'anah al-Nakbah* [The Meaning of the Calamity] (Beirut, 1948).

European Languages

Alami, Musa. *Palestine is My Country* (London, 1969).

Antonius, George. *The Arab Awakening* (London, 1938).

Arab Executive Committee, *Memorandum on the Palestine White Paper of October 1930*, prepared by Aouni Abdul-Hadi (Jerusalem, 1930).

Arab Higher Committee, *The Palestine Arab Case: A Statement by the Arab Higher Committee, April 1947* (Cairo, 1947).

Arab Higher Committee for Palestine, *Memorandum Submitted by the Arab Higher Committee to the Permanent Mandates Commission and the Secretary of State for the Colonies* (Jerusalem, 1937).

Bentwich, Norman. *England in Palestine* (London, 1932).

Bernadotte, Folke. *To Jerusalem* (London, 1951).

Carpi, Daniel. 'The Mufti of Jerusalem, Amin el-Husseini, and His Diplomatic Activity during World War II', *Studies in Zionism*, VII, Spring 1983, pp. 101–31.

Cooley, John K. *Green March, Black September: The Story of the Palestinian Arabs* (London, 1973).

Dann, Uriel. *Iraq under Qassem: A Political History, 1958–1963* (Jerusalem, 1969); *Studies in the History of Transjordan, 1920–1949: The Making of a State* (Boulder, 1984).

Department of State, *Foreign Relations of the United States: 1948, V* (Washington, 1976).

224

Gabby, R.E. *A Political Study of Arab Jewish Conflict: The Arab Refugee Problem* (Geneva, 1959).

Glubb, John B. *A Soldier with the Arabs* (5th edn., London, 1969).

Gomaa, Ahmed M. *The Foundation of the League of Arab States* (London, 1977).

Government of Palestine, *A Survey of Palestine*, prepared in December 1945 and January 1946 for the information of the Anglo-American Committee of Inquiry, II (Government Printer, Palestine: Jerusalem, 1946).

Government of Palestine, *Reports on Agricultural Development and Land Settlement in Palestine by Lewis French* (April 1932).

Great Britain, *Report of Commission on the Palestine Disturbances of August 1929* (London, 1930).

Grobba, Fritz. *Männer und Mächte im Orient* (Göttingen, 1967).

Hasan, Reyazul. 'The Islamic Summit Conference', *Iqbal Review* (Iqbal Academy, Pakistan), XV, No.1, April 1974, pp. 43–4.

Haydar, Afak. 'The Islamic Summit Conference of 1974: An Assessment', *Asian Profile* (Hong Kong), III, No.4, August 1975, pp. 391–404.

Hurewitz, J.C. *The Struggle for Palestine* (New York, 1950).

Jbara, Taysir. *Palestinian Leader Hajj Amin al-Husayni: Mufti of Jerusalem* (Princeton, NJ, 1985).

John, Robert and Sami Hadawi, *The Palestine Diary, I* (Beirut, 1970).

Kedourie, Elie and Sylvia G. Haim (eds.). *Zionism and Arabism in Palestine and Israel* (London, 1982).

Kedourie, Elie. *The Chatham House Version and Other Middle-Eastern Studies* (London, 1984).

—. 'Sir Herbert Samuel and the Government of Palestine', *Middle East Studies* (*MES*), V, No.1, January 1969, pp. 44–68.

Khadduri, Majid. *Arab Contemporaries* (Baltimore, 1973).

—. *Independent Iraq 1932–1958: A Study in Iraqi Politics* (2nd edn., London, 1960).

Khalil, Muhammad. *The Arab States and the Arab League, II* (Beirut, 1962).

Kiernan, Thomas. *Arafat: The Man and the Myth* (New York, 1976).

Kimche, Jon and David. *Both Sides of the Hill: Britain and the Palestine War* (London, 1960).

Kirkbride, Alec S. *A Crackle of Thorns* (London, 1956).

Kramer, Martin. *Islam Assembled: The Advent of the Muslem Congresses* (New York, 1986).

Kurzman, Dan. *Genesis 1948: The First Arab–Israeli War* (New York, 1970).

Laffin, John. *Fedayeen: The Arab–Israeli Dilemma* (London, 1973).

Landau, Julian J. *Israel and the Arabs; A Handbook of Basic Information* (Jerusalem, 1971).

Levtzion, Nehemia. 'International Islamic Solidarity and its Limitations', *Jerusalem Papers on Peace Problems*, No. 29, 1979.

Luke, Harry Charles and Edward Keit-Roach, *The Handbook of Palestine and Trans-Jordan* (London, 1930).

MacDonald, Robert W. *The League of Arab States* (Princeton University, 1965).

Maine, Ernest, *Palestine at the Crossroads* (London, 1937).

Marlowe, John. *Arab Nationalism and British Imperialism* (London, 1961).

—. *Rebellion in Palestine* (London, 1946).

—. *The Seat of Pilate* (London, 1959).

Mattar, Philip. 'Amin al-Husayni and Iraq's Quest for Independence, 1939–41', *Arab Studies Quarterly*, VI, No. 4, Fall 1984, pp. 267–81.

—. 'The Role of the Mufti of Jerusalem in the Political Struggle over the Western Wall, 1928–1929', *MES*, XIX, No. 1, January 1983, pp. 104–18.

Mayer, Thomas. 'Egypt's 1948 Invasion of Palestine', *MES*, XXII, No. 1, January 1986, pp. 20–36.

—. 'Arab Unity of Action and the Palestine Question, 1945–48', *MES*, XXII, No. 3, July 1986, pp. 331–49.

Mitchell, Richard P. *The Society of the Muslim Brothers* (London, 1969).

Morris, Benny. 'The Causes and Character of the Arab Exodus from Palestine: The Israeli Defense Forces Intelligence Branch Analysis of June 1948', *MES*, XXII, No. 1, January 1986, pp. 5–19.

The National Associates. *The Arab Higher Committee: Its Origins, Personnel and Purposes*. The Documentary Record submitted to the United Nations, May 1947 by the National Associates (New York, 1947).

Nevo, Joseph. 'The Arabs of Palestine 1947–48: Military and Political Activity', *MES*, XXIII, No. 1, January 1987, pp. 3–38.

Perlman, Maurice. *Mufti of Jerusalem: The Story of Haj Amin El-Husseini* (London, 1947).

Plascov, Avi. *The Palestinian Refugees in Jordan, 1948–1957* (London, 1981).

Royal Institute of International Affairs, *Great Britain and Palestine, 1915–1939* (London, 1940).

Schechtman, Joseph B. *The Mufti and the Fuehrer: The Rise and Fall of Haj Amin el-Husseini* (New York, 1965).

—. *The Arab Refugees Problem* (New York, 1952).

Al-Shuqayri, Ahmed. *Liberation – Not Negotiation* (Beirut, 1966).
Sinai, Anne and Allen Pollack (eds.). *The Hashemite Kingdom of Jordan and the West Bank* (New York, 1977).
Stein, Leonard. *The Balfour Declaration* (London, 1961).
—. *The Truth about Palestine* (London, 1922).
Taggar, Yehuda. *The Mufti of Jerusalem and Palestine Arab Politics, 1930–1937.* Unpublished Ph.D. Thesis (University of London, 1973).
United States Department of State. *The Quest for Peace: Principal United States Public Statements and Related Documents on the Arab–Israeli Peace Process 1967–1983* (Washington, 1984).
Vatikiotis, P.J. *Arab Regional Politics in the Middle East* (London, 1984).
—. *Conflict in the Middle East* (London, 1971).
—. *The Modern History of Egypt* (London, 1969).
Waters, M.P. *Mufti Over Middle East* (New York, 1942).
Wisenthal, Simon. *Grossmufti – Grossagent der Achse: Tatsachenbericht mit 24 Photographien* (Salzburg, 1947).
Zeine, Zeine M. *The Emergence of Arab Nationalism* (Beirut, 1966).

Hebrew

Abu Iyad. *Le-Lo Moledet* [Without a Homeland], translated into Hebrew from Arabic by Norit Peled (Jerusalem, 1979).
Al-Tal, Abdullah. *Zikhronot Abdullah Al-Tal* [The Memoirs of Abdullah al-Tal], translated into Hebrew from Arabic by Yehoshua Halamish (Tel Aviv, 1964).
Amitai, Yossef. 'Medinot Arav U-Milhemet Yisrael: 1945–1948, Mi-Me'oravut Medinit Le-Hit'arvut Zvai't' [The Arab States and the War over Palestine: 1945–1948, From Political to Military Involvement] *Iyunim Be-Heker Ha-Mizrah Ha-Tikhon* (Haifa University), April 1976.
Arnon-Ohanah, Yuval and Arieh Yudfat. *Ashaf: Diyukano Shel Irgun* [PLO: Portrait of an Organisation] (Tel Aviv, 1985).
Arnon-Ohanah, Yuval. *Harav Mi-Bayit: Ha-Ma'avak Ha-Penimi Ba-Tenuah Ha-Palestinayyit 1929–1939* [Destruction from Within: The Internal Struggle Within the Palestinian Movement, 1929–1939] (Tel Aviv, 1981).
—. *Felahim Ba-Mered Ha-Aravi Be-Eretz Yisrael: 1936–1939* [Felahin in the Arab Revolt in Palestine: 1936–1939] (Tel Aviv, 1978).
Asaf, Michael. *Toledot Hit'orerut Ha-Aravim Be-Eretz Ysrael U'Verihatam* [History of the Awakening of the Arabs of Palestine and their Flight] (Tel Aviv, 1967).
Bar, Gabriel. *Aravi'ey Ha-Mizrah Ha-Tikhon, Ukhlusiyyah Ve-Hevrah* [The Middle East Arabs: Population and Society] (Tel Aviv, 1960).

227

Bari, E. *Ha-Ketsunah Ve-Ha-Shilton Ba-Olam Ha-Aravi* [Officers and the Regime in the Arab World] (Tel Aviv, 1966).

Bar-Lavi, Ze'ev. 'Ha-Mishtar Ha-Hahashami 1949–1967 U-Ma'amando Ba-Gadah Ha-Ma'aravit' [The Hashemite Regime 1949–1967 and its Status in the West Bank], *Sekirot*, September 1981.

Ben-Elkanah, Shlomo. 'Mimtsa'im Hadashim Le-Motsa'ah Shel Mishpahat Al-Husayni Ha-Yerushalmit' [New Findings Concerning the Origins of the Jerusalem Al-Husayni Family], *Keshet*, 1973–74, pp. 121–35.

—. 'Aliyato Shel Haj Amin Al-Husayni El Rashut Ha-Hanhagah Ha-Datit Shel Ha-Eydah Ha-Muslemit Be-Eretz Yisrael' [The Rise of Haj Amin Al-Husayni to the Head of the Religous Leadership of the Muslim Community in Palestine], *Sefer Ha-Shanah* (Bar Ilan University), 10, Part 2 (Ramat Gan, 1972), pp. 83–7.

Ben-Gurion, David. *Pegishot Im Manhigim Araviyyim* [Meetings with Arab Leaders] (Tel Aviv, 1967).

Ben-Zvi, Yitzhak. *Eretz Yisrael Ve-Yishuvah Bi-Yemay Ha-Shilton Ha-Ottomanee* [Palestine and its Settlement During the Ottoman Rule] (Jerusalem, 1962).

Cohen, Aaharon. *Yisrael Ve-Ha-Olam Ha-Aravi* [Israel and the Arab World] (Merhavia, 1964).

Cohen, Amnon. *Miflagot Ba-Gadah Ha-Ma'aravit Bi-Tkufat Ha-Shilton Ha-Yardeni (1948–1967)* [Political Parties in the West Bank During the Jordanian Rule, 1948–1967].

Danin, Ezrah (ed.). *Te'udot U-Demuyot: Mi-Ginzey Ha-Kenufiyyot Ha-Araviyyot Be-Meora'ot 1936–1939* [Documents and Portraits: Archives of the Arab Bands from the 1936–1939 Disturbances], Tel Aviv, 1944).

Dann, Uriel. 'Emirat Ever Ha-Yarden 1921–1946' [The Transjordanian Emirate], *Sekirot*, February 1982.

Dayan, Moshe. *Yoman Ma'arekhet Sinai* [Diary of the Sinai Campaign] (Tel Aviv, 1967).

Eilat, Eliyahu. *Haj Muhammad Amin al-Husayni: Mufti Yerushalayim Li-She'avar* [Haj Amin al-Husayni: Ex-Mufti of Jerusalem] (Tel Aviv, 1968).

Elpeleg, Zvi. 'Meor'aot 1936–1939: Pera'ot o Mered' [The Disturbances of 1936–1939: Riots or Rebellion], *Sekirot* (Shiloah Institute, Tel Aviv University), January 1977.

—. 'Palestin Atsma'it Bi-Svak Ha-Yerivut Ha-Bayn-Aravit: 1946–1948' [An Independent Palestine in the Web of Inter-Arab Rivalry, 1946–1948], ibid., February 1982.

—. 'Tokhnit Ha-Federatsiyyah Shel Husayn: Gormim U-Teguvot'

[Husayn's Federation Plan: Factors and Responses], ibid., December 1977.

Frumkin, Gad. *Derekh Shofet Bi-Yerushalayim* [A Judge's Path in Jerusalem] (Tel Aviv, 1954).

Gilad, Zrubavel (ed.). *Sefer Ha-Palmah*, II [History of the Palmah, Vol. II] (Tel Aviv, 1955).

Goren, Asher. *Ha-Leegah Ha-Aravit* [The Arab League] (Tel Aviv, 1954).

Granovsky, A. *Ha-Mishtar Ha-Qarqa'i Be-Eretz Yisrael* [The Agrarian Regime in Palestine] (Tel Aviv, 1949).

Gurni, Yossef. *Ha-She'elah Ha-Aravit Ve-Ha-Ba'ayah Ha-Yehudit* [The Arab Question and the Jewish Problem] (Tel Aviv, 1985).

Habas, Beracha (ed.). *Sefer Meora'ot 1936* [Book of 1936 Disturbances] (Tel Aviv, 1937).

Harkabi, Yehoshua. *Emdat Yisrael Be-Sikhsukh Yisrael–Arav* [Israel's Position in the Israel–Arab Conflict] (Tel Aviv, 1968).

—. *Emdat Ha-Aravim Be-Sikhsukh Yisrael–Arav* [The Arabs' Position in the Israel–Arab Dispute] (Tel Aviv, 1968).

— (ed.). *Arav Ve-Yisrael* [Arabia and Israel], collection of translations from Arabic, No. 3–4 (Tel Aviv, 1975).

Hirshowitz, Lucas. *Ha-Reich Ha-Shlishi Ve-Ha-Mizrah Ha-Aravi* [The Third Reich and the Arab East], translated into Hebrew from Polish by A. Cana'ani (Tel Aviv, 1965).

Kazzaz, Nissim. 'Du'ah Va'adat He-Hakirah Mi-Ta'am Memshelet Iraq Al Meora'ot 1–2 Be-Yuni 1941' [Report of the Iraqi Government's Commission of Inquiry into the Events of 1–2 June 1941], *Pa'amim*, 8, 1981, pp. 46–59.

Me-Ahorey Ha-Pargod, Va'adah Ha-Parlamentarit Iraqit Al Ha-Milhamah Be-Yisrael [Behind the Curtain: The Iraqi Parliamentary Commission on the War Against Israel], translated by S. Segev (Tel Aviv, 1954).

Meinertzhagen, R. *Yoman Mizrah Ha-Tikhon 1917–1956* [Middle East Diary 1917–1956], translated into Hebrew by Aaharon Amir (Haifa, 1973).

Nevo, Yossef. *Abdullah Ve-Aravi'ey Eretz Yisrael* [Abdullah and the Arabs of Palestine] (Tel Aviv, 1975).

Niv, David. *Ma'arakhot Ha-Irgun Ha-Zva'i Ha-Leumi*, III [The Campaigns of the Irgun Zva'i Leumi Group, III] (Tel Aviv, 1967).

Porat, Yehoshua. *Be-Mivhan Ha-Ma'aseh Ha-Politi: Eretz Yisrael, Ahdut Aravit U-Mediniyyut Britaniyyah 1930–1945* [The Test of Political Action: Palestine, Arab Unity and British Policy 1930–1945] (Jerusalem, 1985).

229

—. *Mi-Mehumot Li-Meridah: Ha-Tenuah Ha-Leumit Ha-Aravit-Pales-tinayyit 1929–1939* [The Palestinian Arab National Movement: From Riots to Rebellion] (Tel Aviv, 1978).

—. *Tsemihat Ha-Tenuah Ha-Leumit Ha-Aravit-Palestinayyit 1918–1929* [The Emergence of the Palestinian Arab National Movement 1918–1929] (Jerusalem, 1971).

Rosen, S. *Sefer Ha-Hozim La-Mizrah Ha-Tikhon: Osef Heskemim, Amanot U-Veritot-Zva'iot* [Collection of Agreements, Charters, and Military Alliances of the Middle East] (Tel Aviv, 1956).

Safran, Nadav. *Ha-Imut Ha-Aravi-Yisraeli, 1948–1967* [The Arab–Israeli Confrontation, 1948–1967] (Jerusalem, 1969).

Sa'id, A. *She'elat Palestin* [The Question of Palestine] (Jerusalem, 1981).

Sassar, Asher. *Bayn Yarden Le-Palestin: Biyografiyyah Politit Shel Wasfi Al-Tal* [Between Jordan and Palestine: A Political Biography of Wasfi al-Tal] (Tel Aviv, 1983).

Sela, Avraham. *Ahdut Mi-Tokh Pirud Ba-Ma'arekhet Ha-Bayn-Aravit* [Unity Amongst Division in the Inter-Arab Arena] (Jerusalem, 1983).

Shamir, Shimon. *Toledot Ha-Aravim Ba-Mizrah Ha-Tikhon Ba-Et Ha-Hadasha* [History of the Arabs in the Middle East in the New Age], I (Tel Aviv, 1965).

Sharett (Shertok), Moshe. *Yoman Medini* [Political Diary], I (Tel Aviv, 1968), II (1971), III (1972).

Sherf, Ze'ev. *Sheloshah Yamim* [Three Days] (Tel Aviv, 1959).

Shihada, 'Aziz. '*Megamot He-Hakikah Ha-Yardenit Ba-Gadah Ha-Ma'aravit*' [Trends in Jordanian Legislation in the West Bank], *Ha-Mizrah Ha-Hadash* 20, pp. 166–70.

Shim'oni, Ya'acov. *Aravi'ey Eretz Yisrael* [The Arabs of Palestine] (Tel Aviv, 1947).

—. *Medinot Arav* [The Arab States] (Tel Aviv, 1977).

Slutsky, Yehuda, *et al.* *Sefer Toledot Ha-Haganah* [History of the Haganah], I (Tel Aviv, 1956), II (1963), III (1972).

Sykes, Christopher. *Mi-Balfour Ad Bevin* [From Balfour to Bevin], translated into Hebrew by S. Gonen (Tel Aviv, 1966).

Vashitz, Yossef. *Ha-Aravim Be-Eretz Yisrael* [The Arabs of Palestine] (Merhavia, 1947).

Ya'ari, Ehud. *Mitsrayim Ve-Ha-Fedayeen: 1953–1956* [Egypt and the Fedayeen: 1953–1956] (Giva'at Havivah, 1975).

—. *Fatah* (Tel Aviv, 1970).

Yizhar, Michael. *Artsot Ha-Brit Ve-Ha-Mizrah Ha-Tikhon* [The US and the Middle East] (Tel Aviv, 1973).

Yudfat, Arieh. *Brit Ha-Moatsot Ve-Ha-Mizrah Ha-Tikhon* [The Soviet Union and the Middle East] (Tel Aviv, 1973).

Index

Abaqarius, Michel, 114
'Abd al-Baqi, Ahmad Hilmi see al-Baqi
'Abd al-Hamid II, Ottoman Sultan, xi
'Abd al'Illah, 56, 58, 60, 62
'Abd al-Majid, deposed Turkish Sultan, 27
'Abd al-Samad Ibn 'Abd al-Latif, 2
'Abdah, Muhammad, 37
Abdullah Ibn Hussein, King of Jordan, 28, 35, 44, 51, 92, 171, 177; Haj Amin's confrontation with, 84, 85, 88–9, 90, 95, 97–8, 99–101, 120; and invasion of Israel, 92, 93, 94, 95, 97; and All-Palestine Government, 99–118 passim; annexation of West Bank by, 121–4, 126–7; murder in Jerusalem of (1951), 125–6
'Abidin, Sabri, 31
Abu Iyad (Sala'ah Khalaf), 162, 178
'Ajrudi, General, 130
'Alami family, 2, 4
al-'Alami, Musa, 43, 59, 81
'Alawi revolt (1920), 37
Alexandria, 78–9; Arab League preparatory conference (1944), 80; Arab Summit meeting (1964), 146
Alexandria Protocol (October 1944), 81
'Aley Conference of Arab League Council (1947), 85, 86, 87, 88, 89, 90, 92
Algeria, 136, 137, 138
'Ali Ibn Husayn, 28
'Ali, Shawkat, 26, 27, 29
All-Palestine Government (*Huqumat 'Ummum Filastin*), 99–118, 119, 120, 121, 124, 125, 127, 128, 131, 169; setting up of (1948), 206–9; provisional basic law of, 210–13
'Alubah, Muhammad, 'Ali, 48
al-'Amari, Iranian Foreign Minister, 64

Amman, 90, 114, 121, 140, 141, 142, 146, 147, 149, 151, 155, 156, 158, 159, 160, 161; First Palestinian Congress (October 1948), 105, 112; World Islamic Congress (1967), 154; Muslim Christian Conference (1967), 154; memorial to Haj Amin in Jordanian University, 164
amnesty for political prisoners, 6, 7, 160
'Ana'an, 'Ali Rushdi, 77
Andrews, Lewis, murder in Nazareth of (1937), 48
Antonius, George, 62
'Aqashah, General Mahmud Fahmi, 130
Aqil, Amin, 114
al-Aqsa mosque see *al-Haram al-Sharif* mosques
Arab Brigade, 69
Arab Congress, Paris (1913), xii
Arab Higher Committee (*al-Lajnah al-'Arabiyyah al-'Ulia*), 42–3, 44, 46, 48, 51, 79, 81, 82, 83, 117, 167, 175; rejection of 1939 White Paper by, 52–4, 201; proclamation of independence of Palestine by (1948), 209–10
Arab Higher Front (*al-Jabhah al-'Arabiyyah al-'Ulia*), 81, 82, 83
Arab Higher Institute (*al-Hyah al-Arabiyyah al-'Ulia*: established 1946), 84, 85, 86, 87, 90–103 passim, 108, 109, 115, 118, 119–20, 123, 124, 128, 130, 131, 134, 135, 136, 138, 140–51 passim, 159, 160, 162–3, 167, 169, 170, 171, 173, 175
Arab Home Treasury (*Bayt al-Mal al'Arabi*), 174
Arab–Israeli wars, 129, 164, 169; War of Independence (1948), 173, 175, 176–7,

INDEX

Damascus, 49
Chamoun, Kamil, 163
Chancellor, Sir John, 20, 22
Chou En-lai, 132
Churchill, Sir Winston, 76, 84, 175
Ciano, Count Galleazo, 65, 69
Civil Guard (*al-Haras al-Ahali*), 131
Congress of the Palestine Islamic Nation, 27
Creech Jones, Sir Arthur, 85
Czechoslovakia, Egyptian arms deals with, 131, 132

al-Dajani family, 5
Damascus, xiii, xiv, 4, 6–7, 125
Danin, Ezra, 92
Dar al-Dawa wa al-Irshad, academic institute, Cairo, 2
Darwaza, Muhammad 'Izzat, 7, 19, 20, 43, 86, 201
Darwish, Ishaq, 58, 131
Da'ud, Muhammad (Abu Da'ud), 160
Day of Atonement (Yom Kippur), Western Wall incident on (1928), 16, 18–19, 20; see also Yom Kippur War
Deedes, Sir Wyndham, 13
Deutsch–Arabische Lehrabteilung (DAL), 69
al-Din, Sa'id 'Ala', 141
al-Din, Sala'ah, 5
al-Din, Dr Sala'ah, 127
Dome of the Rock see *al-Haram al-Sharif* mosques

Egypt, 2–3, 27–8, 39, 53, 63, 84, 87, 88, 89–90, 91, 92, 97, 99, 100, 102, 103, 104, 106, 107, 109, 110, 111, 113, 115, 120–1, 122, 124, 127, 130–9, 140, 141, 147, 148–9, 150, 152, 155, 169, 203, 209; Haj Amin's escape from France to, 76–9; Israeli 'Operation Yoav' against (1948), 110–11; Rhodes agreement (1949), 109, 113, 114, 115, 133; Free Officers' coup and overthrow of Farouk (1951), 127–8; arms deals with Czechoslovakia, 131, 132; Suez/Sinai War (1956), 132–3; Iraqi relations with, 133–5, 136, 137, 138, 160; Jordanian agreement with (1967), 152–3; Six Day War (1967), 153; October War (1973), 161
Eichmann, Adolf, 77
elections, local municipal (1934), 33–4, 35

Fadil, Munir Abu, 120–1
Faisal I Ibn Husayn, Amir, King of the

Hejaz and Iraq, xiii, xiv, 4, 6, 28, 202–3
Faisal of Saudi Arabia, Amir, 131–2
Faisal, King of Saudi Arabia, 147, 164
Faranjieh, Suleman, President of Lebanon, 163
Farouk, King of Egypt, 63, 77, 78, 110, 120, 121, 127
Farraj, Ya'qub, 33
al-Faruqi, Suleman Ta'aji, 105
Fatah, 139, 143, 144, 147–8, 155, 156–7, 178
al-Fatah al-Islami, 155–6
Fatma, daughter of Muhammad the Prophet, 1
fedayeen (Palestinian 'suicide-fighters'), 131, 132
Federation Plan (1972), Husayn's, 159, 160
Filastin (Jaffa-based newspaper), xii
Filastin (Haj Amin's Beirut-based newspaper), xviii, 145, 178
Filastinina (Fatah official newspaper), 148
First World War (1914–18), xi, xii, 177
Fox Scott, 122
France and French Mandate, xiii, xiv, 5, 37, 49, 56, 59, 132, 175, 202, 203; Haj Amin's internment in and escape from, 74–9
Free Officers coup, Egypt (1951), 127–8
Freij, Dr Futi, 114
French, Lewis, 31
Fu'ad, King of Egypt, 27

Gaulle, General Charles de, 75
Gaza/Gaza Strip, 97, 98, 108–9, 111, 112, 114, 115, 118, 127, 130, 132, 154, 169; Palestine National Council Conference in (1948), 102–5, 106, 109, 110, 117, 119, 120, 169, 209–10; IDF's raid into (1955), 132, 133; and IDF's withdrawal from (1957), 132, 133; Israeli occupation of (1967), 153, 154
General Islamic Congress: Jerusalem (1928), 20; Jerusalem (1931), 26–9, 167, 172; Karachi (1951), 124–5; Baghdad (1962), 137; Amman (1967), 154; Rabat (1969), 161; Lahore (1974), 161–2
Geneva Conference, 20; 1973: 161
Germany, Nazi, xvii, 39, 40, 56, 58–9, 60, 63–73, 75, 80, 81, 178–80
al-Ghouri, Emil, 82, 131, 136, 140, 141, 142, 146, 147, 156
al-Ghusayn, Ya'qub, 36, 37, 48, 52, 79, 80
Glubb Pasha, 126, 190

233